Henry James Coleridge

The ministry of St. John the Baptist

A new edition

Henry James Coleridge

The ministry of St. John the Baptist
A new edition

ISBN/EAN: 9783743329416

Manufactured in Europe, USA, Canada, Australia, Japa

Cover: Foto ©Lupo / pixelio.de

Manufactured and distributed by brebook publishing software
(www.brebook.com)

Henry James Coleridge

The ministry of St. John the Baptist

THE MINISTRY
OF ST. JOHN BAPTIST.

BY

HENRY JAMES COLERIDGE,

OF THE SOCIETY OF JESUS.

A NEW EDITION.

LONDON:
BURNS AND OATES.
1882.

✝

JOANNES · BEATISSIME
PRÆCURSOR · CHRISTI · PRÆCO · JUDICIS
AMICE · SPONSI · VOX · VERBI · DIVINI
QUI · SOLATIUM · NOSTRÆ · REDEMPTIONIS
NUNTIARE · MERUISTI
IMPETRA · MIHI · MISERO
APUD · EUNDEM · DOMINUM · NOSTRUM
JESUM · CHRISTUM
TUIS · SANCTISSIMIS · PRECIBUS ·
UT · PURGATO · VITIIS · PECTORE
ET · ORNATO · VIRTUTIBUS
PAREM · SECUNDUM · SALUBRIA · TUA · MONITA
VIAM · DOMINI
ET · RECTAS · FACIAM · SEMITAS · EJUS
QUATENUS · IN · EXTREMO · JUDICIO
CUM · AREAM · ECCLESIÆ · SUÆ · MUNDAVERIT
ET · TRITICUM · A · PALEIS · SEPARAVERIT
MEREAR · INTER · GRANA · TRITICI
ET · ELECTOS · SUOS · INVENIRI
ET · IN · HORREUM · CÆLESTIS · MANSIONIS
CUM · EIS · REPONI.
AMEN.

(Ex Ludolpho.)

PREFACE TO THE FIRST EDITION.

No kindly disposed reader of the following pages will, I hope, be inclined to blame a writer who has long desired and meditated the composition of a Life of our Lord of considerable length and compass, if he breaks up his work into parts, each of which may be to some extent complete in itself, and if he avails himself of this method to publish the several portions in an order not exactly corresponding to the order of time. All the reasons which have induced me to select that instalment of the present work which is now put before the reader as the first in order of publication need not be now stated; but it must be obvious to any one well acquainted with the literature of the subject, that the Public Ministry of our Lord is that part of His Life upon earth which is set before us at the greatest length by the Evangelists, while at the same time we have more available histories of the Passion or of the Sacred Infancy than of the Public Life. In the English language, in particular, the beautiful series of works begun but not finished by the late Father Faber, has left this central part of the Gospel history untouched; and although the work which I have long contemplated is not exactly of the same character with his volumes, I am very glad rather to attempt to fill up the gap in another way, than at once to go over the same ground with a writer whose memory is so dear to English Catholicism. I have therefore chosen the Public Life as the portion of our Lord's biography to which to devote myself in the first instance, hoping, if God so wills, to be allowed in due time to complete the whole narrative by the Infancy, Hidden Life, Passion and Resurrection.

If I might venture to utter a criticism on the many excellent works which already exist on the Life of our Lord, I should be inclined to add that it is just as to the arrangement and gradual unfolding of the providence of God as to the Public Life of our Lord that I have been accustomed to find them least satisfactory. It is pre-eminently as to that arrangement and unfolding that the true principles of what is called the Harmony of the Gospels need to be ascertained and applied, and yet it seems as if, even after the lapse of so many centuries, these true principles were but little attended to. The great St. Augustine, whose work on the *Consensus Evangelistarum* is so full of various merit, has yet given all the authority of his name to a principle which can be shown to be altogether a misconception in this subject-matter, and which, if a misconception, cannot be practically applied without producing confusion. For he has taken St. Matthew's Gospel as the basis to which to conform the statements of the other Evangelists, it being now generally admitted by students on the subject that the order of St. Matthew's Gospel is not chronological. In modern times there is a tendency to distinguish between the three first Evangelists, who go by the name of the Synoptists, and the fourth, who is supposed to fill up the gaps left in the history by his predecessors.

This principle, as far as it applies to St. John, is un-doubtedly true. But criticism must be carried much further than this, and the relations of the three first Evangelists to one another must be carefully ascertained. It will thus, perhaps, become manifest that St. Luke is quite as much a 'supplementer' as St. John, and that St. Mark as well as St. Luke wrote with a distinct refer-ence to the Gospel of St. Matthew. Again, a great deal has been excellently said about the scope and character of each of the four Evangelists, but comparatively little attention has been paid to the kindred subject of the internal structure of their works—a kindred subject, because that very structure owes much of its detail to that scope and that object. The idea that there is a great importance in the order of our Lord's Life, apart from the order in which parts of it had been represented by this or that of His historians, seems hardly to have impressed itself on the minds of modern critics with sufficient force, and we consequently find the most arbitrary arrangements of certain incidents in some of the Harmonies, or in some of the narratives which pre-suppose them. In such arrangements the order of the Evangelists is sometimes violently dislocated, to a degree which almost implies the opinion that they put their materials together, as it were, by accident. And, on the other hand, no attempt is made to trace the onward march of the manifestations of our Lord, the gradual training of His Apostles, the development, so to speak, of His moral or doctrinal or ascetical teaching, and other elements which do not perhaps lie on the surface, but which are still certain enough and precious enough when they are discovered to repay with abundant interest the patient labour which may have been spent upon them. It has been said that the science of New Testament criticism is as yet in its infancy, and I cannot help thinking that a great deal more general knowledge than is at present common concerning matters such as those just now indicated might be acquired without any great difficulty, if only a right method were carefully adhered to in the reverent examination of the fourfold record in which it has pleased God that the Life of our Lord should come down to us.

No perfect Life of our Lord can ever be written by human hand, because very large portions of it are entirely hidden from us, and, even as to those parts which we know most about, there is much more that we do not know. What Christian criticism can do is to attempt, as far as may be, to restore, if the expression may be used, out of the materials which are furnished by the Evangelists, the Life of our Lord as it was known, in its external facts, to the Apostles and those who were familiar with Him, before the Gospels were written, to shed upon it the light which is furnished by Christian theology, from St. Paul and St. John to the Catholic writers of modern times, and then, to go on to point out the purpose and method in accordance with which each several Gospel was composed. This may be a difficult task, a task which it is impossible, perhaps, to accomplish completely ; but it does not follow that it should not be attempted, or that nothing short of perfect success can be valuable and profitable in advancing our knowledge of our Lord. Anything of the kind that is true and sound as far as it goes must be very precious, and it would almost seem as if Christian students were intended to exercise their minds and powers in industry of this kind, by the very fact that it has pleased God that the records of our Lord's Life should be divided, as they are, between four several witnesses. A French infidel of the present day has said that a visit to the Holy Land is like a fifth Gospel in the intelligence which it conveys concerning our Lord's Life; but, without undervaluing that local knowledge and acquaintance with biblical scenery and antiquities which are so highly prized by the men of our time, we may surely give the name of a 'fifth Gospel' with far more justice to a Life of Christ which should bring out the arrangement and development of the whole in the manner spoken of above, helping us, at the same time, by this very background to their pictures, to understand better the works of the four Evangelists separately.

It is, as has been already said, the Public Life of our Lord which chiefly requires treatment of this kind; and if Catholic students, well armed with critical scholarship as well as accurate and deep theology, should be led by the example and even the failure of the present attempt to labour in this vast field, it will have been worth the while that the attempt should have been made. We have already some most precious monuments of the theological contemplation of the mysteries of our Lord's Life in St. Thomas and in his commentators, especially in Suarez, who has introduced a number of subjects into his work on the mysteries of our Lord's Life which are not treated of in the *Summa.* But Suarez passes over the whole Public Life in one or two disputations. Other Catholic writers of the same or later date who have dwelt more upon the Life as a whole, such as Jansenius (of

Ghent) and Barradius, have left us works which contain very great treasures of devotion and doctrine, but the arrangement of time and order is uncritical. Salmeron's great work on the Gospels is, in like manner, a store-house from which most abundant materials may be drawn, but he has not attempted any continuous narrative, and has left the criticism as to the Harmony almost untouched. These statements are made merely for the sake of giving instances, for the number of great Christian works on the Gospel is untold, and what has been said is enough to indicate the extent to which the field lies open to modern Catholic writers, some of whom, in Germany particularly, have already laboured with much success, but without exhausting its resources.

The Introduction to the present work, which until lately I intended to publish first in order, was meant to contain a brief summary of the whole Life of our Lord, without going into details, but in the order in which its events appear really to have succeeded each other, and, as a sequel to this, a careful account of the work of each Evangelist, his scope and method, as determined in the first instance by the object he had in view and the persons to whom he immediately addressed himself, and then the relation of his narrative to the Life of our Lord in general, as well as to the narratives of his brother Evangelists. This Introduction was partly written when it seemed to me better to postpone it, and to begin the fuller narrative of the Public Life at once, as has been done in the present volume. The first part of the Public Life, as it is set forth in the Latin Harmony of the Gospels published some years ago by the present writer, under the title of *Vita Vitæ Nostræ*

Meditantibus Proposita, embraces the whole of the first year of our Lord's Ministry, down to the time when, as it appears, soon after the second Pasch, He began to meet with fierce opposition from the Jewish authorities on account of His supposed laxity as to the observance of the Sabbath Day. The bulk of the present volume would have been swollen inconveniently if the whole of this period had been commented on fully in it. It includes, among other matters of the highest importance and interest, the long Sermon on the Mount, a summary of our Lord's teaching at this period, which would of itself require a large volume if it were to be treated with due fulness. The treasures of doctrine which are, if the words may be used, compressed and packed so closely in that discourse, require ample space if they are to be even partially unfolded, and thus the comparative dearth of incidents which characterises this first year of our Lord's teaching is abundantly compensated and counterbalanced by the great store of doctrine which belongs to this time. As it was necessary to divide the commentary on this part of the Public Life, I have ended the present volume with the imprisonment of St. John, the point of history at which the active evangelical preaching of our Lord in Galilee seems to have begun. The part of the work, therefore, which is now put before the public is coextensive in subject with the preaching of St. John, and has thus received its name from that preaching.

It has not been my object to make the present work either a record of all the opinions which have been maintained on the various points treated in it, or a book of reference for authorities. I have given the name of the author whom I have followed in cases where a reference to the work will be of advantage to the student, but otherwise I have been content with the result of researches which I trust have been sufficiently wide and industrious to render it safe to say that no important opinion or authority has been altogether neglected. The readers of many modern books on the Gospel History may well be frightened at the immense number of names of authors and books which meet their eyes at the bottom of the page, and they will sometimes be wearied at the long discussions in which all conceivable opinions and conjectures are dealt with and discussed. The truth is, that the field has been overgrown with critical writings without, as I venture to think, any proportionate benefit to true criticism, and it would be a real loss to the cause of truth if it were to be considered an established rule that no one should deal with the critical questions connected with the Gospel History unless he had read all that has been written before him. Many authors merely repeat, either at second hand or as the result of their own speculations, opinions which have been put forward over and over again, and perhaps as often answered; and the same may be, in its degree, said of the interpretations of the words of our Lord or of others which are recorded in the Gospels. I have endeavoured to keep down, as far as possible, anything that may interfere with the direct onward flow of the narrative or the commentary, by such discussions as rather exhibit the process by which a conclusion has been arrived at than add anything to the clearness of the doctrine or the history. Moreover, every one who has studied the Gospels continually and critically will be aware that he is often unable to trace to its right author a view of facts or an interpretation of words which has fixed itself on his mind after much reading and thought, and I trust that this will be an excuse for the paucity of acknowledgments and of references to authorities in the present volume. It has been written in the midst of occupations and distractions, such as would certainly have prevented me from undertaking it, if I had not thought it better to do what I could rather than wait for greater leisure which might never come.

It only remains for me to commend it, such as it is, to the kind consideration of the Christian reader, and to lay it at the feet of Him who vouchsafes to allow His glory to be advanced even by the puny efforts of the weakest and unworthiest of those whom He has called to His service.
H. J. C.

London, Feast of St. John Evangelist, 1874.

PREFACE TO THE SECOND EDITION.

In sending forth the Second Edition of this volume I have but little to add to what is said above, except to express my thanks for the kind welcome which the work, as far as it has gone, has received from those for whom it is written. I hope that, if I am allowed to complete the book as it is designed, it will be found that the kindness thus shown has borne its fruit in encouraging the writer to spare no toil to make it as little unworthy as possible of the aim which he has in view. With regard to the present volume, I have revised it very carefully, and I trust that some of its original defects have been removed. The corrections are mostly verbal, and such as have been made with a view to render the meaning clearer and more easy to grasp. No alteration of any importance has been made in the substance. There are here and there a few additional sentences. In one case, that of Note VII., I have considerably expanded the argument. I have hitherto been careful to avoid, as far as possible, discussions on questions as to the arrangement of the Harmony which is followed in *Vita Vitæ Nostræ*, on which this work is a commentary, because I hoped that I might have an opportunity of discussing all such subjects in one volume. But it appears to be better, at least as to questions of such great importance, as that which is treated of in the Note just named, to insert in the body of the work the arguments on which what appears to be the soundest conclusions are founded.

H. J. C.

London, Feast of St. Gabriel, 1876.

CONTENTS.

—o—

Contents. xxi

CHAPTER XV.

True and false Miracles.

St. John ii. 21 ; *Vita Vitæ Nostræ,* § 22.

CHAPTER XVI.

Miracles and Faith.

St. John ii. 12 ; *Vita Vitæ Nostræ,* § 22.

CHAPTER XVII.

Capharnaum.

St. John ii. 12 ; *Vita Vitæ Nostræ,* § 22.

CHAPTER I.

Mission of St. John Baptist.

St. Matt. iii. 1–12; St. Mark i. 2–8; St. Luke iii. 1–18;
Vita Vitæ Nostræ, § 16.

THIRTY years form a long space in the ordinary life of a man, and to many of us what is separated from us by so great an interval seems hardly to belong to our present existence. We usually reckon such a period as the life of a generation, because, within such a space of time, almost the whole outward aspect of the human world changes, as far as those elements of it are concerned which are variable. New men are in power or in vigour, or in possession of influence, wealth, estates, and other things which pass from hand to hand because they survive the frail strength of the children of Adam. The thirty years that intervened between the Birth and the Baptism of our Lord Jesus Christ had not been less fruitful of change and succession than any others. While He had been advancing so gradually 'in wisdom and age and in grace before God and man,'[1] and hiding Himself so completely in His life of obedience and silence at Nazareth, the world had been rushing on in all its flurry and tumult, and the memories of those wonderful manifestations by which the Providence of the Father had honoured His Birth had almost died away. The great Emperor Augustus, whose edict had

---

[1] St. Luke ii. 52.

forced St. Joseph and our Blessed Lady to go up to Bethlehem, and who had thus unconsciously served the true Master of the world by occasioning the fulfilment of the prophecies concerning the spot of His Birth, had passed away from his place of power, asking of his friends as a last homage the acknowledgment that he had played his part well.[2] Some two years before his death,[3] he had associated his stepson Tiberius with himself in his Imperial power, and we find St. Luke dating the preaching of the Baptist from the reign of Tiberius thus raised to the throne as colleague of Augustus. Herod, the wicked and cruel King, had gone to meet his Judge at no great interval of time after the massacre of the Holy Innocents. Archelaus had succeeded him, but after nine years of reigning he became intolerable. He was accused at Rome, summoned before the Emperor, and banished to Vienne. Herod's kingdom was then divided, as St. Luke's description intimates; and, at the time of which we are speaking, Judæa and Samaria were a part of the Roman province of Syria, governed separately by the sixth of the series of Roman procurators, Pontius Pilate. Certain portions of the former kingdom of Herod were retained by his children under the name of tetrarchies. ‘Herod’ Antipas ‘was tetrarch of Galilee (and Peræa), his brother Philip was tetrarch of Ituræa and the region of Trachonitis, Lysanias was tetrarch of Abilene,’ a territory lying about the Lebanon.[4] The last-named province alone of those enumerated by St. Luke does not meet us in the Gospel history, as having something to

---

[2] Sueton. *Octav.* 99.

[3] It was either in A. U. C. 764 or 765. Augustus died in August 767.

[4] For a summary of the difficulties raised by the mention of this tetrarch, and their answer, the reader may be referred to Andrews' *Life of our Lord*, pp. 123–125.

do with the career of our Lord or His blessed Precursor. 'Annas and Caiaphas were the High Priests'[5]—the mere statement tells us of the degrading change which had come over the High Priesthood, which was now given from time to time, in defiance of the Law, to the favourites, the partisans, or even the purchasers, of the Roman Governor.

Thus, at the time of which we are speaking, there were new rulers and even new systems at Jerusalem and all over the Holy Land. Death had removed most of the early witnesses to our Lord. Simeon was gone, and Anna; so also, we must suppose, were St. Zachary and St. Elisabeth. If the parents of our Blessed Lady had been alive at the time of our Lord's Birth, they also were now dead. Our Lady herself was a widow, though we are in ignorance of the date of the death of St. Joseph. And the changes which had come over the Holy Family and the nation at large, had been paralleled in every family in the country. The shepherds who had seen the vision of angels, the people at Jerusalem or at Bethlehem who had guided or waited on the Eastern kings at the Epiphany, the neighbours of Zachary who had been filled with wonder at the marvels which had been seen at the birth of the Baptist, many even of the doctors at Jerusalem whom our Lord had astonished by His learning, His answers and questions, when He had remained in the Temple for three days at the age of twelve years, were now dead. The birth of the marvellous Child at Bethlehem, the King's ruthless murder of the other children for His sake, the witness borne to Him in the Temple at the Purification of our Blessed Lady, had become matter of tradition, carefully

---

[5] Caiaphas was the actual High Priest, but St. Luke may mean that Annas was the only lawful one, or that he held some high office, such as that of President of the Sanhedrin.

nursed and preserved, no doubt, in the hearts of many who were 'looking for the redemption of Israel,' but the length of time which had passed since hopes were first raised concerning Him must have been enough, in many cases, to turn those hopes into disappointment. Meanwhile, all around, the moral and religious atmosphere seemed to grow darker and darker, the sceptre had more clearly than ever before been taken away from Judah, the signs of dissolution and desolation in the chosen nation became more conspicuous, and the heathen world all around it seemed sinking deeper and deeper into the gulf of the foulest moral degradation, less and less illumined, as time went on, by rays of hope, less and less startled by voices which bare witness to yearnings after better things.

The preparations of God are patient and leisurely, and when the moment comes, He acts strongly, quietly, and swiftly. Never since the creation of the universe had there been on the face of the earth creatures of God so dear to Him, never had there been such mighty spiritual forces and such consummate beauties and glories of the highest sanctity to delight the gaze of heaven, as during this interval when all seemed outwardly so dead and hopeless. During all those years, Nazareth had been in the eyes of God and His angels a focus of the intensest and purest light, in which Jesus, Mary, and Joseph, lived and moved in the constant practice of the loftiest virtue : and their whole life was the preparation and the foundation of the coming kingdom of God. The Incarnate Son was there in all the fulness and glory of the perfect grace with which His Sacred Humanity was endowed, and pouring Himself out in constant prayer for the advancement of the work committed to Him. And it cannot be doubted that His presence must have made itself felt on many good and simple souls around, near or far off, among Jews and Gentiles, in holy illuminations and inspirations, drawing them nearer to God and further from the world and from sin, and preparing them by silent touches and supplies of spiritual strength for a part in His kingdom. His everlasting intercession in heaven kindles at the present moment the whole Church with life and vigour, and so at that time His life and toils and prayers and obedience and humiliations were the support and spiritual health of numbers of souls, who were afterwards to be addressed by the external calls so soon to be made upon men by our Lord and St. John the Baptist. Thus it always is. That part of the work of God in the world which meets the eye and leaves its mark in human history, rests upon the interior preparation which has preceded or, which underlies it, and the active influence of the Church and the ministers of God's Word is the fruit of her interior life, of the prayers and penances and silent religious sacrifices of the hidden saints and of those whose vocation it is especially to perpetuate the imitation of the life at Nazareth. There were then, no doubt, many Jewish homes where aged saints like Anna served God in retirement or prayer, or where the future Apostles and martyrs were being trained. There were many holy virgins brought up in the Temple, or pious communities in the desert where the ascetic life was practised after the imitation of the prophets. On all these, fresh blessings daily descended in answer to the prayers of the Sacred Heart which beat for them with so much love at Nazareth. But we cannot doubt that one glorious soul above others was all this time the object of the special care of our Blessed Lord—the soul of him who had leaped in his mother's womb for joy when the sound of Mary's salutation fell upon her ears, who, as it is believed in the Church, was then sanctified from original sin and filled with the gifts of the Holy Ghost, in order that no time might be lost in his preparation for the high perfection and great work for which he was destined.

The Evangelist St. Luke, to whom we owe the history of the birth of St. John and our Blessed Lord, tells us that the former was from his early years 'in the desert, until the day of his showing unto Israel.' It is well known that the word desert in the Gospels does not mean an arid waste of rock and sand, in which human life can hardly be sustained, and in which in consequence there are no settled human habitations, but that wild and uncultivated country, in which there were but few farms or villages, through which the Jordan flows between the Lake of Gennesareth and the Dead Sea, and which lies also between the western shore of the last-named sea and the cultivated portion of Judæa properly so called. A veil is drawn over the whole youth and training of this great Saint. We know from the announcement of the angel that he was to be a Nazarite from his youth. He comes before us in the Gospel narrative very much as Elias, his prototype in the history of the Old Testament, a full-grown man, ripe in sanctity, which had been gradually mounting higher and higher by continual communion with God. 'The word of the Lord was made unto John the son of Zachary in the desert. And he came into all the region of Jordan preaching the baptism of penance for the remission of sins—as it is written in the book of the words of Isaias the Prophet, " A voice of one crying in the wilderness, Prepare ye the way of the Lord, make straight His paths : every valley shall be filled up, and every mountain and hill brought low, and the crooked shall be made straight, and the rough places made into smooth paths, and all flesh shall see the salvation of God."'[6]   To this prophecy, which St. Luke gives at greater length than St. Matthew, St. Mark prefixes the words of Malachias, which are also applied to St. John by our Lord Himself,[7] 'Behold I send my messenger (angel) before Thy face, who shall prepare Thy way before Thee.'[8]   These passages serve to show us the importance of St. John's mission as a preparation for our Lord, or rather as the last stage of that long preparation which had been going on from the beginning, which embraced all the various dispensations of God, His methods of dealing with men, and revelations of Himself to them.   And to give ourselves as full an idea as may be of the several Scriptural declarations concerning that mission, we may remind ourselves once more of the words of the Archangel Gabriel to Zachary at the time of the announcement of his miraculous conception—'He shall be great before the Lord, and wine and strong drink he shall not drink, and he shall be filled with the Holy Ghost even from his mother's womb, and many of the children of Israel shall he convert to the Lord their God, and he shall himself go before Him in the spirit and power of Elias, "that he may turn the hearts of the fathers unto the children," and the incredulous unto the wisdom of the just, to prepare for the Lord a perfect people.'

These predictions certainly prepare us to find that the mission of St. John Baptist filled a large and important place in the divine plan for the redemption of the world by our Lord Jesus Christ, and that his office ranks exceedingly high, higher than that of any of the prophets, inasmuch as he was more near to our Lord and had to perform a more personal work in His regard, both in pointing Him out, in fitting people to

---

[6] Isaias xi. 3–5.   [7] St. Matt. xi. 16; St. Luke xii. 27.
[8] Mal. iii. 1.

receive Him, and also in baptizing Him in order that all justice might so be fulfilled. It turned out, in fact, that our Lord's own ministry was inaugurated, if we may so speak, by His reception of the baptism of St. John, that the mass of the people, as well as His chosen disciples, were prepared for Him by his Forerunner, that St. John designated Him to the emissaries of the Jewish authorities who were sent to question him, that he pointed Him out to his own followers as the Lamb of God, that our Lord formally appealed to him and to his baptism as an appointed testimony to Himself, and that the classes of men who accepted the one accepted the other, while those who rejected St. John's teaching also rejected that of our Lord. Yet the teaching of St. John was only for a short time, his work was soon done, his course soon over, and, if it is to be considered independently of its effect in preparing for our Lord, it certainly ended in a failure according to all human measures of estimation. And yet, when we examine it more closely, we see how perfect and beautiful his work was, and how much it teaches us of the ways of God in manifesting His Incarnate Son.

We cannot doubt, that notwithstanding all the long preparation of the world and of the chosen people for the coming of our Lord, men's hearts were in general altogether unready for Him when He came. At the time of His Birth that characteristic feature of His treatment at the hands of men which St. John has expressed in the words, 'He came unto His own, and His own received Him not,' was figured in the poor welcome with which His Blessed Mother in her hour of need was met by the people of Bethlehem. 'There was no room for them.' The few who received Him and acknowledged Him, as the shepherds, the Eastern sages, Simeon, Anna, and the like, were all simple unworldly hearts which had been prepared for Him by the grace of God. To others the Star shone in vain in the heavens, nor could the songs of the Angels penetrate their ears. No class was exempt from this blindness. Herod on his throne, and the Priests and Doctors at Jerusalem, could help others on their way to Him, but they felt no need of Him themselves. Their hearts were not ready—and we have no reason for thinking that the great mass of mankind or of the Jews were more ready for Him than their Rulers, lay and ecclesiastical.

In the mission of St. John Baptist, God mercifully chose the most fitting way for that preparation of the heart for our Lord, without which His manifestation would be in vain. In the first place, it is a part of the Providence of God that when He is to do a great work in the world, He sends a great Saint, or a number of great Saints, to do it. They receive their gifts, in proportion to their mission, out of His inexhaustible treasures, and thus it is that at any crisis He is able to revive and reinvigorate His Church. St. John was himself a person of the loftiest sanctity. The process of his sanctification had been begun, as has been said, in the womb of his mother at the time of the Visitation, and it is the common feeling of the Church that it went on from that moment with steady and ever-increasing rapidity. The Fathers, as well as the Church in her services, apply to him the words which properly belong to the Prophet Jeremias, 'Before I formed thee in the bowels of thy mother, I knew thee, and before thou camest forth out of the womb, I sanctified thee, and made thee a prophet unto the nations.'[9] In the same way, Christian theology puts together the several

[9] Jer. i. 5.

scattered sayings of our Lord and of the Evangelists concerning him, and thus peering, as it were, through the veil which half conceals the great Forerunner of our Lord, forms to itself an idea of his perfection and of the graces vouchsafed to him to enable him to fulfil his lofty office.   Original sin, as has been said, he had, but it was washed away through the merits of our Lord at the moment of the Visitation.   His leaping in the womb for joy shows the existence of another gift, the acceleration of the full use of his reason and intellectual faculties, and a corresponding endowment of sanctifying grace and illumination.   If he was not entirely free from that infirmity of our nature which theologians call the 'fomes peccati,' at least he was always preserved from mortal sin, and confirmed in grace, though he may have been liable to imperfections and distractions not fully voluntary.   His continual growth in grace and in divine knowledge is witnessed to by St. Luke. [10]   His abstinence, mortification, and solitude were the external conditions of an existence which was in constant and close union with God, Whose Holy Spirit, rather than any outward instructor, was the teacher and guide of that privileged soul.   His great mission was one of enlightenment, [11] and so he must be supposed to have had wonderful communications of divine knowledge granted to him in his long years of preparation in the desert, because, as Suarez says, 'He was a prophet and more than a prophet, sent by God to bear witness to

---

[10] ἐκραταιοῦτο πνεύματι. St. Luke i. 80.

[11] As the *Benedictus* says, 'Ad dandam scientiam salutis plebi ejus' —and although in the following verses, the ' illuminare his qui in tenebris et in umbra mortis sedent,' etc., belongs rather to our Lord, the Ἀνατολὴ ἐξ ὕψους, still the office of St. John is spoken of as connected with and subservient to that of our Lord, and so is of the same character.

Christ. Therefore he had whatever was necessary to be a witness worthy of belief; but for this it is necessary not only to have innocence and goodness of life, but also knowledge of those things concerning which testimony is to be given. Therefore, since St. John was to bear witness concerning Christ, the kingdom of heaven, and the grace of the Holy Ghost which was to be poured out upon men, and as he was to show them the straight path to God, it was due that he should have perfect knowledge of all these things.' [12] He possessed therefore sanctifying grace in the highest degree, the infused virtues, and the gifts of the Holy Ghost. Of the graces which are known to theologians as 'gratiæ gratis datæ,' he had those which were necessary to fit him for his office, such as that of prophecy, a gift distinctly attributed to him by our Lord Himself, of interpretation of Scripture, of discernment of spirits, enabling him, not indeed to read all hearts with that clearness of sight which belongs to God, but to help those who came to him in a pre-eminent degree, as well as the faith, know-ledge, and wisdom which were among the graces re-quired by him as a teacher and preacher. Miracles, as we know, he never worked, that grace being reserved, as it seems, for our Lord, as one of the great evidences of His divine mission, to which St. John himself would refer when the time came to send his own disciples to Him. [13] And the Church has always believed that these wonderful gifts of St. John on earth corresponded to a singular exaltation of glory in heaven, enhanced by the triple *aureola* of virgin, doctor, and martyr, which he has won in so eminent a degree.

---

[12] *De Mysteriis Vitæ Christi*, Disp. xxiv. § 4. n. 5.

[13] Cf. St. Matt. xi. 2, where the words τὰ ἔργα τοῦ Χριστοῦ do not simply mean 'what Christ was doing,' but the 'wonderful works which belonged to the office of Christ.'

It is not unfrequently the way in which God proceeds in His greatest works, to employ, for missions of severity and stern witness, men who are either naturally shrinking and retiring, or whose training has been such as might seem to make the undertaking of such an enterprise as that which is committed to them uncongenial in the highest degree. We cannot tell, certainly, much of the natural dispositions of St. John Baptist, so entirely is his personal character hidden in the light of his prophetical mission. But there is a marked contrast—a contrast, however, found in other great Saints who have had work of the same kind to perform—between his more private utterances and the scorching fire of his preaching. When he has to speak of himself or to his disciples, he is the gentlest and humblest of men. We picture him to ourselves as a man of the utmost recollection, delicacy of soul, and modesty, so absorbed in God as to make it seem an effort to him to leave his contemplation. And certainly his many years of uninterrupted prayer and tranquil communing with heaven must have made it a strange task for him to undertake to preach penance and reprove vice, and spend his days in healing the wounds of the souls of one crowd of grievous sinners after another. Such, however, was the work for which the pure silent angelical life which he had led, more in heaven than on earth, prepared the Baptist. Outwardly, his power lay in the unearthly purity and majesty of grace which marked him as one far above the rest of mankind, sent on a mission of keen reproof indeed, but also of ineffable mercy. Men felt that they were in the presence of a prophet and a saint. His garb and life were alike austere, speaking of the utmost mortification and self-abnegation. 'He had a raiment of camel's hair, and a leathern girdle about his loins,' exactly as the great Elias whom he represented, 'and his food was locusts [14] and wild honey.' This was his only external sign of sanctity, entirely in harmony with the stern lesson of penance which he came to preach. But the power of his sanctity, itself the choicest gift of God, was the power which had been exercised by Elias, and to which his great achievements were due—the power of perfect self-devotion, and of prayer with God. The power of Elias was rather with God than with men, though the fruits of his power with God were for the benefit of men. St. James speaks of him as the pattern of effectual prayer, [15] and the same account is given of him in the book of Ecclesiasticus, [16] where, moreover, it is said of him, in words some of which are applied to St. John Baptist by the angel, that he is 'registered in the judgments of times to appease the wrath of the Lord, to reconcile the heart of the father to the son, and to restore the tribes of Jacob.' Such is the high and quasi-mediatorial office which is still reserved for Elias, and which was a part of the office of St. John Baptist.

This great Saint, then, so dear and so united to God, so powerful with Him by virtue of his prayers and austerities, his perfect humility and burning charity, was sent in the first place to preach two simple truths, which, when set forth by those whose character and mission give them authority, and whose labours are assisted and prospered by a large outpouring of divine grace on the souls of their hearers, are always enough to work great conversions and even lasting changes in large bodies of men. These two cognate truths were the necessity of penitence and the near approach of the

---

[14] It seems better to understand that the insects themselves, and not the fruit so called, were the food of St. John.

[15] St. James v. 17.

[16] Ecclus. xlviii. 1–10.

kingdom of God. For these were the things wanting in men's minds, without which our Lord's manifestation would have appealed to them as vainly as the warnings of the Magi or the oracles of the prophets appealed to Herod and the Chief Priests at Jerusalem—the spirit of penance, contrition, compunction, and the penetrating sense of the nearness of the unseen world and of the great account which all have to give to the coming King. Without a feeling of these truths, men's hearts are utterly hardened to all that is above or beyond the world of sense.

These truths lie at the bottom of every human conscience, though they are in some more than in others overlaid by worldliness, or by human affection, or by that ignorance of God and His truth which, in persons outside the pale of the Church and without the light of faith, often becomes almost a positive system of falsehood which stifles man's inborn instincts as to higher things. These truths lie more or less dormant in every human conscience, and the near presence of sanctity, which makes itself felt as an invisible silent power in a manner of which we can give no account, seems to quicken them into action and energy. It thrills the heart and soul as with an unearthly touch, and makes them tremble as men have trembled and cowered when angels have appeared to them. It rouses all the good elements in the soul, and disturbs and frightens all that is bad. Then, again, in the mouth of one who is closely united to God, the word of God has that power and penetrating keenness of which St. Paul speaks,[17] and there is nothing on earth more forcible than the clear, simple preaching of the great truths to which conscience bears witness, by the mouth of such a person, from whom it seems to come forth almost as a personal

[17] Heb. iv. 12.

utterance of God. And, again, it is the method which God very constantly pursues in such cases, to pour forth His graces largely on those who hear such preaching, so that such assistance on His part may almost be called a rule in His kingdom—though it is indeed only a rule the application of which depends in each case on His good pleasure, nor is it ever His wont to apply it in such a way as to do violence to the free will of those who are obstinately wedded to their worldliness or who hug the chain of shameful sins which keeps them down.

These seem to have been the elements which made the mission of St. John so wonderful and so fitting a preparation for the reception of our Lord. There are times in the experience of those who have to preach the great truths of faith to masses of men—though there may be many among the hearers who have little faith, and who come to listen either out of curiosity or to follow the crowd, and though the preachers themselves may be full of imperfections—when they feel that a large effusion of grace has been given to help them, and that the souls of men are stirred by a mighty movement towards penance and amendment which can be nothing but the working of the free mercy of God. Such seems to have been the case with large masses of the Jewish nation when St. John began to preach. The consummate sanctity, the burning words, the authority of the preacher, found a ready echo and answer in the hearts of the people, who flocked from cities and towns and villages, first to listen to the warning voice, upbraiding them with their sins, and bidding them flee from the wrath which was to come, and then to confess their sins with humble contrition and receive baptism at St. John's hands as a mark of their public profession of penance and of faith in his mission. 'Then there went forth to him all the country of Judæa, and all the people of Jerusalem, and all the region about Jordan, and were baptized by him in the river Jordan confessing their sins.' It was eminently a popular movement, but it reached to all classes. St. Matthew mentions that many of the Pharisees and Sadducees came out to St. John's baptism ; but it appears from St. Luke [18] that as a class they did not submit themselves to it. The fact that many even of the class which as such was opposed to St. John, came out to hear him, proves the universality of the movement as to the other classes, who accepted him as a prophet. This enables us to understand how it was that in the few months of his preaching and baptism he really performed the work which was committed to him, that of preparing the way for our Lord. An almost universal stir of the people in the direction of penance, humiliation, the confessing of sins, and the rite of baptism as a pledge of repentance—such was the immediate preparation which God devised for the advent of His Son.

[18] St. Luke vii. 29, 30.

CHAPTER II.

Preaching and Baptism of St. John.

St. Matt. iii. 1–12; St. Mark i. 1–8; St. Luke iii. 1–18;
Vita Vitæ Nostræ, § 16.

THE Evangelists give us an account of St. John's preaching, both general and particular—that is, as addressed to the world in general or to men of several classes in particular. The general preaching is summed up in words which are given both by St. Matthew and St. Luke, though the former tells us that they were in the first instance addressed to some of the Pharisees and Sadducees, probably taken as representatives and leaders of the rest. 'Generation or children of vipers,' the stern preacher called them, 'who hath shown you to flee from the coming wrath?' He spoke as if in surprise, and as if it were their affair rather than his, as if they had sought him out rather than he them. The crowds thronging to him could only be brought thither by a motion from God. He it must be Who had put it into their hearts to come. If their desire to escape His judgments came from God, they must take God's way of securing their safety—the way of penance, not that of reposing in foolish confidence on the external privileges of their nation as inheriting the covenant which God had made with Abraham. 'Bring forth therefore worthy fruits of penance, and do not begin to say, We have Abraham for our father: for I say to you, that God is able from these stones to raise up children to Abraham.'

It is a consequence from the fact that God has from the beginning to the end of His dealings with. mankind used the method of selecting persons, families, or nations, as the objects of particular bounties, either entirely external, or in such manner external as to convey the greatest opportunities and facilities for internal grace, that the possession of such privileges should be perversely regarded by some as a sure passport to salvation without further trouble. The Jews regarded their position as the chosen people of God and the depositaries of His truth with intense pride and self-satisfaction, and the more gross-minded among them had no idea of the spiritual needs of their souls. They looked for the Messias to come and deliver them from the Roman yoke and establish a glorious kingdom for the throne of David. But that they were in bondage to sin and had need of divine grace to turn away from their past transgressions and reconcile themselves to God, thus to save themselves from the wrath to come, was a thing which they never thought of, and in consequence they were certain not to receive the teaching which offered them such grace. This very thought against which St. John warned the Jews meets us afterwards in their dealings with our Lord.[1] He had promised them liberty through the truth. 'You shall know the truth, and the truth shall make you free.' They answered Him, 'We are the seed of Abraham, and have never been in bondage to any man : how sayest Thou, Ye shall be free?' And our Lord answered them, 'Amen, Amen, I say to you, that every one who committeth sin is the slave of sin.' It is clear that they must have thought themselves safe in this world and in the next on account of their descent from Abraham, quite apart from their personal observance of God's law—much as if Christians

[1] St. John viii. 31.

or Catholics were to think themselves safe by virtue of their baptism or their external communion with the Church, without any regard to purity of conscience. They may also have reasoned that they must be safe, because if the promise were not kept to the children of Abraham, God would have no people to call His own. St. John reminds them, in his forcible image of the stones, that the external gifts of God, however precious in themselves and in what they might lead to, might be transferred from one people to another, and that as for their descent from Abraham, God could make any whom He chose their substitutes in the privileges which that descent involved. In the judgment for which they were to prepare themselves the test would not be descent, or external position in God's kingdom, or anything else but the good or bad works which they had to show. 'For now the axe is placed at the root of the trees: every tree therefore which brings not forth good fruit, shall be cut down and cast into the fire.'

These general exhortations to penance, enforced by the authority which the great sanctity and austerity of the speaker gave to them, and brought home to each man's conscience by the abundant grace which attended on his mission, produced the fruits of compunction and contrition of heart, evidenced, as we are told by the Evangelists, in two ways: by the confession of sins, and by the reception of baptism at the hands of St. John. It would appear that the particular confession of sins was not in practice among the Jews before this time. They probably accused themselves as sinners in a general form, such as that used by the Publican in our Lord's parable.[2] Nor, of course, had the priests any power to absolve them, and the confession which they made was not made to the priests, either in general or in

[2] St. Luke xviii. 13.

particular. The words, however, in which the practice introduced by St. John is described, seem to point to the particular confession of sins. And although Christian baptism remits all sin, original or actual, whether confessed or not, it seems to have been customary for adults in the early ages of the Church to make particular confessions before receiving it.[3] And some have gathered that the confession made to St. John was particular, from the directions which he gives as to the duties of the states of the several classes who applied to him. This confession, then, was an act of great self-humiliation, and, in a great number of cases, would be blessed and rewarded by God by the gift of contrition, on which the perfect absolution of the penitent would depend, the baptism of John having no sacramental efficacy of that kind. The ceremony of baptism was not, however, a mere empty rite, for it was at the least an act of religion, in which all the penitent's interior sorrow for sin and resolutions of amendment would be gathered up and solemnly expressed, and this would in most cases imply a special gift of grace. Moreover, the reception of baptism, as administered by St. John, was a distinct profession of faith in his mission, and, as St. Paul says in the Acts,[4] of belief in 'Him Who was to come after him,' and this could not but be fruitful of grace. The rite of baptism was by no means unknown to the Jews, and seems to have been a rite used on a great many different occasions. The spiritual meaning of each was special in each, much as the 'imposition

---

[3] S. Chrysost. *Hom. in Matt.* x. 5; Cyrill. Hierosolym. (ad Catech.) *Cat.* i. § 1, 2, 5; S. Gregory Nazianzen, *Orat.* 40 *in S. Bapt.*; and Tertullian, *de Baptismo.* c. 20, speak of this confession before baptism as representing the baptism of John. See Patrizi, *in Evang.* t. iii. p. 470.

[4] Acts xix. 6.

of hands' is a general rite with various particular effects under the Gospel law.[5] Baptism was particularly used on the admission of a proselyte, after circumcision, and in this case had a special significance as implying the profession of a new religion, the entering into a covenant with God:[6] and it was supposed that it would be used for this purpose when the Messias came, according to the prophecies of Ezechiel and Zacharias.[7] On this account the administration of the rite by St. John was made a subject of question by the authorities at Jerusalem, as if it implied—as it was meant to imply—that his taking on himself to confer baptism was to assume some office belonging either to a prophet or to some one connected with the new kingdom of the Messias.[8] Thus, although the language used by St. Peter of Christian baptism,[9] which implies its sacramental effect in the remission of sins, could not be used of St. John's baptism, it was still something more than a mere ceremony, and placed those who received it in a new relation to God as prepared to receive that teaching and to enter into that new covenant for which St. John was preparing the way. And thus, again, the Evangelist speaks of the Pharisees and lawyers as 'despising the council of God in their own regard,' because they did not submit to this baptism.

Thus, at the very outset of the preaching of the new

[5] The places in which the rite is mentioned, are Lev. xiv. 8, 9 ; xv. 5, 8 ; xvi. 24, 26, 28; xvii. 15, 16; xxii. 6 ; Numb. xix. 7, 8, seq. ; Deut. xxiii. 11 ; Ecclus. xxxiv. 30 ; Exod. xxix. 4 ; xl. 12, &c. There were other 'baptisms' of the Pharisees. St. Mark vii. 10; St. Luke xi. 48.

[6] Cf. in the Old Testament, Gen. xxxv. 2, Exod. xix. 10, where something of the kind is implied.

[7] Ezech. xxxvi. 26 ; Zach. xiii. 1.

[8] St. John i. 25.

[9] Acts ii. 38. Cf. also the words of Ananias to St. Paul, as related by the latter, Acts xxii. 16.

kingdom, while as yet our Lord Himself was still keeping in the background, and living the hidden life by which He had been glorifying God for eighteen years since His first public appearance in the Temple at Jerusalem, the thoughts of men were being revealed, and men themselves divided into two camps. The humble, the penitent, those who were ready to embrace with grateful hearts the offer of better things made to them in the baptism of St. John, were ranging themselves on one side, and on the other were already found many of the men who were afterwards to become the bitter opponents and persecutors of our Lord Himself. The baptism of St. John was not obligatory as a condition to salvation, but it was the appointed symbol of that spirit of penance and contrition which was absolutely necessary in all those who were to benefit by the Gospel preaching. It was the issue and fruit of a special time of grace and visitation, a means of preparation arranged by God's Providence which could not be deliberately neglected without danger, indeed, the deliberate neglect and rejection of which showed pride and hardness of heart. There are many seasons of grace, devotions given by God at various times to the Church, calls to repentance, or preparation for death, or greater strictness of life, or particular methods of honouring Him in regard to this or that mystery, and the like, which seem to come to her children from time to time with some special mark of appropriateness or some special sanction. As to these, any singularity or isolation from the feeling which is breathed as by a heavenly instinct over the Christian community in general, is a sign of danger, secret pride, or coldness of charity. Those who hold aloof may not suffer immediately the forfeiture of any Christian grace, but the issue may show that it cannot be without great peril to their souls that they turn away from what may be as the baptism of John was, the good counsel of God in their regard.

St. Luke, who fills up the picture which has been drawn in a few strokes by St. Matthew and St. Mark, adds to the foregoing instruction of St. John the teaching which he gave by way of explanation of his own words about worthy fruits of penance. 'The multitudes asked him, saying, What then shall we do?' You speak to us of works of penance, and of the tree which brings not forth good fruit being cut down; what are the good works, the fruits of penance, which you enjoin upon us? St. John's answer, given at the very beginning of what we may call the Gospel preaching, may be compared to the wonderful description of the conditions of the future Judgment which our Lord gave in His last parable on the Mount of Olives. There He, the appointed Judge of all, speaks of nothing but works of mercy or the neglect of works of mercy as the grounds then to be given for the two different sentences of reward or punishment, and here St. John, when asked about works of penance and good fruit, speaks of charity as the one great work which he recommends. 'He answering them, said, He that hath two coats, let him give to him that hath none, and he that hath food, let him do likewise.' It is not necessary to recite here the many places in Holy Scripture in which alms-deeds are spoken of as having a special power for the satisfaction for sin. It seems as if this were the reason why they are particularly insisted upon by St. John. He, the severest and most austere of men in the treatment of his own innocent body, still does not urge the practice of penitential exercises and corporal mortification upon the crowds that came to him for advice. He taught his own disciples to fast as well as to pray, as we learn from later passages in the Gospel history : but he recommends the crowds to take up the practice of giving in alms their superfluities. So it is often found that the spiritual guides who are the strictest in the treatment of themselves are the most indulgent in dealing with others.

St. Luke gives us also two particular instances of his teaching with regard to certain classes of men. The penitential movement produced by his appearance and preaching extended, as has been said, to all sorts and conditions of persons, and among them to the despised class of the publicans, the farmers of the revenue, and the soldiers—as it seems, the soldiers in the army of Herod.[10] Each of these two classes might fairly be numbered among the most hopeless and the least religious of the community, and, as is often the case under such circumstances, each had contributed largely to the number of St. John's penitents. To each he gave, as a special instruction, the careful observance of justice in the discharge of the duties of their calling. 'Now publicans also came to be baptized, and said to him, Master, what shall we do? And he said to them, Exact nothing more than what is appointed to you. And the soldiers also asked him, And we also, what shall we do? And he saith to them, Use extortion to no one, nor accuse any one falsely,[11] and be content with your wages.' Both publicans and soldiers had many opportunities of such injustice as that here forbidden. The taxpayers and traders were very much at the mercy of the former, and the latter had it often in their power to frighten people into purchasing their silence, or to threaten them with false charges : while, on the other hand, they felt their

[10] The original word implies that they were on some active service.

[11] μηδένα διασείσητε, μηδὲ συκοφαντήσητε. The first word seems to apply to violence or threats used to extort plunder, the second to false information lodged against persons with the same ultimate object. The same word is used by Zacchæus, St. Luke xix. 8.

own power over their masters, and were often tempted either to demand an unjust increase of pay or to help themselves to whatever they might covet. St. John's instruction in each case contents itself with keeping them to their duty.

To these instructions of St. John must be added the further fact which is gathered from several passages in the Gospels, that, like the prophets of old, he had a school of more intimate disciples whom he trained in the practice of virtue, prayer, fasting, and the ascetic life more strictly so-called. They formed a distinct body even after his imprisonment, and perhaps were not altogether disbanded by his death, though we find more than one indication of his desire to pass them over to our Blessed Lord Himself, to Whom they had recourse after that final blow. That St. John retained them at all after our Lord began to preach, is a conclusive proof that there was no difference between his teaching and that of our Lord.

It remains to us now to turn our thoughts briefly to the second part of St. John's office, that of bearing witness to and even pointing out our Lord. For it was his mission not merely to prepare men's hearts generally for the reception of Jesus Christ, but still further, he had a personal office to perform to Him of so definite a character that it could be appealed to afterwards as one of the several kinds of witness which God had provided for His Incarnate Son. And this witness of his was to be so clear and undeniable, that it would be enough for our Lord to ask them whether they acknowledged the heavenly mission of the Baptist, in order to put His own questioners into an inextricable difficulty.

We may gather from St. Luke that the fact that St. John administered baptism was the main ground on which the surmise that he might himself be the Christ was founded. 'When all the people were considering, and thinking in their hearts concerning John, whether he were the Christ, he answered them, saying to all'—answering, as it seems, rather their thoughts than any direct question—'I indeed baptize you with water, but there shall come a stronger than I, of Whom I am not worthy to loose the latchet of His shoes; the same shall baptize you with the Holy Ghost and with fire; Whose fan is in His hand, and He shall purge His threshing-floor, and shall gather the wheat into His barn, but the chaff He shall burn up with unquenchable fire.'

Thus did St. John at once turn away their thoughts from himself, to Him Who was to come after him, a mightier and worthier than he. The strong parabolic or proverbial language which he had before used, now becomes personal, and he speaks of our Lord's dignity and office, not only as the baptizer with the Holy Ghost and fire, but also as the appointed Judge Who is to come a second time and cleanse His threshing-floor, gathering up the wheat into His barns, and burning the chaff. It is habitual in the prophetic writings and in the language of the saints, who speak as the prophets, that the two comings of our Lord should be blended as in one and the same image. Thus we find the prophecy of Malachias applied to St. John, the precursor of our Lord's first advent. 'Behold I send My angel, and he shall prepare the way before My face. And presently the Lord Whom you seek, and the Angel of the Testament, Whom you desire, shall come to His Temple, behold He shall come, saith the Lord of Hosts'—and immediately the prophet adds, 'And who shall be able to think of the day of His coming, and who shall stand to see Him? for he is like a refiner's fire, and like the fuller's herb.'[12]   It may indeed be said, that even in our Lord's first coming, there was an awful and searching character, as holy Simeon said when he addressed our Lady on the very occasion of the Presentation of the Child Jesus in the Temple, that He was to be for the fall and rising again of many in Israel, that the thoughts of many hearts might be revealed.   There was something terrible as well as something winning, salutary, lovely, about the near coming of One so infinitely Holy and Pure, so keen a searcher of consciences, so ineffably severe in His hatred of sin at the very time that He was full of love, gentleness, and compassion for sinners.   But it can hardly be a mistake to apply the words of St. John Baptist more directly to His second coming, especially as such is the aspect of our Lord which belongs most naturally to the preaching of penance and satisfaction.

This mingling of the two advents of our Lord in one image gives us the explanation of St. John's expression, that He is to baptize with the Holy Ghost and with fire. As he is contrasting this baptism of our Lord's with his own, which was with water, it cannot be doubted that what water was in the one baptism, that the Holy Ghost and fire were to be in the other or in the others, that is, the instruments and means of purification and change.   It is not only that men were to be baptized by our Lord in the power of the Holy Ghost.   In the Christian baptism given by our Lord, then, the Holy Ghost was to be the source of regeneration and renovation, the author of the new creation and of all the benefits which we shall see represented in the actual Baptism of our Lord Himself.   That is to be the Baptism of which in this world He is to be the minister.   And in the next world He will baptize with fire, because those who have not availed themselves of

12 Mal. iii. 1, 2.

the blessings offered by Him, those who will be as the chaff and not as the wheat in the threshing-floor, shall be burnt up in inextinguishable fire. It may also be remembered, as involved in the same interpretation, that our Lord will baptize with fire, in another sense, those whose lot is to be for a time the objects of His wrath and chastisement, inasmuch as the flames of Purgatory will be the place of the full cleansing and purification of such as belong to Him indeed by Christian baptism, but who may be found, when they stand before Him as their Judge, to have stained their robes of innocence and not sufficiently cleansed them by holy penance. In both these cases, fire will be the instrument used in the baptism, though the sinner and reprobate will be burnt in it without purification, while those who are in His grace will find in it their perfect cleansing and restoration to spiritual health and beauty.

NOTE I.

On the Baptism by fire.

The interpretation which is given above of the difficult expression of St. John, is that maintained by Toletus in his work on St. Luke, *ad loc*, and is supported by St. Basil, St. Hilary, and St. John Damascene. The modification of this opinion by the addition of the application to Purgatory has also considerable support among Christian writers. There are several other opinions. According to some, tribulations, afflictions, and even martyrdom endured for the sake of our Lord, are signified by the baptism of fire, and it is certain that martyrdom was anciently called a baptism of blood, and sometimes a baptism of fire (see Mazochi's *Spicilegium Biblicum*, t. iii. on this place, as well as his dissertation on the baptism of blood, on St. Mark x. 48). It may be remembered that one very probable interpretation of the difficult words of St. Paul about the practice of 'baptism' for the dead (1 Cor. xv. 29) is that which understands the word to speak of penance, sufferings, and the like, endured as satisfaction for the dead. It is certain that the words 'baptism,' 'baptize,' are used in more than one sense in the New Testament, as when our Lord tells the Apostles, speaking of the day of Pentecost, 'You shall be baptized with the Holy Ghost not many days hence' (Acts i. 5); or when He says to the sons of Zebedee, 'Can you drink the chalice which I drink, or be baptized with the baptism with which I am baptized?' (St. Mark x. 38); or, again, of Himself, uniting the two ideas of fire and baptism, (St. Luke xii. 49, 50): 'I am come to cast fire upon the earth, and what will I, but that it be kindled, and I have a baptism, wherewith I am to be baptized, and how am I straitened until it be accomplished?' There are other interpretations also, understanding the 'fire' to refer to the tongues of fire seen on the Apostles at the Day of Pentecost, of the fire, fervour, charity, and zeal kindled by the Holy Ghost in the heart, or of the efficacy of divine grace ; and, lastly, the two expressions, Holy Ghost and fire, are taken simply for the fire of the Holy Ghost. It must be noted, in conclusion, that St. Mark, who, alone of the three Evangelists who mention these words of St. John, leaves out the image of the fan and the purging of the floor, also leaves out the mention of fire in connection with baptism, simply saying, He shall baptize you with the Holy Ghost. It would seem, therefore, that there is an antithesis carried out in both clauses, as given by St. Matthew and St. Luke, and that the baptism in the Holy Ghost and the baptism in fire are contrasted one to the other in the first clause, in the same way as the gathering of the wheat into the barns is contrasted with the burning up of the chaff in the second clause. On this account, among others, the interpretation given above seems, on the whole, to be preferred to the rest.

CHAPTER III.

Baptism of our Lord.

St. Matt. iii. 13–17 ; St. Mark i. 9–11 ; St. Luke iii. 21–23;
Vita Vitæ Nostræ, § 17.

THE preaching and baptism of St. John had continued, as it seems, for several months, and must have moved a large portion of the Jewish nation, at all events to a temporary return to God from sin, and to a more eager expectation of the coming Messias, of whom the Baptist had spoken so plainly. Powerful as was the impulse given by St. John to all the better and higher elements in the public mind, he was yet in great measure and professedly only a teacher who was preparing the way for One greater than himself, by the perfect innocence and lofty purity of his example, as well as by his preaching of penance and administration of baptism. The expectation and longing desire of so many souls was now to be answered, but in the way which characterises the great works of God. There was to be a great manifestation, and yet it was to be a manifestation which it required purity of heart and a discernment of spiritual greatness to recognise : a manifestation which, like those which had preceded it in the economy of the Incarnation, was to be addressed to those only who could, to some extent, weigh things in the scales of heaven. St. Paul more than once speaks as if it were the counsel of God that the mysteries of our Lord and of His Church should be unfolded before the angels for their wonder and instruction as much as, if not more than, to men,[1] and we may certainly believe that the true greatness and magnificence of the manifestation which was now to take place on the banks of Jordan, were far more truly understood and adored by the angels who witnessed the mystery than by any others, unless we except the blessed Baptist himself, who was the minister in this great work of God.

Holy contemplative souls have often loved to dwell on the leave-taking which passed between our Lord and His Blessed Mother at Nazareth, when the moment had come at which it was the will of the Father that Jesus Christ should take His departure from the home where He had so long dwelt in humility, obedience, and obscurity. Our Lady was now alone; her Blessed Spouse had some time before breathed out his soul in the arms of Jesus, and with Mary praying by his side, dying the most blessed of deaths, and winning, by his perfect resignation to the sacrifice entailed on him by such a parting, the prerogative which belongs to him in the Church as the patron and father of all holy deaths. Many of our Lady's relations lived in Nazareth, and it seems as if that family of cousins of our Lord, who go in the New Testament by the name of His brethren, either now or before this had come to live with her or near her. What we know about her at the departure of our Lord rests upon the pious instincts of the Christian imagination as well as on the theological belief of all ages as to our Blessed Lady's consummate perfection of sanctity, and the absolute union of her will with that of God. But on neither ground are we to conclude that the separation was not a matter of intensest pain, or that our Lady's heart was steeled against the suffering natural on losing the

[1] 1 Tim. iii. 16. ὤφθη ἀγγέλοις. Eph. iii. 10.

constant companionship of a Son between Whom and herself there was a bond of love, the tenderness of which was in proportion to the sanctity and lovableness of both, or against the apprehension of what might happen when He was exposed to the rude indifference of men who knew Him not.   Now was the time for the fulfilment of Simeon's prophecy of the sword which should pierce her heart, or rather that prophecy had already had its fulfilment in anticipation when our Lord had remained alone in the Temple.   The three days during which our Lord had left her when He was a lad of twelve years, had prepared her for this parting. The three days were to become three years—not indeed of separation, for she was constantly with Him, and her heart was most closely united to His—and then she was to see Him, not in the full beauty and vigour of perfect manhood, passing with grave joy along the path over the hills which led towards the Jordan valley, but hanging in the agony of death and in the extremest dishonour and suffering upon the Cross, which was the instrument of the redemption of the world.

'Bethany,[2] beyond Jordan,' the spot where St. John was baptizing, seems to have been near the fords by which travellers passed from the eastern bank to the neighbourhood of Jericho, on their way to Jerusalem. As this was the common and easiest route even from Galilee, and much more from Peræa, to Jerusalem, it was a convenient spot for the multitudes who came to St. John from all parts, as we cannot doubt, though the Evangelists speak directly of Jerusalem and the region of Judæa only.

[2] Bethany, the reading of the Vulgate, is now generally received as the better reading on the authority of the uncial manuscripts. The meanings of Bethany and Bethabara—which used to be the received name—apply equally well to the place, as the first is 'the house of the ship,' or ferry-boat, the other ' the house of the ford.'

From what we know of the disciples of St. John, among whom were numbered many who had certainly come to him from the distant part of the Holy Land in which Nazareth lies, we gather that the fame of the new preacher had reached Galilee, and that our Lord may not have been alone in the pilgrimage to the Jordan. The Evangelist speaks as if He approached the Baptist in the midst of the crowd. He presented Himself, like any one else, but the spiritual discernment of St. John at once recognised Him, 'I have need to be baptized by Thee! and dost Thou come to me? But Jesus answering, said to him, Suffer it now; for thus doth it become us to fulfil all justice. Then he suffered Him.'

St. John's perfect intelligence concerning the dignity of Him who thus came to receive baptism at his hands cannot be questioned. The words show that he recognised the universal necessity of the baptism which our Lord was to establish and administer—a necessity arising out of the positive arrangement of God, as well from the immense spiritual benefits which He had attached to Christian baptism as their ordinary and appointed vehicle. St. John had been sanctified and filled with the Holy Ghost even in his mother's womb, but this did not exempt him from the general law as to baptism. We may notice also the modesty and gentleness of his humility, remonstrating with our Lord rather by a simple question than in the abrupt, positive manner afterwards used by St. Peter when he refused to let our Lord wash his feet at the Last Supper. Nothing more was required to make him yield to perform an office in itself so repugnant to his knowledge of his own lowliness and of the high dignity of our Lord, than the simple words which the latter addressed to him. 'Suffer it now! it is true, as thou sayest, that I have to baptize thee, that I am above thee and before thee, that thou art My

minister, and that any rite or gift that confers or represents sanctification ought to pass from Me to thee and
not from thee to Me. It is true that I am He that
baptizeth in the Holy Ghost, and that thou must be
made partaker of My baptism. But this which thou art
to do is what is becoming and right in order that we
may fulfil all justice—that nothing may be omitted which
perfect obedience to My Father and the practice of
perfect virtue under our circumstances make requisite.'

The baptism of St. John was, as we have seen, an
ordinance of God, an arrangement of His providence
with special reference to the dispensation of the Incarnation and of the redemption of the world thereby.
It was right, therefore, that all reverence should be
shown to it, and that as our Lord had humbled Himself
to undergo the rite of circumcision, to be presented in
the Temple, and there redeemed by an offering, so He
should also honour the appointment of the Father by
the devout reception of the baptism of St. John. If it
had led to nothing and implied nothing but itself still,
as the ordinance of God, it deserved reverence, and it
became all to receive it. When anything of the kind
springs up in the Church or in the order of Providence,
we are not to inquire whether we ourselves have special
need of it, or whether it is a matter of obligation, but
only whether the simple truth, that it comes, even
indirectly, from God, and has become for the time a part
of the system, or at least a thing in accordance with the
spirit, of the Church, which is His Spouse, does not
make it unfitting for us to hold ourselves aloof from it.

In the second place, our Lord, by receiving circumcision, and by the other legal observances and ceremonies
which He allowed to be performed in His regard, sanctioned and blessed them, and imparted to them, as it
were by His own touch—the touch of the Incarnate

Godhead—whatever power of sanctification, of conjunction with God, of remission of sins, and the like, which they possessed.   So also by receiving in His own Person the baptism of St. John, He gave to it from Himself the power, not indeed to act as a Christian sacrament, but to be the occasion of grace, reconciliation, sanctification, to those who had received it, or might receive it, in the dispositions which are the conditions of such spiritual benefits.   In this sense, again, it was a part of the fulfilment of perfect justice that He should receive that baptism, for it was His mission and work to be the source and fountain of all means and occasions of grace to the children of Adam from the beginning to the end of time.

In the third place, our Lord was about to begin the work of teaching, and take upon Himself the Evangelical and Apostolical functions of His ministry as the Master as well as the Redeemer of mankind.   And it was and is the will and the rule of God that all teaching must be begun and founded in humiliation, as the means and safeguard of that humility, without which no one can be trusted by God with any commission to work for His glory.   But the receiving of the baptism of His Forerunner was a great and further act of humiliation on the part of our Blessed Lord.   In His Circumcision and in His Presentation in the Temple He had gone through certain rites and observances, the significance of which was that He was to pay the penalty of original sin, although no such stain could possibly fall upon Him. But by receiving the baptism of St. John He went still further, because that baptism was a public profession and confession that His state was that of an actual sinner. It implied that He had sins to confess and penance to do, whereas He had indeed penance to do and sins to confess, but they were the sins of the whole world, not

His own, and their chastisement and penance were to be upon Him. And as there is always to be the closest union between our Lord Himself and all those who in any way or measure have to carry on in the Church and to share His holy work of teaching mankind, He was, in this mystery, both setting them the example of the constant uniform practice of self-humiliation as the fit and appointed preparation for the exercise of such functions, and also blessing their humiliations, in His own, strengthening them and giving them virtue thereby, making them the occasions and conditions of success and of exaltation to be granted them on the part of His Father, and warning all that they must never shrink from such, as if the authority of a teacher and his fruitfulness in teaching could ever suffer thereby. These are some of the reasons for this action of our Lord, considered in itself as an act of simple humiliation, in obedience to what at that time was the arrangement of His Father's Providence.

But the Baptism of our Lord had also another aspect. It was not merely that He received the baptism of St. John as He received the rite of circumcision, which was to be entirely done away with under the New Law. He was to take up the rite which St. John had adopted as the symbol of his mission and as a profession of penitence and faith, and make it into a Christian sacrament, and that sacrament the most fundamental and essential of all. And this was to be done at the moment when He Himself was to be solemnly and manifestly anointed for his own office as Redeemer and Prophet. Thus, in the Christian scheme our Lord's Baptism has a twofold character, as it refers to Himself and as it refers to the work which He came to do and the kingdom which He came to found. The description given by the Evangelists refers principally to the first part of this twofold aspect: the writings of the Apostles and the theology of the Church instruct us as to the second.

The accounts given by the Evangelists, when they are put side by side, tell us three principal things concerning this mystery. In the first place, we are told that at the time of His Baptism ('while He was praying,' St. Luke adds, in accordance with one of the leading ideas of his Gospel), our Lord, 'as He was going up straight out of the water,' beheld the heavens opened; 'the heavens were opened unto Him.' Secondly, 'He saw the Holy Ghost descending in bodily form like a dove, and abiding on Him.' Thirdly, a Voice came from heaven, 'Thou art My Beloved Son, in Thee I am well pleased.' These then are the features in this mystery, on which Christian contemplation must feed itself.

The opening of the heavens is said by the Evangelists to have been seen by our Lord; but this, as well as the visible descent of the Holy Ghost and the Voice from heaven, may have been perceptible to others also, as we certainly know to have been the case, at least as to the descent of the Holy Ghost, with St. John himself. The other manifestations must be understood as implying each a particular spiritual truth with regard to our Lord's office in the kingdom of God. To His beatified Soul the heavens were always open: He was always living in the full possession of the vision of God, nor could heaven ever have been closed to Him from the moment of the Hypostatic Union. The opening of the heavens must therefore be considered either as a manifestation of what always had been the case, and of this He Himself, to Whom the manifestation was primarily made, could have had no need. Or it must have had reference to some power and privilege conferred upon Him with reference to the office which He was then taking upon Himself, and thus there would be a reason why such a visible declaration should have been made at that time. His Sacred Humanity was the connecting link between heaven and earth : there could no longer be any division, any shutting out from the earth of the sight of heaven, when God was Incarnate upon earth, and a human soul and body personally united with the Godhead. There had been a vision of old of one of the ancestors of our Lord, in which a ladder had been seen reaching from earth to heaven, and making a pathway along which the angels of God passed to and fro, ascending with prayers from earth and descending from heaven with blessings. Such a ladder our Lord soon after this time declared that He the Son of Man was to become : 'Ye shall see the heavens opened, and the angels of God ascending and descending upon the Son of Man' as upon the ladder of Jacob. This union of the two natures in His Divine Person is the foundation of the other mysteries which were sensibly represented in the further unfolding of this wonderful manifestation. The Humanity of Jesus Christ opens heaven, not to Himself alone, but to all those to whom the fruits of the Incarnation are communicated by the exercise of His Mediatorial Office.

The descent of the Holy Ghost in a visible shape upon Him was a manifestation of the same kind as the opening of the heavens. From the first moment of the Union, the Soul of Jesus Christ had been filled to overflowing and without measure by the Holy Ghost. It was not possible that this fulness could be increased at any time, any more than that it could begin at any moment later than that of the Union or ever cease. But here again, without being merely a manifestation, symbolising what always had been the rich endowments of His Soul, the visible appearance of the Holy Ghost at this moment signified that the anointing and consecration of our Lord had been for the special purpose of the office of which He was now about to undertake the external functions. 'Jesus of Nazareth, how God anointed Him with the Holy Ghost and with power,' were the words in which St. Peter afterwards spoke of our Lord and His word to the first Gentile converts.[3] This was the visible fulfilment in Him of the twofold prophecy of Isaias,[4] that the 'Spirit of the Lord should rest upon Him, the spirit of wisdom and understanding, the spirit of counsel and fortitude, the spirit of knowledge and piety, and He shall be filled with the spirit of the fear of the Lord,' and that other which He Himself quoted in the synagogue at Nazareth, 'the Spirit of the Lord is upon Me, because the Lord hath anointed Me, He hath sent Me to preach to the meek,' and the rest. This descent of the Holy Ghost represents that fulness of His of which we have all received, the grace first bestowed upon Him in order that from Him it may overflow to all others who are joined to Him. And the outward form of the dove seems to have represented the tenderness, simplicity, and gentleness, which are the characteristic qualities of the dispensation of the Incarnation and of the first advent.

The Voice from heaven which declared our Lord to be the well-beloved Son of the Eternal Father, in Whom He was well pleased, did not of course confer any new Sonship or adoption upon our Blessed Lord. As to this again, all had been perfectly accomplished at the moment of the Hypostatic Union, when the human nature was assumed by the Son of God. What took place now was a solemn declaration of His Sonship, but a solemn declaration which was at the same time the inauguration of His Office as Mediator, whereby He was to be the author and giver of the adoption of sons to those who

---

[3] Acts x. 38.   [4] Isaias xi. and lxi.

belong to Him.   'For to as many as received Him, to them gave He power (authority[5]) to become the sons of God,' the Eternal Sonship was communicated to them in such way as it was possible for it to be communicated. He imparted to them His own relationship to the Father in such a manner as it is possible for sons of adoption to share that filiation.   Thus, to open heaven to mankind by means of His own Humanity, to be anointed with the fulness of the Holy Ghost as the Head of mankind, the new Adam, the source from which the graces of the Holy Ghost were to be communicated to men, and to place them in the dignity of the relation of sons to the Eternal Father, were three prerogatives of His mediatorial office which were solemnly confessed, manifested, and proclaimed in the mystery of His Baptism.

This manifestation of the dignity of His Humanity is considered by many holy writers as corresponding to the great humiliation by which our Lord lowered Himself, as has already been said, in submitting to seek baptism at the hands of His Forerunner—as if in this too were fulfilled the saying of St. Paul to the Philippians,[6] that inasmuch as 'He humbled Himself, being made obedient,' therefore hath God highly exalted Him.   And the Fathers remark, both that our Lord always signally humbled Himself before any great stage or act of His Ministry, and that the Father in His Providence always answered such humiliation by a great exaltation.

It remains to point out the further significance of the several parts of the mystery of our Lord's Baptism in relation to the sacrament which He was now to institute as the fundamental source of grace in the Church.   In the first place, the Fathers tell us that in His own Baptism He sanctified the element of water that it might become in His own sacrament the instrument

---

[5] ἐξουσίαν.   St. John i. 12.   [6] Philip. ii. 9.

of that regeneration and of that adoption of sons which were to be conferred upon mankind. Thus they say that the old Adam was buried in the waters of His Baptism, which, as Suarez explains, may be understood in three ways. For that mystery was a representation and figure, showing how human nature was to be washed from sin in Christ and through Christ. Again, the merit of the humiliation which our Lord then underwent was applied to the destruction of the sins of mankind, which were thus, as it were, buried in the waters of Jordan. And lastly, as has been said, our Lord then gave to the waters the power of sacramentally healing and cleansing our poor human nature, the old Adam, which is thus buried, as St. Paul says, together with sin by baptism unto death. Again, the sacrament of regeneration, which by the institution of our Lord is to be accomplished in the name of the Father, the Son, and the Holy Ghost, was founded and instituted at the moment of this great manifestation, in which the Three Persons of the Ever Blessed Trinity were each singly revealed, the Father in the Voice from heaven, the Son in the Person of our Blessed Lord Himself, declared to be so by the Voice of the Father, and the Holy Ghost in the visible appearance of the dove. Again, the threefold privilege which is attributed in this mystery to the Sacred Humanity of our Lord, as has been pointed out above, is as it were stored up in the Sacrament of Baptism as the means of grace by which that privilege is conveyed. For in it men are admitted again to have access to heaven, and are indeed made its heirs; they are enriched in their new birth with the gifts and presence of the Holy Ghost, and they are made the children and the sons of God the Father. Thus in this mystery we have both the meritorious cause, and the form, and the matter, and the effects and fruits of the great sacrament of regeneration set forth and manifested—that is, the action and Person of our Blessed Lord, the invocation of the Three Divine Persons, the water sanctified by our Lord's touch, and the threefold privilege which has already been named more than once.

It is, moreover, the doctrine of many of the Fathers that the great Sacrament of Baptism was at this time not only virtually and meritoriously established, but also positively instituted by our Lord. For, they say, a sacrament may be established by act as well as by word, and there is a clear analogy between this mystery and that of the Last Supper in this respect, that in each our Lord did two things: first, He approved and sanctioned what was old and figurative, that is, the legal Paschal supper in the one case and the baptism of St. John in the other; and, secondly, He established what was new and true and far more perfect, that is, in the one case, the Sacrament of His own Precious Body and Blood, and in the other the Sacrament of Baptism. Moreover, it seems clear that Christian baptism began to be administered very early in our Lord's teaching, and indeed soon after this, and from this it is gathered that it must have been already instituted. And it could at no time have been more fittingly instituted than at this. It must, however, be understood, that the obligation to Baptism as the door to the kingdom of heaven and the means of admission to the blessings of the Christian covenant, and of regeneration in particular, did not become obligatory on men until after our Lord's Ascension into heaven and the descent of the Holy Ghost on the Day of Pentecost.

It is clear from the words of the Baptist to his disciples shortly after this, that he at least, as has been said, saw the visible sign of the descent of the Holy Ghost upon our Lord in the form of a dove, and we

may thus fairly presume that he heard the Voice of
the Father, and saw the heavens opened. And yet it
seems also to be the truth, that these marvellous signs
were lost upon the great mass of the bystanders, and
the whole manifestation passed away without leaving any
great impression upon the multitude to whom it yet was
of so transcendent an importance. The silence and
outward hiddenness which shroud so many of the
great acts of God, had their place in some measure
here, although the whole scene was essentially a manifestation, and a manifestation which was the object and
end of the baptism of St. John, as he said himself,
'that He may be made manifest in Israel, therefore
am I come baptizing in water.'[7] And yet we cannot
contemplate the Baptism of our Lord without being
struck with the magnificence and grandeur of the manifestation. It was no longer a star in heaven, testifying
to the homage which the visible creation owed to its
Master, Who had now become a creature, nor were the
voices of the angels heard, to show that they too owned
allegiance to the Child of Bethlehem. The shepherds
and kings, who were His earliest earthly visitors, the
ancient oracles of the prophecies which were consulted
and gave so true an answer as to the place of His Birth,
were as nothing compared to the witnesses who here
testified to the dignity of the Lord of the new Creation.
The scene was thronged with penitent crowds, the
saint higher in office than all the prophets of the Old
Testament stood by our Lord's side, the appointed
minister of the holy rite which was made the occasion
of so great a display of supernatural majesty. Never
since the beginning of time had the Three Divine
Persons manifested themselves so clearly, never had
Man been so solemnly proclaimed as the beloved

[7] St. John i. 31.

Son of God, never had benefits so immense been conferred on the human race as those which, as has been seen, were then granted to it through and in Jesus Christ, and represented by the circumstances of the manifestation itself.

Henceforth the earthly Life of our Blessed Lord becomes distinctly the Life of the Anointed One, the Messias, the Christ. Mystery after mystery is now to succeed, manifesting and exercising the attributes and prerogatives which belong to Him by virtue of that unction which is here sensibly represented. The whole Public Life is founded on the mystery of the Baptism. Its culminating point, in which it issues in the foundation of the Church, which, in a certain sense, is a continuation of our Lord's Life on earth, is the confession by St. Peter of his faith in that declaration concerning our Lord which is here made by the Voice of the Father, and in which St. Peter answers in the name of all, 'Thou art the Christ, the Son of the living God.' And the final act of our Lord, in regard to the application to the world of all that He had done and suffered, is His commission to the Apostles to 'go and teach all nations, baptizing them in the name of the Father, and of the Son, and of the Holy Ghost.'

CHAPTER III.

Fasting of our Lord.

St. Matt. iv. 1 ; St. Mark i. 12, 13; St. Luke iv. 1 ; *Vita Vitæ Nostræ*, § 18.

IMMEDIATELY after the great mystery of His Baptism, our Lord, as the three Evangelists tell us, entered into the desert, and was there tempted by the deviL The language used by the Evangelists is very remarkable, inasmuch as they all expressly state that this withdrawal into the desert was made under the special direction of the Holy Ghost, Who guided the Sacred Humanity of our Blessed Lord in all the steps of His Life in accordance with the will of His Eternal Father. St. Matthew tells us that Jesus 'was led into the desert by the Spirit ;' St. Mark uses a stronger word, and says that immediately 'the Spirit cast Him forth' into the desert, and St. Luke says that our Lord returned from the Jordan full of the Holy Ghost, and was 'driven by the Spirit' into the wilderness for forty days and forty nights. As there never was a time at which the blessed Soul of our Lord was not under the special direction of the Holy Ghost, it is natural to suppose that it is meant that on this occasion, as on others when similar language is used, some very extraordinary instinct suggested this particular step, which might not have been taken but for that instinct.

Many reasons may be assigned, in harmony with the usual dictates of Christian prudence, why, at this conjuncture, our Lord should ·have retired from the Jordan. He was about to begin His great work as the Teacher of mankind, and He had inaugurated it, as we may say, by a very signal act of humility in seeking for baptism at the hands of St. John, as has been seen in the foregoing chapter. But as was so often the case, this self-humiliation had been met and crowned, in the Providence of His Father, by a far more signal exaltation, for the heavens had been opened to Him, the Holy Ghost had descended and remained upon Him, and the voice of His Father had been heard, declaring Him to be the Son of His love and predilection. After this, it was natural for our Lord, in His constant practice of the most exquisite and consummate humility, to wish to withdraw from a spot in which He had no longer any occasion to remain, and where so striking a manifestation of His dignity and excellence had been made. Such must also have been His desire for the sake of the Apostolical life which He was now beginning and founding for those who were to come after Him, for which nothing can be more injurious or dangerous than applause, honour, and the like, so that Apostolic men are ever desirous to leave the spots where they have had great success, unless indeed, it is for the greater glory of God and greater service to souls that they should remain there.

Again, our Lord may have now desired to commence His active life by a long season of rigorous fasting, of uninterrupted prayer and communion with His Father, for which purpose no place could be better fitted than the wilderness into which He retired. Certainly, there can be no doubt that the long years of the Hidden Life had been years of preparation and forecasting to the Sacred Heart of our Lord, as to the work which He came to do and the kingdom which He was com-

missioned to found. Still, as we have considered the
mystery of the Baptism as the solemn inauguration of
our Lord in His mediatorial office, as the beginning
and foundation of the new order of things which was to
arise from the Incarnation, it is natural to see in the
retirement for the purposes of prayer and fasting which
immediately followed it a more special devotion of
Himself on the part of our Lord to immediate preparation for the work which He was now actually to
take in hand. There was another period like to this
in our Lord's sojourn upon earth before His Ascension,
a period also of forty days, during which His main
occupation, as far as it is revealed to us, was the consoling, strengthening, and conversing with the friends
whom He was to leave behind Him to carry out the
work of the foundation of His Church, and 'speaking
of the kingdom of God.' There may perhaps have
been something parallel to His occupation in those
last forty days, in the preparation for the immediate
work of the three years of His Public Life which our
Lord may be thought to have made during the forty
days' retirement in the wilderness. Now, however, He
was conversing with His Father alone, and negotiating,
if we may use an expression found in some holy writers,
the great business of His preaching, the formation of
His disciples, His miracles, His dealings with and
attitude towards the authorities at Jerusalem and the
people at large, as well as with those single souls whom
He already counted as His own, whom His Father was
to draw to Him, and of whom He was to make the
future princes and apostles of His kingdom. We shall
find our Lord more than once retiring, in the midst of
His active work, to spend the night in 'the prayer of
God,' as the Evangelist calls it, and these occasions
are usually connected with the taking of some step in

advance in the formation of His Church, the fore-shadowing of some great sacrament, and the like. And here again we may see that our Lord would also desire to set an example of such retirement and preparation to those who were to follow Him in the same sort of work for God, as Moses and Elias had shared in the same work in their day, and prefigured His fast and solitude. In the Old Testament, as well as in the history of the Church, those have been the most powerful instruments for good in the work of the con-version of souls or of the advancement of the glory of God in other ways, who have spent a long time in retirement, and who come forth from the wilderness or the cloister fresh, as it were, from long solitude, penance, and prayer. Such was the training even of St. Paul, who spent three years in Arabia before he began his Apostolic career, such that of St. Benedict and St. Ignatius, and of thousands of others who have followed in the footsteps of our Lord in this respect. And it may be fairly said that no activity, in the way of preaching or working, no close and familiar dealing with the souls of men, have any real strength, or stability, or blessing, unless they be well founded on that union with God and that elevation above earthly things which are the fruits of long solitary and penitential prayer, and unless, either virtually or actually, they are prepared beforehand.

And, once more, our Lord may have intended, not merely that the benefit of His own example and of the strength which He left behind Him for His children in whatever holy practice or counsel which He adopted, should be won for those who were to follow Him as preachers of God's Word and teachers in His Church, but also that all those who were to belong to Him might be instructed to attach a very high value to the exercises of prayer, contemplation, and self-mortification, whatever might be the line of life in which they were to have to imitate His virtues. In particular, we can hardly help seeing that our Lord was here taking possession, as we may say, and blessing by His own contact, both of the solitary eremitical life in general, whether it be practised perpetually or only for a time and occasionally, and of those most famous deserts which were in after ages of the Church to be peopled with Christian solitaries and ascetics. All of these must have looked to the mystery of His fasting and sojourn in the wilderness as one of those points in His Divine Life upon earth which were at once the example, the sanction, and the strength of that kind of service to which they were themselves to be impelled by the guidance of the Holy Ghost. Thus the desert, as well as the Christian home, the cave or cell of the solitary ascetic, as well as churches or crowded cities, have been blessed by the footprints of our Divine Lord, and in each of the varied paths along which His children have to walk, secular as well as religious, ecclesiastics as well as laymen, those who live the common life as well as those who are called to the state of perfection, or the observance of the Evangelical counsels, or who have some of the more extraordinary vocations of which the history of the Church affords us so many instances,—all are able to encourage themselves by the thought that His pattern is before them, and that each particular lot out of the whole multitude has His blessing and His grace.

And again, the holy weapon of fasting, which from the beginning of time had been used by the servants of God and enjoined at certain special times by the Synagogue as a part of public religion, was now to be taken up and sanctified by our Lord in His own Person, that He might hand it over with His blessing and strength upon it to His Church. In her system the sacred season of Lent was to become a perpetual ordinance in honour of these forty days of His retirement, and there were to be other holy seasons and days spent in the same observance, which her children were to practise continually along with their prayers and almsdeeds, according to His own precept given in the Sermon on the Mount. All the countless privileges and graces which are connected with this blessed practice and others which resemble it in their effects, the satisfaction for sins, the repression of all that is vicious, the elevation of the mind to God, the impetration of virtue and grace and of spiritual rewards—all these have their source in the fasting of our Lord, and it was to secure them all to us that He undertook this long and rigorous fast of His own. In our prayers, in our good works, in our sufferings, we are to look to Him, and so also are we to do the same in our fastings and penances. It was not to be the order of the Providence of His Father that in His Public Life He should be conspicuous for austerity or penance or solitude, as His Forerunner had been. For our Lord was to make Himself the companion of all, to condescend to ordinary modes of life, and to hide all that might seem severe or scare away sinners from His burning and most tender love. But fasting, penance, mortification, and austerity were to have their part in the system which He was to introduce : the children of the bride-chamber were to mourn when the Bridegroom was taken from them,[1] and therefore in this, as in everything else, He was to go before them.

Two circumstances are added by the Evangelists in their statements concerning this retirement of our Lord which serve to make more complete the picture which they set before us. St. Luke tells us that our Lord

[1] St. Matt. ix. 15.

'ate nothing' during the forty days, which may, perhaps, be intended to signify that His fast was a perfect natural fast, as had been the fasts of Moses and Elias, and not only an ecclesiastical fast, which permits of some sort of refection at a certain time in the day and of a certain kind. The other circumstance is mentioned by St. Mark, that our Lord 'was with the wild beasts,' and this seems meant to show how entirely He was cut off from the haunts of men and without shelter of any kind, such as might have been open to Him in the few huts or cottages which might have been found in the less entirely wild parts of the country called the desert of Judæa. He had never hitherto been away from the care of Mary and the home at Nazareth, and now His abode was in one of the caves in the wild and almost inaccessible mountain which still keeps the name given to it in commemoration of His sojourn there.[2] And ' He was with the wild beasts '—renewing, as it appears, that peaceful companionship with and dominion over the animals which Adam enjoyed in Paradise, which he had lost through his self-indulgence, and which our Lord, therefore, resumed, at the time of His fasting, as the Lord of the new Creation. For the consequences of the Fall extended both to the brute creation and the physical universe, as St. Paul tells us, and the redemption and renovation of all things by our Blessed Lord are to reach as far as and further than the fruits of the sin of Adam.

---

[2] Djebel Kourontoul (Quarantana). M. l'Abbé Verrier (*Journal d'un Pèlerin*, t. ii. p. 78) speaks of the chapels—now in ruins—which mark the traditional spots of our Lord's fasting and temptation as very difficult of access.

CHAPTER IV.

Temptations of our Lord.

St. Matt. iv. 2–10; St. Mark i. 13; St. Luke iv. 2–12;
Vita Vitæ Nostræ, § 18.

THESE, as we have seen, are reasons for the retirement into the desert which may be considered as general in character, and as suggested by what may be called the ordinary maxims of spiritual prudence. But holy writers have seen in the strong expressions of the Evangelists of which mention has already been made, an intimation that our Lord was now guided, as has been said, rather by an extraordinary and singular movement of the Holy Ghost than by more usual motives, and they have connected the mention of such a movement with that which is also assigned by the Evangelists as the particular end of His retirement into the desert, that is, 'that He might be tempted of the devil.' For He Who has taught us to pray that our Heavenly Father may not lead us into temptation, and Who has given us so many holy warnings about the avoidance of all that may be an occasion of sin to ourselves, may have wished us to understand, that although temptations are inevitable, although we are not to be surprised at them or fear them, or even be sorry for them when they come to us unsought, although we are to resist the devil and he will flee from us, and the like, still we are not to seek them out and, as it were, go forth to defy the devil and try our strength with him, unless it be under some very special and extraordinary impulse from the Holy Ghost, the guide of our souls. Theologians are wont to distinguish between various motive powers for good and holy actions, some of which proceed from the ordinary use of reason, some from the principles of an acquired or infused virtue, as temperance, courage, faith, or hope, while others are caused by the special influence of the gifts of the Holy Ghost—wisdom, understanding, counsel, fortitude, and the rest.[1] And it certainly belonged to our Lord as a part of His special office, in the carrying out of the dispensation of the Incarnation and of the Redemption of mankind as to the second Adam, to fight with and overcome the great enemy of the human race, whose wiles had seduced our first parents, and whose temptations have ever since been the chief occasions of the sins of their children. It was therefore a work, not of ordinary Christian virtue, or even one in which all Christians would be called upon to imitate our Lord, willingly to undertake such a conflict. This doctrine of the special guidance and impulse of the Holy Ghost, does not of course exclude the truth that this conflict of Satan was willingly undertaken by the Sacred Humanity of our Lord, Who would have seen in it no danger to Himself, and on the other hand immense glory to His Father, wonderful benefit to mankind, and a great humiliation and confusion to the enemy both of God and man.[2]

We are thus led to consider the temptation of our Blessed Lord as one of those great mysteries of His Life which are for ever to be commemorated and honoured and contemplated in the Church, and from which we are to derive continual strength and support, light, and

[1] See St. Thomas 2. 2æ, q. 52, art. 1, and Lanuza, *Serm. in 1 Dom. Quadrag.*

[2] See Suarez, *De Mysteriis*, disp. xxix. 1, 6.

life. We are taught to consider it as one of the great actions which belonged to Him in the character, as we have said, of the second Adam, the new Head of our race, the first-born of the new creation. All through the mysteries of the Incarnation and of our Redemption, there runs a perpetual reference to the history of man in his original condition in Paradise, and our Lord is continually doing this or that, or suffering this or that, which is a counterpart to something which is found in the history of Adam. In the present case it is obvious that as Satan had tempted our first parents in Paradise, and as this temptation of and victory over them had been the turning-point in their history, and in the history of their race, so it was right and fitting that the second Adam should also fight with and overcome the same adversary, and that by means of His victory the race of which He was the Head should win blessings and crowns which might more than compensate for the losses which they had incurred by the weakness of Adam and Eve. Thus the outset of the new dispensation is marked by a triumph of Man, as the outset of the history of the human race had been marked by a triumph of Satan.

Another consideration which we find in the Fathers is somewhat different from this, namely, that as mankind had become in a certain sense, and to their own inexpressible misery, the subjects of Satan by means of his victory over our first parents, it was fitting that our Lord, Who was now beginning the work which His Father had committed to Him of 'bringing many sons unto glory' and making men partakers of the kingdom of heaven, should in the first instance fight with and overcome him, who by means of sin held mankind in bondage to himself, and thus begin the work of redemption by the destruction of our bondage.

It must be further added, that our Lord's temptation and victory over Satan were intended in the providence of God, not so much to free us from temptation as to make it easy for us to endure it and to conquer it. As our Lord knew how terribly those who were to belong to Him were to be tried in this way and how entirely their salvation would depend upon their faithfulness under the trial, we must suppose that in this mystery He was providing for each one of us in that loving and complete manner in which all our needs and dangers and sufferings have been guarded against by Him. Thus we are led to understand that, as St. Paul tells us, His temptation is the mystery on which His power to help us under temptation rests, not as if He had not that power otherwise, but because such is the harmony and correspondence between what He has done for us and the blessings which we derive from Him. 'For in that He Himself hath suffered and been tempted, He is able to succour them that are tempted.[3] Thus, also, His temptation is an instruction as well as an encouragement to us—an encouragement, because it teaches us that to be tempted is not necessary to fall, nor any mark of God's displeasure with us; an instruction, because, as we shall presently see, our Lord has so arranged His own temptations, and His conduct under them, as to provide for us most perfectly an example how to bear ourselves under such trials and how to conquer whatever assaults may be made against us. And again, Satan no longer approaches us with the strength and vigour and audacity which he used of old, after he had conquered man and had established his kingdom well-nigh over the whole world. He is intensely proud as well as intensely malicious and cunning, and as pride is so great a cause of blindness in him, so also to have his pride broken down

<hr>

[3] Heb. ii. 18.

and utterly confounded by defeat weakens him. But this is not the only cause of the comparative weakness of his temptations to man after our Lord's victory. The strength of Satan has been immensely weakened, but also, on the other hand, the strength of our human nature has been immensely increased by the Incarnation, and especially by the triumph of that nature in our Lord's Person in this mystery of the Temptation. Our Lord has the right of a conqueror over Satan, and we have conquered in Him.

These general reasons throw light on the importance as well as the position of this mystery in the Life of our Blessed Lord. It is put at the very outset of His Apostolical and Public Life, immediately after His Baptism, as if to show us that the very first condition of the Christian life is conflict and temptation. And the particular circumstances under which our Lord's Temptations took place are further understood by the Fathers as signifying that no one can press on generously in the path of His imitation without at once meeting with the opposition which comes from temptation. It is when we set ourselves to 'the service of God,' as the Song of Sirach tells us,[4] that we are to prepare our souls for temptation, and when men have cleansed their souls in Baptism or in the Sacrament of Penance, when they aim at higher things, and fast and pray and seek to keep themselves in retirement or at least in innocence from the world, then it is that the tempter is certain to assail them. Then it is that he is alarmed, because he sees them endeavouring to follow our Lord more and more closely, and then it is that they must study our Lord's example, have recourse to Him in humble prayer, and trust in the victorious strength which trampled Satan down in the desert, and by that triumph

[4] Ecclus. ii. 1.

weakened him for future assaults and provided for us a store of illumination and grace with which it is easy for us to conquer also.

The words of the Evangelists seem to imply that the temptations with which Satan beset the Sacred Humanity of our Blessed Lord were continued without intermission during the forty days during which His stay in the wilderness lasted. If this was the case, we must then understand that the three remarkable temptations, which are specially related by the Evangelists, took place at the close of the time, when our Lord allowed Himself, with full deliberation and will, to suffer the extreme pangs of hunger natural after an unbroken fast of forty days and forty nights. Satan, as is implied in the narrative of the Evangelists, took occasion of this extreme hunger to begin his final and most subtle temptations.

It must be remembered that according to the doctrine of the Fathers,[5] the manner of temptation which was possible in our Lord was not the same as that of which we ourselves have experience. We are tempted both externally and internally, that is, by words, suggestions, or objects addressed to the exterior senses, and also by evil thoughts, which can be shot into our minds, even when there has been nothing voluntary on our part, as is so often the case, on which they may be founded or grafted, as well as by our sensual concupiscences, which can also be inflamed even against our own will. This state of things in us is the consequence of sin, primarily of original sin, but also practically of our actual sins. The lower part of our nature is no longer held in that obedience to the reasonable will which ruled it in the case of our first parents before the Fall. Thus Adam and Eve were tempted externally, but not interiorly. There was as yet no internal discord or rebellion in

---

[5] See St. Greg. *Hom. in Evang.* 16 ; Toletus *in Luc.* c. iii. n. 7.

their nature. Our Blessed Lord's Sacred Humanity could not, of course, be subjected to an interior evil or defect of this kind. There could be no disobedience of the sensitive part of His nature to the rule of reason, and, in consequence, the temptations with which He was assailed, violent and subtle as they were, were entirely external.

In order to understand fully the doctrine of the Fathers as to the particulars of the temptations addressed to our Blessed Lord by Satan, it must be remembered that the ancient writers suppose, what is indeed suggested by the very words used by him in the temptations, that he was ignorant, or at least doubtful, as to the Person of Jesus Christ. There is great ground for thinking that it was the revelation of the future mystery of the Incarnation, as it was set before the angels at the time of their probation, claiming their allegiance and homage for their God in a nature inferior to their own, which was the occasion of that first miserable revolt of the will of His creatures in heaven which was punished by Him by the banishment of the rebel spirits from His presence and their condemnation to the eternal torments of hell. Thus the Incarnation had been the occasion to Satan of his own irremediable fall, and was in consequence the peculiar object of his hate, while at the same time he was aware that it was also to be the instrument of the redemption of that inferior order of God's spiritual creatures whom he had induced in some sort to imitate and share his own rebellion. He had known and most carefully watched from the beginning every step and stage in the counsel of God for the restoration and redemption of the human race. He had noted the first promise made to Eve of the seed of the woman who was to crush the serpent's head, and no intimation of type or prophecy concerning the carrying out of that promise in the fulness of time had been lost upon him. If the Scribes and Priests at Jerusalem could tell Herod where the Saviour was to be born, if they could have calculated the weeks of the prophecy of Daniel, or the note of time given in the last promise of Jacob, if they knew that our Lord was to be the Son of a Virgin, and of the house and lineage of David, much more could the arch-enemy of mankind have told all these things concerning the one future event which he dreaded above all others, the coming of the Son of God in human flesh to redeem the world. If Simeon and Anna, and others with them, were looking for the redemption of Israel at the time of our Lord's birth, it is certain that the same expectation must have been entertained with far different feelings by Satan and his angels.

There were many things about our Lord's birth and infancy which may have filled them with alarm, because they seemed to be so clearly the fulfilment of. notes which were attached to the promised Messias. Occurrences like the testimony of Simeon in the Temple, or the visit of the Eastern Sages at the Epiphany, might have made Satan suspect that the wonderful Child to Whom such honour was done might be more than human, but he seems all through to have been baffled and fooled by the humility, poverty, meekness, and entire hiddenness of the life of our Lord and His Blessed Mother. When our Lord left Nazareth and presented Himself at the Jordan, Satan may have been again alarmed at the singular and magnificent honours which were then paid to Him, and this may have been the reason why he assailed Him when in the desert, with every kind of temptation which it was. permitted to him to use, with the twofold object of discovering who He was, and at the same time of inducing Him to sin. If it be thought that it would have been impossible that a creature with all the wonderful natural gifts of intellectual discernment which are possessed by the fallen angels, should have been deceived as to the Person of our Lord, we must remember that in the use of their natural powers to hurt and deceive us the devils are not left to themselves, but are only allowed to do what it pleases God to permit, and that in the same way there may have been many circumstances in the divine dispensation of the Incarnation which Satan was not allowed to know, even though he might perhaps have known them; notably the virginal conception of our Blessed Lord in His Mother's womb. Again, pride, whether in devils or in men, has the property already noted, of blinding the intellect to many things which it might otherwise know, especially if they are presented under the form of humility.

Tradition has fixed on the mountain tract which lies somewhat to the south-west of Jericho as the scene of the forty days' fast and temptation of our Lord. The mountains are pierced by many caves, and there are some lofty peaks. In the early ages they became the habitation of hermits and monks, who sought this desert for the purpose of leading the life of Christian ascetics near the actual spot which our Lord had sanctified by His long sojourn in the wilderness. Here it was then that the tempter, appearing as it seems in the form of a man, approached our Lord in the extreme state of weakness to which He had allowed Himself to be reduced, with the suggestion, 'If Thou be the Son of God, command that these stones be made bread.' The suggestion was a temptation in the first place to a sort of infidelity, as if our Lord could doubt that He was the Son of God, as He had lately been declared to be by the Voice from heaven at the time of His Baptism. Satan's hatred is ever most intense against God Himself, and he here insinuates a question as to the truthfulness of God, as if He could not really have left the Son of His love in such a condition of famine and hunger in the wilderness, and in this respect the words recall to mind the manner in which he also called in doubt the veracity of God in his temptation to Eve. All his temptations indeed have this in view, to make God's creatures disbelieve and distrust Him, and then to substitute himself and his own lies as the object of our confidence and faith. In the second place, his suggestion was an appeal to the sensual appetite, because it promised a relief to the terrible hunger with which our Lord had now allowed Himself to be afflicted. But it was not simply an appeal to the appetite, inasmuch as he might have made such an appeal by presenting our Lord with delicate viands, such as he might doubtless have produced, and which might have been in our Lord's case what the forbidden fruit was to Eve. He does not tempt our Lord to eat when it was forbidden Him or what was forbidden, but he says, 'If Thou be the Son of God, command that these stones be made bread' —that is, show Thy Sonship by using the power of miracles, which cannot but be attached to such a dignity, by commanding stones to be made bread so that Thy hunger may be satisfied. He does not say, Ask Thy Father or pray to Thy Father. For prayer, humility, the loving petitions of a Child to God the Father are things which Satan hates and can never recommend, and his one idea of Divine Power is that which St. Paul speaks of when he seems to allude to him in contrast with our Blessed Lord, saying that Jesus Christ did not think it a thing 'to be seized on, clutched, and used as a prey,'[6] as a robber uses the riches of which he gets possession, r as a tyrant uses his usurped power, at his own caprice and fancy, without regard to justice or decency, and

[6] Philipp. ii. 6. οὐχ ἁρπαγμὸν ἡγήσατο τὸ εἶναι ἴσα θεῷ.

merely to show that he has it. Certainly, if our Lord had so chosen He might have made the stones become bread, as He soon after this time turned the water into wine. Or again, if He had chosen, He might no longer have permitted the pangs of hunger to afflict Him, or in many other ways, even without having any recourse to supernatural means, He might have obtained relief. But our Lord was fasting in obedience, as is clear from the whole history, to the guidance of the Holy Ghost; and as His Sacred Humanity was ever perfectly obedient to and dependent upon that guidance, it would have been against what we may call the law of His life to supply His temporal needs by a miracle without such guidance. Again, in the case of any one in His position, saint or prophet or apostle, to whom the gift of miracles had been granted, that gift would have been granted not to be used arbitrarily or on every possible occasion or for the relief of himself or others, but only in accordance with the will of God in each particular case. And Catholic theologians tell us that there would have been something inordinate in the working of a miracle in such circumstances—of course, without the express direction of God—because relief might have been had in other ways, natural and human.

These considerations explain the intention of Satan, in so far as he was bent on inducing our Lord, if possible, to sin, while his design in the temptation before us as to finding out whether our Lord were truly the Son of God, is too obvious to need explanation. We see at once that his desire was to induce our Lord to do something disrespectful, and, as it were, to take some liberty with God: and his words express clearly that arrogance and scorn which characterise him, for they remind us of no other words so much as of those of the Chief Priests who mocked at our Lord on the Cross, 'If He be the

King of Israel, let Him come down from the Cross—let Him save Himself, if He be the Christ, the chosen of God.' Our Lord's answer may be considered under three aspects—as restoring the honour to God which was impaired by the proposal of the tempter, as giving a reason for His own refusal to accede to that proposal, and as baffling the desire of Satan to discover Who He was. As to the first, the answer, ' It is written, Not on bread alone doth man live, but on every word that proceedeth out of the mouth of God,' was directed to give honour to the Father, first in the reverence which it expressed for the Word of God as the rule and authority of human conduct, and then as expressing that entire dependence upon God which is the true life of man. To know the will of God, to do His work, to be as He wills, to take the appointments of His Providence as they come, good or bad, hard or pleasant, without moving a finger to extricate himself or going a hair's breadth off the path along which he is put to walk, that it is which makes a man live more truly than bodily food. It is better to be thus without bread, than without any intimation from the mouth of God to work miracles in order to supply bread. ' I am without bread, but I do not want it, because I am doing the will of God.' Then, as to the second aspect of these words, they convey the full explanation and reason of our Lord's conduct in enduring His long fast without any relief. And in the last place, they leave the tempter in entire ignorance as to the Person Whom he was assailing, because they give from the Scriptures a rule of action which applies to the humblest child of Adam as well as to the Incarnate Son.

The same intention of the baffling of the tempter may be considered as influencing our Lord in the method of His answers, which in all the three cases which are recorded for us by the Evangelists are taken from the Sacred Scriptures and the Book of Deuteronomy. For the shield which St. Paul bids us take in all our conflicts with the principalities and powers with whom we have to fight is the shield of faith,[7] and faith rests upon the authority and witness of God, whether in the Holy Scripture or in the Church. Faith is the virtue of souls who have not sight, who do not yet possess the vision of God and therein the clear knowledge of all things which they now take upon trust, and thus our Lord's answer, being an appeal to the Word of God, was one which we might give as well as He Himself. And again, to allege the authority of Scripture was, as some of the Fathers point out, a modest, humble, and gentle way of making His reply, when He might, if He had so chosen, have made the tempter feel His power and majesty. It was an answer founded on reason, not on might, and breathing perfect tranquillity, without any mark of anger or indignation. All these circumstances are full of instruction for us, for our Lord not only thus baffles His enemy, but sets us a perfect example of the method by which we are to baffle him in our turn, by the exercise of faith, especially by the use of short ejaculations or maxims of divine truth, and by a fearless tranquillity and humble reliance upon God.

Again, we shall usually find that when our Blessed Lord quotes the Sacred Scriptures, there is, when the passage is examined, a reference to the context as well as to the particular words which form the quotation. Certainly it seems so to be in the case before us. For this passage from which His answer is taken is one in which Moses reminds the Israelites of their trials and wanderings in the desert, of the marvellous food

[7] Ephes. vi. 16.

with which they had been fed, and of the lesson which God meant them to learn from all that happened to them, of their perfect dependence on Him and of His power to sustain them in any way that He chose. It was a passage which any one in our Lord's position might most lovingly dwell upon as applied to his own case. 'Thou shalt remember all the way through which the Lord thy God hath brought thee for forty years through the desert to afflict thee and to prove thee, and that the things that were in thy heart might be made known, whether thou wouldest keep His commandments or no, He afflicted thee with want, and gave thee manna for thy food, which neither thou nor thy fathers knew, to show that not in bread alone doth man live, but in every word that proceedeth from the mouth of God.'[8] The tender care which God had taken of the chosen people in the wilderness, a tender care which did not exclude the holy discipline of affliction and want and trial to which He subjected them, was, like the whole of His dealings with them, typical both of the history of our Lord and of His method of perfecting one by one souls which are dear to Him. The very words which our Lord quotes refer immediately to the miracle of the daily manna by which the Israelites were fed, and with a God of so much power and tenderness to care for Him there was certainly little reason for taking it on Himself to change stones into bread. And, in truth, when the temptation was over, the angels of God came and ministered to Him, as 'angel's food' had been given day by day to the people in their sojourn in the wilderness.

Our Lord's answer to the first temptation had thus baffled Satan in his attempt to discover who it was with whom he was dealing, while at the same time it

----

[8] Deut. viii. 2, 3.

furnished a simple reason against his proposal, inasmuch as it showed it to be utterly superfluous and inconsistent with perfect reliance on God. Thus we are provided for by our Lord, not only in His example, but also in the instruction conveyed in His answer. The temptation with which, if we follow the order of the more historical of the two Evangelists on whom we are dependent as to this mystery, he next assailed our Lord, seems at first sight to have so gross, palpable, and outrageous a character of wickedness about it, as to make it almost a matter of wonder that even Satan should have the insolence to propose it to one whom he must at least have known to be a very holy man, or the folly to suppose that it could be proposed with success. 'And the devil led Him into a very high mountain, and showed Him all the kingdoms of the earth in a moment of time, and he said to Him, To Thee will I give all this power, and the glory of them, for to me they are delivered, and to whom I will I give them. If Thou, therefore, wilt adore before me, all shall be Thine.' It is also to be noted that in this temptation he no longer uses the form, 'If Thou art the Son of God.' Gross indeed and outrageous was such a temptation as addressed to our Blessed Lord; but it must be again remembered that Satan is eaten up with the most intense pride, skilful and subtle as he is. And we often see in those who are his greatest instruments among men a sort of infatuation, arising from pride, the folly and impolicy of which men of the most ordinary prudence would avoid. There is, therefore, nothing very surprising in the transparent vanity, mendacity, and foolishness of the pretensions which Satan here advances, and of the proposal which he makes. Nevertheless, in dealing with mankind he may often find that such temptations, which appeal to ambition, the love of power and influence, a nobler concupiscence than that of the gratification of the senses on which the first temptation was grounded, may be far more successful than the others. For even spiritual men, men who have conquered the lower passions, and can live above nature in fasting and mortification, are liable to fall before the allurements of ambition, and we see this constantly before our eyes in the history of the Church, some of the most unhappy pages of which are those which record the love of power and the consequent jealousies and rivalries which have ruined lofty souls, and hindered, more almost than anything else, the greater glory of God. Satan could not understand the perfect humility and dependence upon God which breathed in our Lord's first answer, but he knew well enough from experience that when a man has tamed his sensual appetites he has often a yet harder conquest to achieve in subduing his ambition.

Again, many holy writers remark, as to this second temptation, that it does not at all exclude that second purpose which Satan is thought to have conceived in his approaches to our Lord, that is, the purpose of discovering who He was, as well as the purpose of inducing Him to sin. There is, indeed, no open mention of the Son of God, no overt challenge to our Lord to prove His Sonship by this or by that, as in the other temptations, and yet it may well be supposed that Satan hoped in this temptation also to lead our Lord to reveal Himself. He may have imagined, from our Lord's first answer, that He was on His guard, and desirous not to betray Himself, and thus he may have shaped his second attack with the object of forcing Him to declare Who He was, if He were really the Son of God, by claiming as his own the kingdoms of the world, which, in truth, did not belong to him, and by asking Him to pay him that adoration which was rather due from the creature to the Creator than from the Creator to the creature. Certainly if Satan had been challenged himself by some claim or offer which implied his own inferiority, nothing more would have been required to make him boil over with indignation and turn upon his tempter with words of outraged pride. And so, perhaps, he thought that the Incarnate Son of God, if He were there before him, would have disclosed His Majesty in answer to so insulting a proposal, rebuking him for his false claim, and asserting His own right to the kingdoms which were offered to Him on so degrading a condition.

The manner in which this temptation was presented to our Lord is not explained in the narrative of the Evangelists. Both in this and in the following temptation Satan is permitted to go beyond mere suggestions, as he has a certain power allowed him of leading our Lord where he wills, and, indeed, in the other temptation, of transporting Him preternaturally through the air. No mountain, of course, could be found from which any human eye could take in all the kingdoms of the earth and their glory, and yet it would appear that the mountain spoken of here is not as visionary as the representation of 'all the kingdoms' must have been. Little, indeed, must the sight, however dressed out and magnified by the preternatural power of illusion which Satan was allowed to exercise, of all the glories of the earth, and all the pomp and splendour of Imperial Rome, of Alexandria, Antioch, Ctesiphon, or whatever other capitals may have been pictured in this vision, with their subject provinces, have seemed to the eye of Him Whose human Soul from the first dawn of its being had been familiar with the blessed sight of God and the glories of His heavenly kingdom, especially when He knew, as none other knows, in the perfection of the gifts of the Holy Ghost, 'what was in man,' and what all this outward show was worth. And strange indeed must it have sounded in our Lord's ears, that the possession of goods so perishable and so unable to satisfy the soul, could be a motive for committing so enormous a sin as that of giving to a creature and to the enemy of God the worship due to Him alone. But our Lord condescended to bear even this insult calmly and meekly, for our sakes, rebuking the tempter, indeed, as was necessary for the honour of God, 'Avaunt, Satan!' but at the same time answering him with a few words of Sacred Scripture, which may serve as a light and a defence to all His children who might be tempted after Him in a like manner.

The answer of our Lord makes no direct mention of the offer which had been made to Him, any more than of the falsehood of Satan's claim to be the master of the world and to have the disposal of its kingdoms and their glory. But though there is no direct mention of the desire of earthly power, wealth, and magnificence, and so no reason given for refusing to gratify it, as was the case in the former temptation, yet our Lord, after restoring the honour of His Father, which had been insulted by the proposal of the tempter, quotes a passage of Scripture which seems not only to give the direct prohibition against the adoration of any one but God, but also, when the context is examined, to point to the danger which worldly possessions and prosperity bring with them of making us forget God, and so in time coming to worship something else, whether it be what is formally called an idol or not. For Moses, in the passage quoted by our Lord, earnestly warns the people against such forgetfulness and the ingratitude which follows upon it. 'And when the Lord thy God shall have brought thee into the land for which He swore to thy fathers, Abraham, Isaac, and Jacob, and shall have given thee great and goodly cities which thou didst not build, houses full of riches which thou didst not set up, cisterns which thou didst not dig, vineyards and oliveyards which thou didst not plant, and thou shalt have eaten and be full, take heed diligently lest thou forget the Lord, Who brought thee out of the land of Egypt and of the house of bondage—thou shalt fear the Lord thy God, and serve Him only, and shalt swear by His name.'[9]   Wealth and power have this inevitable danger as their shadow, of forgetfulness of God and in-gratitude, and when men are once sunk in ingratitude to God, as we know from St. Paul's account of heathen-dom in the Epistle to the Romans, they may soon find their way even to the abominations of idolatry, actual as well as moral.   And if we take our Lord's words as furnishing us with instruction against every kind of worldliness, love of power, ambition, and the virtual worship of the devil, who is so often spoken of in Scripture as the god of this world, the lesson comes to this, that we are to have a pure intention to seek God's glory in all things, to make His service the end of our being and of all our actions, and then even the possession of wealth, material or intellectual, of rank, high estate, influence and power, will be no hindrance to us, but rather the means of fulfilling the end for which we are made, and of glorifying God in the place and time in which He has fixed our lot.

In the third and last temptation Satan went further in two ways than he had ventured in the former, and thus—if such be the true order of them, as to which there can be no perfect certainty—this temptation is

[9] Deut. vi. 10–13.

a sort of climax to which the others lead up. In the
first place, as has been mentioned, he no longer led
our Lord, as to the mountain, but he must have trans-
ported that sacred Body through the air by an exercise
of preternatural power; and our Lord must have submitted to this, knowing that such was the will of His
Father, as He afterwards allowed Himself to be crucified,
as ancient writers say, by the members of the devil. In
the second place he ventured, as it were, to attempt
to turn our Lord's weapons against Himself, and pervert
Holy Scripture to the purposes of his temptation. For
Satan is not deprived, as has often been said, of those
powers which belong to him by nature, and although
in their use as in everything else he is simply permitted
to do what God allows him, still that permission is very
often extended, as we see in the history of Job and in
this instance in the Person of our Blessed Lord Himself,
to limits very far indeed beyond what is ordinarily supposed. It would seem as if our Lord's conflict with
Satan, and His victory in our human nature over him,
would not have been so complete as they are, nor so
full of consolation and strength to His children, if the
enemy had not been allowed in His case what is permitted to him in the case of others, though not ordinarily.
As it is, Satan runs through, in the course of the three
temptations, the whole range of his power of suggestion,
of illusion—for the vision of all the kingdoms of the
world must have been preternatural—and of actual
violence. Something of the same sort may also be
said as to his use of Scripture in the last temptation,
which is full of meaning to those who seek to interpret
the Word of God for themselves, and so incur the most
dangerous temptation possible, that to misbelief. For
Holy Scripture is an authority which can be used for
evil as well as for good, and has often been alleged

to sanction what is erroneous in doctrine as well as what is wicked in practice.

'Then the devil took Him up into the Holy City and set Him upon the pinnacle of the Temple, and said to Him, If Thou be the Son of God cast Thyself down, for it is written that He hath given His angels charge over Thee, and in their hands shall they bear Thee up, lest perhaps Thou dash Thy foot against a stone.'[10] The 'pinnacle' is spoken of by both Evangelists as some well-known part of the Temple, and Josephus has mentioned two such lofty points, one over the valley of Kedron, on the southern front, and another the summit of Solomon's Porch, which is said to have been the spot from which St. James was thrown by the Jews.

There are clear traces of fury, anger, and confusion in the challenge made to our Lord by the tempter, for though it might have served his purpose as to the discovery of our Lord if He had in truth thrown Himself from the pinnacle and been borne up in the air by the angels of God, still this would have tended to the defeat and shame of Satan himself, who, moreover, hates the good angels with a peculiar hatred as the instruments of God in his chastisement and in the prevention of his mischievous designs against men. Yet it is in keeping with the object which Satan had in view all through, that he should even thus be content to find out whether our Lord were the Son of God or not. The other purpose which he pursued in all the temptations, that of inducing our Lord, if possible, to sin, is more palpable and evident in this his last assault. Each of these three temptations suggests some disrespect and insult to God, and in this case it would clearly have been taking a rash liberty with Him for any one wantonly to throw himself off a pinnacle, at the risk of certain death,

10 Psalm xc. 11, 12.

unless God were to interfere miraculously by means of the angels to save him from the natural consequences of his rashness. If such a thing had been possible for the Son of God, it would have been ostentatious and vainglorious, in accordance with the character of Satan himself, to make an unnecessary exhibition of such a kind. It would have been the sort of sign which the Jews were so often to ask of our Lord, the kind of miracle, perhaps, which Herod had hoped to see Him perform at the time of His Passion. And in any ordinary case it would not only have been ostentatious and presumptuous, but it would probably have issued in the death of any one who had committed such a fault. God would not have allowed the angels to support him, and Satan's suggestion was therefore to suicide.

Holy writers have remarked that although Satan quoted the Psalms in this temptation, he did not quote the passage fully or correctly. For the Psalm speaks of the angels having charge over the man of God, ' to keep thee in all thy ways,' which words do not surely mean that if men cast themselves into extraordinary and unnecessary dangers the angels will protect them. But this is left out by the tempter, as well as the verse immediately following what he quoted, in which his own defeat is spoken of, 'Thou shalt walk upon the asp and the basilisk, and thou shalt trample under foot the lion and the dragon.' Our Lord's reply was again a simple quotation from Scripture, taken from the same passage in Deuteronomy which He had cited before, ' It is written again, Thou shalt not tempt the Lord thy God.'[11] The text adds, ' as thou temptedst Him in the place of temptation '—and the reference seems to be to the conduct of the Israelites, at the encampment at Raphidim,[12] where there was no water for them to drink, and they

[11] Deut. vi. 16.   [12] Exodus xvii. 1–7.

showed some signs of distrust of God in chiding Moses for having brought them out of Egypt to die of thirst, as if God could not or would not relieve them in due time. The fault of the people seems to have been an unbelieving impatience and want of confidence in God, coupled with a sort of arrogance, as if they thought they had a right to demand that their wants should be attended to at their own choice,—as if God, Who had just given them the manna, was bound at once to furnish them with water, and that if it were not so, they might find fault with the leaders whom He had given them for bringing them out of Egypt. Such is the presumptuous dealing with God against which the words quoted by our Lord warn us. We see again how our Lord here also corrects the liberty taken with God by the insinuation that His preternatural aid might be called upon at any moment, however wantonly, and how again He baffles the tempter in his design to draw out the secret as to the Divine Person Whom he was addressing.

Our Lord's temptations are our consolation, our strength, and our instruction. Our consolation, because they comfort us when we are under the like interior trials ; our strength, because He has won for us all the graces which are needed to enable us to triumph ; and our example, because He teaches us how to contend with temptations calmly and confidently, resting on our faith and trusting in God. His use of Sacred Scripture and of the truths which it sets forth is a general instruction that in all temptations our great resource must be in what we know by our Christian faith, which St. Paul speaks of as the shield wherewith we may be able to extinguish all the fiery darts of the most wicked one.[13] It may be asked whether, as to the particular temptations

<hr>

[13] Eph. vi. 16.

which are here recorded as undergone by our Lord, there is any analogy or resemblance to the ordinary temptations which beset ourselves?   It is not difficult to see that the three great concupiscences, the love of pleasure, the love of possessions, and the love of honour, are appealed to by Satan in his successive assaults, and that the principles conveyed in our Lord's three answers are adapted to guard us against these three concupiscences.   For the truth, that 'not in bread alone doth man live,' raising us to the thought of a nobler sustenance and higher pleasures than any that have to do with our ordinary appetites, is enough to quench all the fires of sensuality. 'To adore God alone and serve Him alone,' is the key to the true and indifferent use of all the good and great things in this world, and the principle never to tempt God is the proper safeguard against the inordinate love of honour and praise, for all honour and all glory belong to Him, and to seek or take any for ourselves is to tempt Him and provoke His jealousy.   But if we are to consider our Lord's three temptations as particularly representing the dangers of any one class of men more than others, that class would be those who have in any degree a share in the work which He was about to begin, and for which He had just received His solemn unction, when He was driven by the Spirit into the wilderness.   For spiritual men, and men who have to work for God in preaching or in other sacred ministrations, are particularly assailed by three temptations, one of which allures them to bodily comforts and a refined sensuality, another of which puts before them the bait of influence, personal power, wealth to be used for good purposes, and the like, while the third, which has often led to the greatest falls, attacks their personal vanity and pride through the applause which waits upon their success.

NOTE II.

On the action of the gifts of the Holy Ghost.

It has been said above that the language of the Evangelists intimates that our Lord's going to His temptation was one of those actions which are attributed to the gifts of the Holy Ghost. It may be useful to subjoin an abstract of the passage quoted in the footnote from Lanuza, in illustration of this point.

Lanuza's language may be thus epitomised, ' Christ was *led* by the Spirit. Not that He lost His free will, but He was urged by the Spirit as distinguished from going (into temptation) of His own accord. He was urged by a strong internal motion, as the saints sometimes are, without any violence done to the free will; of whom it may be said, *Spiritu Dei aguntur.*'[1]

'To understand this, we may assume the Catholic doctrine, that, besides acquired and infused virtues, which enable us to act rightly, there are also gifts of the Holy Spirit, which excite to more noble acts.[2] A carriage will go down-hill of its own weight, but if it is to go up-hill its wheels must be greased. "A man," says St. Ambrose, "is a carriage: he goes down-hill easily enough; but if he is to resist the tendencies of the flesh, he must have virtues and the gifts of God, by which the wheels of his faculties are lubricated." But what is the difference between virtues and gifts? Both move a man to what is good : but this good is of two sorts, and to both a man can direct his actions. The first sort of good is in accordance with natural reason imprinted in the soul, or supernatural reason as declared to us by God in the Scripture, or by holy mother Church. To attain to this good, virtues are given to us: *e.g.* faith to believe what passes sense ; hope in a future reward ; charity to love God, the chief good ; prudence, to guide the actions of our life ; justice, to give to each one what is his ; fortitude in the irascible part, to meet danger ; temperance in the concupiscible, to lead a man to acts of mortification.

---

[1] Rom. viii. 14.
[2] *Vide* St. Thom. *Summ.* 1, 2, q. 68.

'There is a second sort of good, whose goodness (*bonitas*) is not derived from or dependent on the rules of reason, but on the particular movement of the Holy Spirit—*Aliud quoque datur bonum, cujus bonitas non desumitur nec dependet ex regulis rationis sed ex particulari S. Sp. impulsu.* Instances are, Samson, destroying himself while destroying his enemies ; David, fighting Goliath ; Judith, going through an army of rude soldiers, and passing the night in the tent of the lustful Holophernes ; Apollonia, leaping into the flames out of the hands of her torturers ; Alexius leaving his wife. All this was good, since it is proposed to us as such by the Church and by Scripture—*quum ut tale* (bonum) *nobis proponit Ecclesia et Scriptura ;* still its goodness does not depend on natural or super- natural reason ; for judged by that, it would not only not be good, but worthy of censure ; but it depends on the special impulse of the Holy Spirit, Who in His decrees and acts is not bound by the ordinary rules of reason. "But that a person be impelled to such a good, which is above (*supra*) all rule, the gifts of the Holy Spirit are needed," says St. Thomas ; "and these gifts are nothing else than certain divine qualities which perfect the soul to allow itself to be bound and led to such goods which surpass all reason and law."

'This is what Christ meant when He said to Nicodemus : *Spiritus ubi vult spirat,* and the rest. This "spiratio" is shown in all history, especially in His choice of instruments : for example, Amos, the Apostles ; in His grace, for example, when given to great sinners, Magdalene, St. Paul, the Peni- tent Thief.'

NOTE III.

On the order of the Temptations.

As St. Matthew and St. Luke give the three temptations of our Lord in a different order, it is not easy to decide which of the two ought to be followed, and it is only the necessity of selecting one of the two as our guide on the point, in a work like the present, that has forced us to adopt one arrangement rather than the other, without pretending to settle the question. It is generally decided on internal grounds in favour of the order of St. Matthew, because it is at the close of His temptation on the mountain that our Lord used the words, 'Avaunt, Satan!' and it is supposed that these imply that the tempter was then chased away. But there is no necessary connection between the words of our Lord and the departure of Satan, which took place, as St. Luke tells us, 'when all the temptation was ended,' and he speaks of the withdrawal for a time as if it had been made simply, as far as it depended on Satan himself, because he was completely baffled. It is hardly necessary to add, what must be obvious to every critical student of his Gospel, that St. Matthew and the other Evangelists frequently use the word τότε, 'then,' without any necessary reference, as to order of time, to what has preceded. The common use of the word, at the beginning of a sentence, is something like that of the words, 'In illo tempore,' which are placed in the Missal at the beginning of the 'Gospels' for the several Masses, meaning, 'At a certain time,' 'Once upon a time.' No argument can therefore be drawn from the use of this word by St. Matthew, as an apparent conjunction between what is to him the third temptation and the departure of Satan. If this is the case, there seems no reason left for preferring the order of St. Matthew. On the other hand we have a general principle to guide us which it is important to follow throughout, and which has therefore been followed in the present case here. That principle is twofold. First, it is clear from an examination of St. Matthew's Gospel that he does not as a rule follow the order of time, but rather the order of ideas, in the arrangement of his Gospel. Secondly, it is also clear that the later Evangelists, and especially St. Luke, writing with a knowledge of the earlier Gospels, as well as an independent acquaintance with the facts, sometimes change the order, add, and by addition seem to correct, not the statements of the previous writers, but the impression that might arise from such statements. The whole intelligence of the arrangement of our Lord's life depends mainly on the knowledge of the scope and method of each Evangelist, and also of the relations, usually tacit but obvious, of the narratives to each other. It is almost a principle that St. Luke always adheres to the order of time, and whenever he or St. Mark seems to differ from St. Matthew, it is safer to follow the later writer, because he could not have inverted the order but for some good reason. It is on this general principle that the arrangement of the Gospels in the *Vita Vitæ Nostræ* has been based.

It may also be added that there is some internal probability in favour of St. Luke's arrangement. Certainly, a greater exertion of his natural powers was permitted to Satan in the temptation on the pinnacle of the Temple than before, and the mention of the angels in his quotation from the ninetieth Psalm, seems to lead naturally to the approach of the angels after his defeat to minister to our Lord. Some critics have said that the Evangelists have of set purpose told the temptations in a different order, that we may understand that temptations of various kinds do not always succeed in the same order; for example, that avarice may sometimes lead to vainglory, and vainglory may sometimes lead to avarice.[1] It is also worthy of notice that when St. Ignatius, in his *Spiritual Exercises*, describes the method of warfare pursued on the one hand by Satan and on the other hand by our Lord, in his meditation of 'Two Standards,' he seems to follow the order, as we may call it, of St. Luke rather than that of St. Matthew. For he describes Lucifer as bidding his emissaries tempt men first to the love of riches, and then to lead them, through the love of human honour, to pride, from which it will be perfectly easy to plunge them into any vices whatsoever. Jesus Christ, on the other hand, adopts the corresponding method, desiring to lead men first to poverty, spiritual or actual, then to the love of dishonour, and so to humility. St. Ignatius leaves out in both cases the field of the lower temptations to sensuality, as he supposes those who are desiring to follow our Lord's example to have no need to be warned concerning them, and on account of his extreme reluctance even to touch those subjects, of which St. Paul says,[2] 'Let them not be even so much as named among you.'[3]

These are reasons which support the order of St. Luke, by tending to show that the temptation which he puts in

---

[1] See Ludolph's *Vita Christi*, p. i. c. 22.
[2] Ephes. v. 3.   [3] See Palma, *Camino Espiritual*, l. iii. c. 2.

the last place is a kind of climax, and that the order of the spiritual conflict usually follows such an arrangement. There are also some authorities who see in the temptation in the pinnacle of the Temple a climax, for another reason, namely, that, as has been hinted in the foregoing chapter, those are the most dangerous of all temptations, which are founded on, or consist in, doctrinal errors, the false teaching of one who apparently supports his error by the Word of God, as Satan used the Psalms to persuade our Lord to tempt God.

It remains to assign, if possible, some reason why, if the temptations really took place in the order given by St. Luke, St. Matthew should have inverted the order. Such a reason may perhaps be found in the fact that it is one of the leading ideas in his Gospel to bring out the kingdom of our Lord, in all its majesty and universality, as conferred upon Him by the Father, and thus he may have been led to regard the temptation in which the kingdoms of the world were offered to Him by Satan on conditions of his own as the climax of all.

Another reason, which is given by some authorities, is founded on the continual though tacit reference made by St. Matthew throughout his Gospel to former events which are connected with what he is relating either as types or as contrasts. His Gospel can certainly never be fully understood unless this part of his method is discerned, and his use of it is very far more frequent than would be supposed merely from the number of his distinct references to prophecy in those familiar words, 'This was done that it might be fulfilled,' and the like. The proper place for drawing out this characteristic of St. Matthew is in another part of this work, and it is enough here to assume that, from the beginning to the end of his Gospel, he has the Old Testament history before his mind, with all its anticipations of our Lord, whether in type or in prophecy, and that his references are sometimes contained in a single word or half sentence.

There can be no question, therefore, about the principle now mentioned, and it only remains · to see how the authors of whom we speak apply it to the present difficulty. The application is founded on the reference to the order of the temptations addressed by Satan to Adam and Eve, for his words in Genesis apply to both. St. Matthew is thought to have had this order before his mind, and to have arranged his narrative of the temptations addressed to our Lord accordingly. 'These authors say,' says Sylveira,[4] 'that St. Luke in his order of the temptations follows the historical truth, but that, because Christ in these temptations intended to overcome the devil in the same things in which he conquered Adam, therefore St. Matthew follows the order of the temptation of Adam ; for the devil said to our first parents,[5] "In the day in which you shall eat thereof," and here is gluttony, "you shall be like God," and here is vainglory, "knowing good and evil," and here is avarice, because there is avarice not only of money, but also of knowledge. And thus according to the intention which Christ had of conquering Satan the order of the temptations is arranged.'

It is, of course, quite out of the question to suppose that either Evangelist was really ignorant of the true order.

[4] In Evangel. tom. i. l. iii. c. 3, q. 21.   [5] Gen. iii. 6.

CHAPTER VI.

The Ministering Angels.

St. Matt. iv. 11 ; St. Mark i. 13 ; St. Luke iv. 13 ; *Vita Vitæ Nostræ,*
§ 18.

THE two first Evangelists add to their account of the
temptation of our Lord the statement, that when Satan
departed, in defeat and confusion, the Angels approached
and ministered to our Lord. And it is remarkable, that
if we had only St. Mark's account, which is a summary
and not a narrative, as he does not give the particulars
of the several temptations, we might imagine that the
ministration of the Angels continued the whole time of
the forty days, like the temptations of Satan, and the
companionship of our Lord with the wild animals in
that rude solitude. We may at all events gather from
the mention of the circumstance by St. Mark that it is
one of the great features of the mystery of the temptation, and that it may well be made the subject of
separate and careful consideration.

St. Luke tells us, in the first instance, that all the
temptations being ended, the devil departed from Him
for a season. Satan had run through the whole range
of his contrivances for the seduction and deception of
mankind in vain, for he had tempted every appetite,
he had tried his power of illusion, he had even been
permitted to transport our Lord from place to place,
and he had also endeavoured to mislead Him by a
false application of that very Word of God which our

Lord Himself had uniformly appealed to, to foil His adversary. In doing this, Satan had covered the whole ground from which he assails the children of the Church, and by being defeated on every point by One Whom he had no right to provoke and assail, he has lost his strength and boldness and freedom in addressing the same temptations to those who are united to our Blessed Lord, Who conquered him everywhere. In the course of the struggle, moreover, Satan had been forced to display his own character : his hypocrisy, and mendacity, and vanity, and pride, his hatred of God, his lust for homage and adoration, and, in the last temptation, his habit of unblushing perversion of sacred authorities, and his cruelty, for if our Lord had been a mere man, the suggestion which he made to Him would have issued in suicide and destruction. It now remained for him, in the counsels of God, to show his cowardice, and how, when he is calmly resisted, he takes to flight, for though his determined and inveterate malice supplies in him the place of patience and perseverance, still there is something womanly, as St. Ignatius has remarked, about his bearing, when he sees that those whom he assails are not afraid of him, and do not intend to yield to him an inch. So he fled away, 'leaving our Lord for a season,' as the Evangelist tells us, for his retirement was not out of any change of purpose or relenting in his hostility, but because he felt himself defeated and was ashamed to run the risk of continual overthrows.

In what way it was that Satan renewed his assaults upon our Lord Himself we are not told, and can only gather from a few words which occur here and there in the Gospels. But we may be certain that he now determined to oppose Him in every way, but by the means of others whom he made his instruments, and that henceforth he was the chief mover in the opposition and persecution which afterwards arose against our Lord, that the calumnies set in circulation against Him were his work, and that such devices as the evil counsel of Caiaphas and the traitorous design of Judas were the masterpieces of his ingenuity. Just before His Passion, our Lord told His disciples, 'The prince of this world cometh, and in Me he hath not anything,'[1] and from this we may conjecture that Satan returned more particularly to attack Him at that time, and that that may be the meaning of the departure for a season of which St. Luke speaks. Then he may have tried once more to molest our Blessed Lord Himself with more direct assaults, though there must have been many before that time, because our Lord, at the Last Supper, also speaks to His disciples as to those 'who remained with Him in His temptations,' as if the whole of His course had been a series of such trials. But now, after the severe conflict which had lasted for forty days and forty nights, the time for peace and consolation had come, and so Satan was chased away to leave our Lord unmolested.

If it be true that the last of the three temptations in order of time is that which St. Luke has placed last, then it would seem as if our Lord had been left by Satan on the giddy pinnacle of the Temple, where he is said to have 'set Him,' as if it were a place that could not be reached in an ordinary way. It was in our Lord's power either to compel the tempter to remove Him from the spot, or to descend of Himself, as He could pass through the crowd or walk upon the waters, or to allow His own blessed angels to assist Him. The words used by the Evangelist, that the angels came and ministered to Him, seem to imply that they were angels who were ordinarily in attendance on our Lord, but

[1] St. John xiv. 30.

that it had been His will that they should withdraw for a time, in order that in the weakness and humility of His Human Nature He might battle with the foe, and triumph over him more gloriously in consequence of the absence of all aid from the angels. For the angels have the power to check and curb the enemies of our souls, who fly away from their presence for fear of punishment from them. Our Lord, Who was the Head of angels as well as of men, Who was perfectly impeccable and in no danger from the assaults of hell, had not, like men in general, a Guardian Angel in the usual sense of the term, but He had a number of angels who were more specially deputed to wait upon Him, and whose services He used at His will.[2] They were, as it were, the immediate servants and guards of His Sacred Humanity, and we may well imagine the burning devotion with which they regarded it, inasmuch as therein was fulfilled that wonderful mystery of God's counsel which had been set before them at the beginning, by allegiance and humble homage to which their own crowns were won, and which was also to be the means through which the ruin which rebellion had brought into their own ranks was to be repaired. These faithful ministers of our Lord's will had watched Him most closely from the first, rendering Him the homage and adoration which were due to Him, and rejoicing in and glorifying God for all the marvels of sanctity and wisdom which were displayed in Him. At the time of His conflict with the Evil One, they had, as has been said, been held aloof, that Satan might be conquered by our Lord alone, and now that the victory was won, they approached in joy and triumph, to bear Him, it may be, from the pinnacle on which He had been placed, and to attend Him on His return to His cave

[2] See Suarez, *De Angelis*, lib. vi. c. 17, n. 21.

on the mountain side in which He had passed the forty days and forty nights.

It seems as if our Lord had now allowed the fatigue and strain and weakness which His long fast and severe temptations would naturally cause Him to have their full effect, and that He condescended, as afterwards in His Agony in the Garden, to receive support and refreshment from the angels. Holy contemplative souls have often dwelt on this scene, and imagined the manner in which His food and refreshment were borne to Him by the angels, and the solemn and calm rejoicings with which they would celebrate His victory. As it is not foreign to the object of this work to assist that use of the Christian imagination, which, though it is not the substantial part of mental prayer, is yet highly valuable as one of its great helps, we may dwell for a moment upon one of the pictures of this mystery drawn by the servants of God. Ludolph, the Carthusian, begins by bidding us 'attend diligently and gaze upon our Lord as He eats in solitude, the angels standing around Him, and consider all things well,' he says, 'for they are very beautiful and devout. And I ask myself, what was it that the angels brought to Him to eat after so long a fast? The Scripture does not tell us, and we may arrange that triumphant banquet as we like. And if we consider His power, He could create what things He chose, or, at His will have taken any created things whatever. But we do not find that He used this power of His for Himself or for His disciples. He used it for the crowds whom He twice fed in great numbers with a few loaves, but of His disciples we read that with Him present with them they plucked the ears of corn from hunger and ate them, and in like manner when, wearied by His journey, He sat by the well talking with the Samaritan woman, it is not said that

He created food for Himself, but that He sent His disciples into the town to seek for it. Nor is it probable that He would provide for Himself by miracle, for He usually wrought His miracles for the edification of others and in the presence of many, whereas here none were present but the angels.' And then he goes on to suppose that as there were no human habitations on the mountain of Quarantana, the angels must have brought our Lord food from a distance, as had been done to Daniel when he was in the den of lions,[3] and so he imagines that our Lord allowed the angels to visit our Blessed Lady and ask her to send by them some food to her Son. 'Look upon Him well,' he continues, 'in each thing that He does and in all that takes place—He sits modestly upon the ground and eats soberly, the angels stand around ministering to their Lord and singing one of the hymns of Sion, rejoicing and keeping festival with Him. But, if we may say so, this festival has to them its mixture of very great compassion, for which we also ought to weep, for they gaze reverently on Him and consider that He Who is their Lord and God, and the Creator of the whole world, Who giveth food to all flesh, is so humbled as to need sustenance for His body, and is eating there like any common person, and so they are moved to compassion concerning Him, and I believe that if thou wouldst look upon Him in this condition with a tender and affectionate heart, and if thou hadst any love for Him, thou also wouldst weep out of strong compassion.'[4]

This mystery of our Blessed Lord's receiving food at the hands of the angels is repeated spiritually over and over again in the souls of His servants and followers, who are tempted and tried and solicited as He was, by Satan, and who overcome the enemy by following His example and by means of the

<hr>

[3] Daniel xiv.   [4] Ludolph, *Vita Christi*, p. 1.

strength and grace which His conflict has earned for them.　　And then, after the trial, comes the consolation, and the angels who waited so joyfully and so reverently upon the Incarnate Son in His Human Nature after He had quelled Satan, are the ministers whom He employs to comfort and solace and refresh, by spiritual light and ineffable peace and joy, the souls which have been proved in trial and have in their turn overcome Satan through Him.　　For, though the angels are always at hand to assist the souls of men in their spiritual trials and temptations, their presence is not always felt as a consolation and a source of joy, it being the will of God that the followers of our Lord should go through the same stages of trial with our Lord Himself.　　There are times, then, in our spiritual warfare, in which the solace of the angels' company seems to be withdrawn from us, and in which, on the other hand, we seem to feel the near presence of the evil angels disturbing us, frightening us, plying us with illusions, and suggesting things against faith or perverse interpretations of Scripture, even if they do not, as is sometimes the case, exercise a sort of power over our lower nature, or go the lengths permitted to them in their assaults against some of the servants of God, in violence analogous to that to which our Lord submitted when He was placed on the pinnacle of the Temple.

In our meditations on the punishment of hell, it is sometimes given us to understand with particular force, depth, and clearness, how intolerable a torment it must be to be the close companions of the wickedest of men, and even of beings so full of malice, fury, pride, envy, and every blackest form of passion as the evil spirits, and these, too, in a state of restless, intense pain, and with their inveterate hatred against God and all His creatures lashed into madness by their knowledge of all that they have lost, and of the utter hopelessness of their eternal doom. At the times of temptation of which we are now speaking, there is a sense in the soul of some approach to such a misery as this companionship, though it is almost infinitely mitigated, in comparison to what it might be hereafter, by the actual presence of the grace of God with His servants, however hardly they may be tried, so long as they are faithful to Him. And, on the other hand, it is a part of what we are allowed to anticipate as the blessedness which awaits us in heaven, that we are then to be for ever in the closest companionship with the holy angels—a part of that blessedness which we see to have been familiar to the minds of the holy Christian painters of the middle ages, who represent the servants of God in the pictures of the Judgment as rising from their graves to throw themselves into the arms of the angels who have watched over and guided them in their earthly course. There are few pure spiritual joys more intense on earth than that true companionship with holy souls, servants of God who dwell together 'like brethren in unity,' and this is a sort of foretaste of that special joy which each of the blessed in heaven will have in all his companions, and all in each. And, as to the angels, there are even now times of joy and peace at which they seem to 'approach' nearer to us than at others, at which we are allowed to have a sense of their loving presence with us, after trials and conflicts, during which it may have seemed to us that heaven was far indeed from us and shut against us. We cannot doubt that our Blessed Lord, Who afterwards in the Garden showed so much desire for the companionship of the Apostles, and was comforted by an angel, felt more intensely than we can do the relief and consolation and joy which come from the nearness and familiarity with the angels, and that He has especially gone before us in refreshment and enjoyment of this kind upon this occasion.

CHAPTER VII.

The Testimony of St. John.

St. John i. 19-24 ; *Vita Vitæ Nostræ*, § 19.

IT seems to have been during the absence of our Lord for the forty days of His fasting and temptation, that St. John Baptist was called upon to give a most solemn and formal witness, in answer to questions put to him on the part of the highest ecclesiastical authorities among the Jews, both as to his own person and mission, and as to our Lord. It has been mentioned in a former chapter how the idea that he might be himself the promised Messias had spread among the people, especially, as it would seem, those who had heard his preaching and seen the great austerity as well as the wonderful sanctity of his life, and how he had answered their thoughts by disclaiming the honour, and by preparing their minds for a baptism of more efficacy than his own, and for a Teacher, the latchet of Whose shoes he was not worthy to unloose. At that time he gave no further indication of the Person of Whom he was speaking, because it was before the Baptism of our Blessed Lord, and the sign of the Holy Ghost descending upon Him had not yet marked Him out.

It belonged to the Sanhedrim of the Jews to take cognisance of all persons who taught in public, and all such were in an ordinary sense under the jurisdiction of that great Council. The great popularity of St. John, and the movement produced by his preaching and baptism, may have, at least, hindered any very active measures against him on the part of the rulers at Jerusalem. It is remarkable that it should not have been until after the marvellous manifestation which took place at our Lord's Baptism that the Sanhedrim determined to send a formal deputation to the Baptist, not to forbid him to preach and continue his ministry, but to interrogate him in a manner which could hardly fail to compromise him unless he showed himself ready to submit to the jurisdiction of the ecclesiastical authorities. The great solemnity of the occasion makes it stand out by itself from all other similar questionings which may from time to time have been addressed to St. John, and his disciple and namesake, the Evangelist, here supplies its omission by the preceding three, who had not the same reasons as St. John for relating in detail the whole action of the authorities at Jerusalem in reference to our Lord and His Forerunner.

The Evangelist says: 'This is the testimony of John, when the Jews sent Priests and Levites from Jerusalem to ask him, Who art thou? And he confessed, and did not deny, and confessed, I am not the Christ.' The Messias was in the thoughts of all men, and though there was no mention of Him in the question put to St. John, he was expected either to assert his claim to that character, or to disown any such pretension. 'They asked him, What then, art thou Elias? and he said, I am not.' The last of the prophets had left on record that Elias was to come before the Messias, although his prediction literally and formally referred to the second advent of our Lord—'Before the great and terrible day of the Lord,'[1] and thus the expectation

---

[1] Mal. iv. 1.

of his coming was general among the Jews. There was, as we well know from Scripture and our Lord's own words, a true sense in which the blessed Forerunner was the Elias,[2] who was to come, for he was sent, as the Angel announced to his father before his conception, in the spirit and power of Elias.' But there was also a sense, in which the question was asked, referring to the identity of person and not to the resemblance of office, and in this sense he was not the promised prophet. And as St. John's deep humility prompted him always to disclaim every honour and title of distinction, he denied that he was Elias, although it might even have seemed to be for the service of religion that he should have asserted it.

This was not enough, so the questioners continued, 'Art thou the prophet? And he answered, No.' The prophet of whom they spoke was the guide and leader like to himself, whom Moses had promised them, 'The Lord thy God will raise up to thee a prophet of thy nation and thy brethren like unto me, whom thou shalt hear.'[3] The Jews necessarily identified the promised prophet with the Messias Himself: but the belief concerning his coming was distinct and popular among them, as we see from the words of the multitudes who had been miraculously fed in the desert,[4] 'This is of a truth the prophet, who cometh into the world ;' and it was to this general belief that the Apostles formally appealed after the Day of Pentecost, when St. Peter had worked the first great miracle in the Name of our Lord, as he had appealed to the testimony of David on the Day of Pentecost itself to confirm the truth of our Lord's Resurrection.[5] There

---

[2] St. Matt. xi. 14.   [3] Deut. xviii. 16–18.   [4] St. John vi. 14.
[5] Cf. Acts iii. 22, 23, ii. 24, seq. In the speech after the cure of the lame man at the Beautiful Gate of the Temple, St. Peter adds the threat which is contained in the same passage of Deuteronomy, 'And it shall be that every soul that will not hear that prophet, shall be destroyed from among the people.'

seems also to have been a belief among the Jews that some of the prophets would rise from the dead at the coming of the Messias,[6] and thus we find that after St. John's own death there were some who thought that our Lord was 'John the Baptist risen from the dead, or Jeremias, or one of the prophets.'[7] 'They said therefore to him, Who art thou, that we may give an answer to those that sent us? He saith, I am the voice of one crying in the wilderness, Make straight the way of the Lord, as saith the Prophet Isaias.' The application of this prophecy to St. John Baptist was not made by the Angel when he announced his miraculous conception to his father Zachary, for St. Gabriel dwelt rather on his mission in the spirit and power of Elias, and spoke in words that are partly quoted from the passage in Malachias already referred to. But Zachary himself, whose canticle is almost made up of personal and Scriptural allusions, had adopted the prophecy of Isaias as the distinguishing mark of his son's mission, when he said, 'Thou shalt be called the prophet of the Most High, for thou shalt go before the face of the Lord to prepare His ways;' and very beautifully indeed do the words which follow about the knowledge of salvation (Jesus) given unto the people for the remission of their sins, and the like, express the whole spirit of St. John's preaching and witness. St. John, then, adopted the account given of him by his father, and made it, as it were, the motto of his mission, adding, however, by the gift of interpretation which belonged to him, the title which he particularly clung to—the Voice crying in the wilderness.

---

[6] See Lightfoot in l.

[7] St. Matt. xvi. 14. This seems a more certain interpretation of their meaning than that which attributes to the Jews the doctrine of metempsychosis (Sepp. *Life of Jesus Christ.* French Trans. t. i. c. 8, p. 303).

'They asked him and said to him, Why then dost thou baptize, if thou art not the Christ, nor Elias, nor the prophet?' The administration of baptism, as has been said, was considered as a sort of initiation into a new religious school or state, and as such, to belong only to those who were authorised teachers. The answer made by St. John was indirect, as if he could not refrain on every occasion from putting forward what had reference to the honour and surpassing dignity of our Lord, that being the one thing which it was of paramount importance that he should speak of and that they should hear. 'I indeed baptize with water, but there hath stood One in the midst of you, Whom ye know not.' As if he had said, 'What does it matter to you to know by what authority and for what reason I baptize, when there has been One among you already Who baptizes with the Holy Ghost?' But yet the words of the Baptist do truly contain the answer to their question, and the reason for his own administration of baptism: because the reason for that was that he might prepare the way for Him Who was to come after him, by rousing in the people the spirit of humble penitence, and also by teaching them to look forward to that other Baptizer in the Holy Ghost, Whom it was also his office to point out to such as were fit to receive Him. His teaching about the kingdom of heaven was identical with that of our Lord, and so led people on to Him. His baptism, in connection with the doctrine of the kingdom, was in like manner a preparation for Christian Baptism, the sacrament which our Lord was to give as the means of entrance to His kingdom. If there had been no future Baptism in the Holy Ghost, there would have been no reason for St. John's baptism. All that St. John did had reference to our Blessed Lord; and the near approach, nay, the actual presence of our Blessed Lord, in the midst of a people who were ignorant of Him, and so in danger of losing their opportunity of salvation because they would not receive Him, was the reason and the justification of all that St. John had done and was doing. And the authority and office of our Lord were the foundation of the office and mission which were committed to St. John, just as for ever afterwards the same authority and office of our Lord have been the foundation of all that has been done in the Catholic Church, of all the preaching and teaching and administration of sacraments and exercise of jurisdiction and of the power of binding and loosing and legislating and defining doctrine which have ever been therein. The world of unbelief is perpetually saying to the Catholic Church, Why doest thou this or that? Why dost thou lay down the law as to faith or morals? Why dost thou claim authority to teach infallibly, to absolve men from their sins, to administer the sacraments and the like, seeing thou art not Christ, nor Elias, nor a prophet? And the answer is always in substance the same, Because there hath been One among you Whom you know not.

The remainder of St. John's words are a repetition of his former declaration as to the superior dignity of our Blessed Lord, in words which are to be found as spoken on other occasions by him and recorded partly by St. John, and partly by St. Matthew, and the other Evangelists. 'He it is, Who is to come after me, Who is put before me' — a little after me in time, but immensely before me and above me in dignity; and in the other passage of St. John he adds the reason, 'because He was before me:'[8] He came after me as Man,

---

[8] St. John i. 15. The words which follow v. 16, 17, 'Of his fulness we all have received, and grace for grace. For the Law was given by Moses: grace and truth came by Jesus Christ,' &c., seem to be the words of the Evangelist, not of the Baptist.

but as God He was from all eternity, and it is because He being God hath become Man that His dignity as God made Man is so pre-eminent—'Of Whom I am not worthy that I should loosen the latchet of the shoe.' That is, as has been said before, to Whom I am not worthy to perform the ordinary menial service of a slave. And at the same time that St. John spoke thus humbly of himself, and unconsciously prepared for himself that reward of exaltation, which our Lord was to confer upon him when in His turn He spoke so magnificently of the high dignity of His Forerunner, he declared himself and all others to be indeed that which he said he was unworthy of, that is, he declared himself to have no title to honour and no authority at all save only that which belonged to him as the servant of Jesus Christ. This image then, first used by our Blessed Lady in her *Magnificat* and by St. John here, of the relation in which all stand to our Lord, was constantly employed by our Lord Himself in His parables and other teaching, and passed into the ordinary language of the Apostles in their Epistles, and from them to the Church.

This formal and authoritative delegation from the great Council of the Jewish nation to the chosen messenger of God, sent to prepare the way before our Lord in His Incarnation, was afterwards more than once implicitly and explicitly appealed to by our Blessed Lord in His arguments with the Jews at Jerusalem. Although on this occasion he did not, in our Lord's absence, point Him out personally as the One to Whom he bare this witness, still they could have no doubt that Jesus Christ was the Person of Whom he thus spoke. And thus by their jealousy or suspicion of St. John himself, they had given him the opportunity, which otherwise he might never have had, of witnessing to the official rulers of the holy nation in his character of prophet, and with all the authority which his extraordinary holiness gave him, to the actual presence among them of the Messias. St. John tells us that the deputies of the Sanhedrim were Pharisees, chosen, that is, from the strictest and certainly, as we should say, the best of the sects into which the Jews were now divided, and so persons who might have been expected to profit more than others by the lesson thus addressed to them. At the time of our Lord and St. John it would seem that the great offices and chief power were rather in the hands of the Sadducees or even the Herodians, but that the majority of the Sanhedrim, at least the most generally respected members of it, those who had most personal influence with the people, were Pharisees. They were the leaders of thought, the active zealous partisans of the law, while the other sects were more worldly, men of lower doctrines and lower lives, standing better with the Roman authorities and the princes of the house of Herod. It may be for some reason of this sort that St. John specially mentions that the envoys of the Sanhedrim were Pharisees.

CHAPTER VIII.

The Lamb of God.

St. John i. 29–34 ; *Vita Vitæ Nostræ*, § 20.

THE formal and, as it may be called, the official witness borne to our Lord by St. John in his answer to the deputies of the Jewish Sanhedrim, did not in any way contain all the doctrine concerning the Incarnate Word of God which His Forerunner had to teach. There were truths concerning Jesus Christ which could not have been understood by the Pharisees, and for which a preparation of the heart was required, the most natural fruit of that preaching of penance and arousing of contrition and compunction which had borne so large a part in the mission of St. John. It is possible to conceive the Incarnation of the Son of God without any reference to its remedial effects and atoning character. Indeed, as is well known, there is a great school of Christian theologians who love to dwell on the thought that even without the Fall, God would still have become man, and who make that opinion more or less the foundation of a whole system. They consider that it was for the glory of the Creator, by Whom the whole universe was made with that glory for its end, that there should be a link between Him and the Creation, even the link of Personal Union on His part with that one creature of His, who, being both material and spiritual, summed up in himself the qualities of all the various natures of which creation consists. They argue from the craving that is innate in all men to know God, that He Who implanted that craving intended to satisfy it by Himself being, as the prophet says, 'seen upon earth and conversing with men.'[1] They consider that as God could not have due glory or thanksgiving paid to Him by mere creatures, it was fitting that one of the Divine Persons should take on Him a created nature, and that particular created nature, which, as has been said, sums up in itself all creation, in order that He in it and it in Him might give due, full, and adequate glory and thanks to God. Thus the Church takes up the hymn of the angels at the Incarnation, 'Glory to God in the highest,' and adds, 'We give thanks to Thee for Thy great glory,' as if now at last it had become possible for that honour and praise to be given to God which He deserved. Such are some of the reasons for this opinion, which is quite in keeping with many passages of Scripture, and with much of the language of the Church, as when in the *Credo* she speaks of the object of the Incarnation in two separate clauses, 'for us men, and for our salvation.'

Thus it is quite reasonable to suppose that the great manifestation of our Lord's glory made in the mystery of His Baptism by St. John, which implied the opening of heaven, the new birth by the Holy Ghost, and the adoption of sons as given to men through Him, might have had its counterpart in some scheme of divine love and condescension towards mankind, even if there had been among them no such thing as sin. But, in truth, all these benefits were to be extended to a race stained with sin, under punishment and banishment and a severe sentence of future judgment on that account, and the Incarnation, out of which all the blessings already mentioned were to spring, was to include, even if it could have been without including, the ransom of that race from the penalties which hang over it, and a perfect satisfaction

[1] Baruch iii. 38.

to the justice of God such as could have been made in no other way. And it was the will of God that our Blessed Lord should be pointed out by the chosen Forerunner in the character which belongs to Him on account of this aspect of the Incarnation, as well as in that of the Baptizer with the Holy Ghost and the Judge of all the world.

This manifestation is recorded for us by the blessed Evangelist, the disciple and namesake of St. John, and he tells us that it took place the day after that on which the Baptist had received and answered the deputation from Jerusalem, on which day, as it seems, our Lord must have returned from the place of His temptation. 'The next day John saw Jesus coming to him and said, Behold the Lamb of God, behold Him that taketh away the sin of the world. This is He, of Whom I said, After me cometh a Man, Who is put before me, because He was before me. And I knew Him not, but that He may be made manifest in Israel, therefore have I come baptizing in water. And John bare witness, saying, I saw the Holy Ghost descending as it were a dove from heaven, and It abode upon Him. And I did not know Him, but He Who sent me to baptize in water, the same said to me, On Whom thou shalt see the Spirit descending and remaining upon Him, He it is Who baptizeth in the Holy Ghost. And I saw, and have borne witness that this is the Son of God.'

These words connect the two testimonies of St. John together. Our Lord, he says, is the Son of God and the Lamb of God—the Son of God as manifested by the descent of the Holy Ghost upon Him, and the Lamb of God, Who taketh away the sin of the world. For no one but the Son of God can be the Lamb of God, and it is the work of the Son of God Incarnate as man to take away the sin of the world. The difference between the circumstances of these two manifestations is striking indeed. The manifestation of the Son of God is made, as has been seen, with every circumstance of solemnity, majesty, and spiritual glory. The three Divine Persons, the Father, the Son, and the Holy Ghost, are proclaimed and shown to the world, as in no other mystery even of the Incarnation save in that of the Transfiguration. In the manifestations which took place earlier in our Lord's history, there were not wanting circumstances of glory, as when the angels' voices were heard and the angels themselves seen by the Shepherds, or when the marvellous Star shone in the heavens to tell the Eastern sages of the birth of the King. There had, indeed, even then been indications of the truth which is now declared by St. John, because the angels had spoken to the shepherds of a Saviour as born at Bethlehem, and the gifts of the Eastern Kings had foreshadowed the Passion. The same truth was implied in the very name of Jesus, and in the prophecy of Simeon at the Purification. But now there are no elements at all of magnificence and glory. The declaration is made, as it would seem, to a few, at all events it is made without any outward sign which either marks its significance or is the witness to its truth. It is simply the word of St. John, spoken in language which would convey his full meaning to such hearts only as were prepared for the great doctrine of the Atonement by the intimate consciousness of the need of an expiation and reconciliation with God, such as could only be wrought by One Who was at once the Lamb of God and the Son of God, Who could be the due satisfaction for sin, because His sacrifice had the infinite merit which belongs to the act of a Divine Person. For we see from St. John's last words, as given by the Evangelist, that his teaching concerning Him Who was to come after him reached to the full height of the doctrine of His Divinity; and that being secured, he could go on to teach his disciples about the Atonement. In this we find an exact parallel between the teaching of St. John and that of our Blessed Lord. Up to the time of the confession of St. Peter our Lord never mentioned the Cross or spoke of His Passion; but, as soon as the faith of the Apostles in His Divinity had been made perfect by the teaching of His Father, then He began to tell them how He was to go up to Jerusalem and be crucified there. And again, the comparative privacy and simplicity of this solemn declaration on the part of our Lord's appointed witness may be understood as intimating that the day was not yet come for the full publication and manifestation of this character of the mission of our Blessed Lord. That day was to come after some three years' interval of time, and then our Lord was to be shown to all the world, crucified on the very day of the Feast in which the typical Lamb of God bore so conspicuous a part, in the midst of the whole multitude of the nation who had cried out to heaven, 'His Blood be upon us and upon our children.' Then it was that our Lord was to be fully manifested as 'making peace through the blood of His Cross,' [2] as giving us 'redemption through His Blood, the remission of our sins,'[3] who are 'redeemed, not with corruptible things as of gold or silver, but with the precious Blood of Christ, as a Lamb unspotted and undefiled, foreknown indeed before the foundation of the world, but manifested in the last times for'[4] us.

These words of St. Peter may be said to embrace the whole doctrine concerning our Lord as the Lamb of God—a doctrine which involves the deepest and most fundamental mysteries of our religion. It rests upon the two great attributes of God which are especially called into exercise in His dealings with creatures whom

2 Colos. i. 17.   3 Ephes. i. 7.   4 1 St. Peter i. 18-20.

He has made free, and so capable of choosing themselves rather than Him—His justice and His mercy, and it reaches to the greatest of all His works, the Redemption of the world by the Precious Blood of His Son. Christians are familiar with this doctrine, which is to them the key and interpretation of the Life of our Lord, which is constantly brought home to them in the daily system of the Church's functions and ministrations, and which has been explained with great minuteness in the writings of the Apostles. In order to give ourselves an account of the significance of the title, 'the Lamb of God,' we must begin by reminding ourselves of the meaning which it would convey to a devout few at the time of St. John—to those who, like the Evangelist himself, like Simon Peter and Andrew, were among the disciples of the Baptist, and may have been the very persons to whom the words were spoken which pointed out our Lord by this wonderful name.

The first and simplest notion connected with the name of the Lamb of God is the quality or character which appears to belong to the innocent animal from which the figure is taken. Thus St. Peter speaks of our Lord, in the passage already quoted, as of a Lamb unspotted and undefiled, and Isaias in his prophecy of the Passion speaks of the patience and meekness of the lamb that ' before its shearers is dumb.'[5] Here we have all the meekness and gentle patience of our Lord set before us under this image, on which, as it seems, St. Peter loves to dwell, as in his other Epistle he speaks of our Lord, ' Who did no sin, neither was guile found in His mouth, Who when He was reviled did not revile, when He suffered He threatened not, but delivered Himself to him that judged Him unjustly.'[6] Even here we find ourselves almost at once drawn on to

[5] Isaias liii. 7. [6] 1 St. Peter ii. 22, 23.

the higher associations connected with the image, because it is the lamb as a victim which is set forth as an example of meekness in that passage of the prophet, which, as may be remembered, was the text from which St. Philip began the instruction of the Ethiopian eunuch, which led to his conversion and baptism.[7]   And so we cannot doubt, in the second place, that the next thought to rise in the mind of such a contemplative as we are supposing, would be this, the sacrificial character of the lamb; and he would remember all that Isaias has said in that passage to that effect, that He Who was a lamb before His shearers 'hath borne our griefs and carried our sorrows, and we have thought Him, as it were, a leper, and as one struck by God and afflicted; but He was wounded for our iniquities, He was bruised for our sins, the chastisement of our peace was upon Him, and by His stripes we are healed.   All we like sheep have gone astray, every one hath turned aside to his own way, and the Lord hath laid on Him the iniquity of us all. . . . If He shall lay down His life for sin, He shall see a long-lived seed.'[8]

Thus we are led to the idea of victim and atonement as connected with the image of the Lamb, and the phrase the Lamb of God, the victim, the sacrifice of God, may remind us of those prophetic words of Abraham used to Isaac when they were on their way to the top of Mount Moriah, 'God will provide Himself a lamb.' Then it must be remembered that the Apostles, in whose writings the doctrine of the Lamb of God is drawn out in its practical applications, speak of the sacrifice of Christ as having been determined upon, and, indeed, as having been in a certain sense effected from the very beginning of all things, as St. John says in the Apocalypse,[9] 'that He was slain from the founda-

---

[7] Acts viii. 32.   [8] Isaias liii. 4–10.   [9] Apoc. xiii. 8.

tion of the world.' And St. Peter uses similar language, saying that Christ as the Lamb was 'foreknown indeed before the foundation of the world, but manifested in the last times for us.'[10] The doctrine which is contained in such statements amounts to this, that the sacrifice of the Lamb of God was decreed from the beginning, and that its virtue was applied to all those who approached God in faith and penitence, and made Him some offering, in anticipation of the sacrifice which was to be consummated in the fulness of time, which He decreed and was pleased to accept. Thus we are led to connect the sacrifice of Christ with the ordinance of sacrifice as a means of appeasing God and doing Him homage, an ordinance which is found from the first, and makes a part of every religion that is not the mere creation of human self-will, such as Protestantism. In all religions which, however degraded and distorted, still retain some vestiges of the original tradition out of which they have sprung, there is found something of a sacrifice, which is a witness, however poor and pitiable, to the doctrine of the Lamb slain from the beginning of the world. We cannot doubt that from the very earliest times sacrifices were offered to God and accepted by Him, and that they availed those who offered them in faith and repentance, by virtue of our Lord's future sacrifice. And from the outset of the sacred history we find this system of sacrifice among those who were dear to God. The doctrine was known to Abel, who offered of the firstlings of his flock, it was known to Isaac, to Abraham, to Job—who lived under the natural law alone—as well as to Moses and the children of Israel. Thus there never was a time, there never was a dispensation of God, when there were not sacrifices looking forward

[10] 1 St. Peter i. 20.

to our Lord, and when sins were not forgiven by faith, implicit or explicit, in His sacrifice. And it must be remembered, that although each new dispensation, as it succeeded to those before it, swept them away to a certain extent and annulled them by its presence, still in cases where the new dispensation was not known, or was not extended to those who lived under the former, that former dispensation remained in its first vigour to such persons. Thus not only did God never forsake altogether any child of His, for all had at least the natural law, the voice of conscience, the teaching of nature and of Providence, as well as primitive tradition concerning them, but from the first a holy, simple system of worship and sacrifice had been ordained by Him, the whole of which rested upon the virtue of the sacrifice of the Lamb of God.

God afterwards chose for Himself a peculiar people in which the line of generations which was to issue in the birth of Jesus Christ was to run, and to which were to be confided His 'oracles,' as St. Paul says—the truths concerning Himself and the rules of conduct which He had revealed to men. The system of sacrifice came to form the main part of the ceremonial and positive institutions which He gave to this people, with the express purpose of preparing them and others for the coming of His Son in the flesh, Who was to be the Lamb of God, and consummate the one great sacrifice which was to purchase the peace of the whole world. Everywhere we find the Lamb of God typified, everywhere the nature of the sacrifice is foreshadowed. The deliverance from Egypt was the great type of man's deliverance from the bondage of sin, and that deliverance is connected with the Paschal lamb, which was afterwards to be sacrificed yearly to keep up the memory of the past and the hope of the future and far greater deliverance. Day by day, morning and evening, the lamb was offered in the sanctuary, in the tabernacle, and afterwards in the Temple, for an expiation for the daily transgressions of the people. It is needless to repeat all the numberless types of the sacrifice of the Lamb of God of which the Mosaic system of worship was so full. All would have their virtue through that sacrifice.

By the side of this ceremonial anticipation of the great sacrifice of our Lord we find a constant strain of deep holy teaching in the Psalms and the Prophets, the purport of which was to keep clear in the hearts of the people the all-important truth, that the remission of sins was not to be found in the ceremonial sacrifices, useful and holy as they were, but in the interior dispositions of repentance and compunction of heart, together with a lively faith in the coming Redemption by the Lamb of God. Thus we find the mere outward sacrifices depreciated in comparison with the broken and contrite heart, as in the great psalm of penitence which was written by David after his sin and repentance. And yet, even in this, there is a reference to a sacrificial 'sprinkling' which can be understood ultimately of nothing but of that 'sprinkling of the Blood of Jesus Christ' of which both St. Paul and St. Peter speak. The psalm begins, as we know, with the expression of the most sincere interior penitence, 'Have mercy upon me, O God, according to Thy great mercy, and according to the multitude of Thy tender mercies blot out my iniquity, wash me yet more from my iniquity, and cleanse me from my sin,' and then it continues, 'Thou shalt sprinkle me with hyssop, and I shall be clean, Thou shalt wash me, and I shall be made whiter than snow.' And yet again, towards the end of the psalm, 'for if Thou hadst desired sacrifice I would indeed have given it, with burnt offerings Thou wilt not be delighted; a sacrifice to God is a troubled spirit, a contrite and a humbled heart, O God, Thou wilt not despise.'[11] The sprinkling with hyssop, spoken of at the same time with the relative depreciation of the ceremonial sacrifices, and the declaration of the value and necessity of a contrite heart, seem to refer to that sprinkling of the Blood of the Lamb of God which we have already mentioned.[12] It is at all events certain that it was the faith in the future great sacrifice which, with repentance and contrition, made the ancient sacrifices efficacious as far as they were so, or at least the occasion of the grace of the remission of sins.

It is thus easy to see that when St. John spoke of our Lord as the Lamb of God Who taketh away the sins of the world, he did not open out to his followers an entirely new field of doctrine, but a doctrine which had been the treasure and hope of the faithful children of God from the very beginning, included virtually in the very first promise made to Adam and Eve after their fall about the seed of the woman and the crushing of the head of the serpent. It was a doctrine known to holy Job, who spoke of his coming Redeemer, as well as to Moses and David, a doctrine relating to an act of God which is spoken of as accomplished from the foundation

[11] Psalm l. 1, 2, 3, 9, 18, 19.

[12] In Exodus xii. 22, the Israelites were told to take a bunch of hyssop and dip it in the blood of the Paschal Lamb, and sprinkle the lintel of the door and the two side-posts with it. This was a direct reference to the atonement of our Lord, inasmuch as it was at the sight of the blood thus sprinkled that the destroying angel was to spare the houses of the Israelites. There is the same use of hyssop in the solemn ratification of the covenant between God and His people, 'For when every commandment of the law had been read by Moses to all the people, he took the blood of calves and goats, with water and scarlet wool and hyssop, and sprinkled both the book itself and all the people, saying, This is the blood of the testament which God hath enjoined unto you' (Heb. ix. 19). These passages throw light on the mention of hyssop in the Psalms.

of the world, both because it was decreed from the beginning, and because its efficacy reached backwards to the very origin of human history, as it will reach onwards throughout all eternity in the kingdom of heaven. The Apostles, as has been said, are the great commentators on the meaning of the last words in St. John's saying, in which he declares that the Lamb of God takes away the sins of the world, and the whole system of the Church is a carrying out of their practical application.

That which is chosen and ordained by God as the means for 'taking away' the sins of the world must be absolutely, fully, and thoroughly efficacious for the end for which He designs and gives it. The Lamb of God, therefore, must altogether and to the very roots destroy sin; He must do away with all its effects and consequences on earth and in heaven, in the manner which is required to satisfy the justice of God and perfectly reconcile Him to man and man to Him. Thus in order to measure the meaning of these words of St. John, we must measure the depths of human sin, the injury which it inflicts on God and on man, and its results in God's providence and in the decrees of God's justice. We begin by original sin, which at once deprives man of all that favour of God which he enjoyed in his supernatural elevation in the state of innocence, with all the gifts and graces and hopes which were the effects of that favour. That sin shut heaven against him, made him the prey of internal disorder and rebellion, and changed his sojourn on earth from its original happiness into a state of exile and misery, in which he is afflicted by a whole tribe of penalties external and internal, and from which he has no exit except by death, to which a number of these penalties lead up, and which is itself the doom inflicted upon the whole race for the sin of their father. After original sin comes actual sin, with all its consequences, temporal and eternal, to each child of Adam and to the whole society which is made up of the children of Adam's guilt, the loss of grace, the slavery to the most shameful passions and the most degrading darkness and delusion, the empire of Satan, the eternal fires of hell which were prepared in the first instance for the rebel angels. Terrible as are these effects in single souls, such as they might be if each sinner was a wanderer on the earth like Cain, without contact with or influence on his fellows, far more fearful are the results of these consequences of sin when they are multiplied and intensified in their mischievousness by that mutual interdependence of men and the influence of each one upon his neighbour which are the conditions of human existence in the society which God has made. The history of man upon earth is the history of a plague-stricken community, relieved only by the lines of light which are interlaced in it by the perpetual action of the merciful Providence and never-ending clemency of God, the Father of all, the Father of the race as a whole, as well of each single soul in the myriads of which the race is made up.

These great moral evils are to be atoned for and healed by the Lamb of God. He is to do away with the debt which they involve to the justice of God by His perfect satisfaction. He is to destroy sin and moral disease by the grace which He has purchased and of which His Sacred Humanity is to be the never-failing source, and He is to deliver man from the penalties in the next world which correspond to the guilt which he has incurred. But the work of the Lamb of God extends still further than to the souls of men one by one. Or rather, as men are placed by God in such close union with one another, it is impossible that the healing grace of God should do its work in single souls without a visible and tangible result on the whole mass, a result consisting in the regeneration of the world by new social principles, and in the formation of a new kingdom of which the Lamb is the King. For sin may be considered in a twofold light, whether in the souls of men one by one or in society, as we regard on the one hand the corruption and foulness which it engenders, and on the other the fair growth of beauty and fertility which it impedes. When grace cancels sin it must not merely remove corruption, but it must develope moral perfection and raise it to a higher standard and level than what it might otherwise have attained. Thus it is the work of the grace purchased and communicated by the Lamb of God to do away with all the havoc made by sin, and to render the souls of men gardens full of the fairest flowers of virtue. In the same way it is to transform the howling wilderness of society, and plant it thickly with manners, customs, fashions, and institutions of which charity is the law and the example of our Lord the normal pattern, in which every seed of holy precept or counsel which He has left behind Him is nurtured until its growth resembles that of the mustard seed of which He spake. The result is the formation of a new social world. That is, the perfect 'taking away' of sin. And the complete work of grace in the single soul in saintliness, and in society it is that Christian system of life in all its manifold relations and conditions which is the ideal at which the polity called Christendom aims or aimed.

There are other 'redemptions' spoken of by the Apostles, notably by St. Paul, which must have their place in our consideration of the work of the Lamb of God. St. Paul tells us of two of them in the famous passage with which he closes the first part of his great argument in the Epistle of the Romans.[13] First he speaks of the effects of sin upon the exterior creation, effects which are to be done away with when the perfect triumph of Jesus Christ is accomplished, when the influence of His redemption has reached to its full sphere. 'The expectation of the creature waiteth for the revelation of the sons of God. For the creature was made subject to vanity,' that is, to change and corruption, 'not willingly,' that is, not naturally, 'but by reason of Him that made it subject, in hope; because the creature also itself shall be delivered from the servitude of corruption unto the liberty of the glory of the sons of God. For we know that every creature groaneth and travaileth in pain, even till now.' The truth is indeed written upon the face of the visible creation in the midst of which we live, for the law of change and decay which is upon it has a penal character about it. But it needed a mind like that of St. Paul, inspired by the Holy Ghost, to explain to us this mystery of the universe. And then he goes on to speak of the other redemption, that of our own bodies. 'And not only it, but ourselves also, who have the first-fruits of the Spirit, even we ourselves groan within ourselves, waiting for the adoption of the sons of God, the redemption of our body.'

There is yet another element to be added to the foregoing in the consideration of the redemptive work of the Lamb of God. He it is of Whom the Psalmist sings, 'With Him there is plenteous redemption.' It does not agree with the dignity of Him Who is our Sacrifice and our Redeemer, to place things as they were before and to restore to God and to man what they have lost. He must make all things more beautiful, more stable,

[13] Rom. iii.

more glorious, more heavenly than before. He must give to God, if that be possible, more glory than He has had dishonour. He must give to man nobler graces, a loftier station, a more divine condition, an ineffable bliss instead of a happy familiarity with God. He 'takes away the sin of the world,' and He leaves in its stead a world which has been turned into an ante-chamber of heaven by His grace, in which souls can rise higher than the state from which they fell, in which society is capable of a glorious profession of Christian virtues which represent even the purity of the angelic choirs. He fills the thrones of heaven with the souls that were under sentence of companionship with Satan and his angels. There are future glories to be revealed, especially as to the redemption of the body and the renovation of the world, the new heavens and the new earth in which justice is to dwell, which are as yet unknown to us and which may be as wonderful in their own kind as those spiritual glories and joys prepared by God for those who love Him, as to which the most soaring imagination of saint or prophet must flag and droop. And this is to continue throughout all eternity, while nowhere in the kingdom of God's glory and at no moment throughout the endless ages of the world to come, will there be any happiness or any exaltation among the sons of God of whom St. Paul speaks, or in the creation which is to be regenerated by their adoption, which is not the fruit of the sacrifice of the Lamb of God, 'Who taketh away the sins of the world.'

It is perhaps a mark of the force and beauty of St. John's words, as well as of the marvellous sanctity, which, as it were, gave them wings of fire, that, few of them as have come down to us, so many out of those few have become the household expressions of the children of God. He it is who has given to our Lord the two beautiful names by which He is known as the Lamb and as the Bridegroom. And St. John the Evangelist, who was one of His disciples, and, perhaps, one of the two who first joined our Lord when St. John pointed Him out as the Lamb, uses this name more than any other in the account of the unseen world and its mysteries, which is contained in his Apocalypse. The heavenly visions of that marvellous book are full of the Lamb, He is the centre of all. 'Behold in the midst of the throne, and of the four living creatures, and in the midst of the ancients, a Lamb standing as it were slain, having seven horns and seven eyes, which are the seven Spirits of God, sent forth into all the earth.' And now the seer beholds Him open the book, 'And when He had opened the book, the four living creatures and the four and twenty ancients fell down before the Lamb, having every one of them harps, and golden vials full of odours, which are the prayers of saints, and they sang a new canticle, saying, Thou art worthy, O Lord, to take the book and to open the seals thereof, because Thou wast slain, and hast redeemed us to God in Thy Blood, out of every tribe and tongue and people and nation, and hast made us to our God a kingdom and priests, and we shall reign on the earth.' And then again he hears the canticle of the angels and living creatures and the ancients, 'the number of them was thousands and thousands, saying with a loud voice, The Lamb that was slain is worthy to receive power and divinity and wisdom and strength and honour and glory and benediction,' and then the song is taken up 'by every creature which is in heaven and on the earth, and under the earth, and such as are in the sea, and all that are in them : I heard all saying, To Him that sitteth on the throne and to the Lamb, benediction and honour and glory and power for ever and ever.'[14]

[14] Apoc. v.

But it would not be well here to draw out more fully the whole of the teaching of the Apocalypse of St. John as to the future glories of the Lamb of God, because it may be summed up in the simple truth that the kingdom of bliss throughout all eternity is represented therein as the Kingdom of the Lamb. Meanwhile the Church on earth is what she is and has the privileges and blessings and powers which she has by virtue of Him Who, as St. Paul says in the Acts, hath purchased her with His own Blood, and she repeats below what the Church in heaven practises above, for the sacrifice of the Lamb is the centre of all her worship, the strength of all her prayers, the life and power of all her sacraments, and day by day, before a thousand altars, her children repeat the invocation which St. John has taught them, 'Lamb of God, Who takest away the sins of the world, have mercy upon us, grant us Thy peace.'

The remaining words of St. John's testimony are also full of significance. 'This is He of Whom I said, After me cometh a Man Who is preferred before me.' He states the truth of the superior dignity of our Blessed Lord, Who came after him in time, but was in the providence and order of God 'made higher than me because He was before me,' because though He was born and appeared in the world as Man after me, He was from all eternity before me. The Fathers have remarked on the emphasis with which St. John seems to use the word 'man,'[15] on which they suppose him to insist either on account of the contrast between this title and that of the Lamb, which he has just used, or because there were several prophecies in which our Lord had been particularly predicted under this name. Such was that famous prediction of Zacharias,[16] addressed to Jesus the son of Josedec, the High Priest, 'Behold

[15] ανης.   [16] Zach. vi. 12.

a Man, the Orient is His name, and under Him shall He spring up, and build a temple to the Lord. Yea, He shall build a temple to the Lord, and He shall bear the glory, and shall sit and rule upon His throne, and He shall be a priest upon His throne, and the counsel of peace shall be between them both.' The name of 'the Orient,' or 'Dayspring,' is applied to our Lord in the Canticle of St. John's father Zachary, taken in this respect from the prophecy of the older prophet of the same name, and thus there is another reason for the reference which St. John himself may be supposed to have made. The same designation of the 'Man,' emphatically such, is applied to our Lord in another passage of the same Prophet Zacharias, 'Awake, O sword, against My shepherd, and against the Man that cleaveth to Me, saith the Lord of Hosts : strike the shepherd, and the sheep shall be scattered.'[17] This passage was, as we know, quoted of Himself by our Lord, on the eve of its fulfilment in His Passion, and we have thus good reason for thinking that the title of 'Man,' in its special signification, was one which belonged to Him.[18] For our Lord was in all strength and vigour, in the perfection of intelligence and use of His faculties, mental and spiritual, a Man from the very first moment of His conception, whereas others pass months and years before they attain even to the first exercises of reason and conscience. And though St. John himself had the privilege of sanctification in his mother's womb, and of the accelerated use of his faculties, he was still a child when our Lord was a Man in those respects. And in the last words in which he gives the reason for the higher elevation of our Lord above himself, he points to the whole doctrine of the

[17] Zach. xiii. 7.

[18] It is used of our Lord by the disciples going to Emmaus (St. Luke xxiv. 19).

Person of Jesus Christ, for as Man He is so highly elevated because His Person is a Divine Person, and thus even as Man He is the Son of God.

'And I knew Him not, but that He may be made manifest in Israel, therefore am I come baptizing in water.' It has already been shown, how the manifestation of our Lord was the great object of the whole ministry of St. John; but the Evangelist goes on to repeat, as he so often does, the same witness with still greater emphasis. 'And John gave testimony and said, I saw the Spirit coming down as a dove from heaven, and He remained upon Him. And I knew Him not, but He Who sent me to baptize with water, said to me, He upon Whom thou shalt see the Spirit descending and remaining upon Him, He it is that baptizeth with the Holy Ghost, and I saw, and I gave testimony that this is the Son of God.' St. John had been sent to baptize either by an interior inspiration from God, or by a message delivered by an angel. He had been brought up in the desert, and our Lord at Nazareth, and although Christian art delights to dwell on the two children meeting in their youth, there is nothing to be certainly affirmed as to any personal intercourse between them, either then or later, when they were growing up to manhood, though it seems unlikely that there should have been no communication at all. But St. John had not only to give an authentic, formal, and juridical witness to our Blessed Lord as the Messias, the Incarnate Son of God, but he had also been given a certain definite sign which he was to make the ground of his testimony, and therefore any knowledge which he might have had of our Blessed Lord independently of this sign, was not the knowledge on which this testimony of his as His Forerunner and Prophet, was to be founded. Whether by mere human knowledge he knew our Lord, is what we cannot know; but that he knew Him when He approached to be baptized, is certain from the conversation which passed between them, which St. Matthew has recorded. That knowledge of our Lord may have been given at the moment by an interior illumination, as it was given to holy Simeon and Anna in the Temple at the time of our Lady's Purification. But, still, that illumination was not the sign, but only a knowledge that our Lord was He as to Whom the sign would be given, and so even that illumination did not supply St. John with the evidence on the strength of which he was to bear witness. When the sign was given, then his knowledge came. The words of St. John, therefore, are to be understood as if he had said, It is not on account of any knowledge that I have had either of old or of late, concerning the Person of the Lamb of God, the Man Who is to come after me, Who is the Baptizer with the Holy Ghost, that I bear this testimony to Him, but because I have seen fulfilled in Him that which I was told to take as the sign that was to be given me. When I was sent to baptize with water, I was told that I should see the Holy Ghost descend and remain upon Him. So it has been, and this is the ground of my testimony, which is the object and end of my mission. The mission and the testimony rest on the same authority, and as I have obeyed Him Who sent me by baptizing, so now have I obeyed Him also by testifying, on the authority of the sign which was given me.

Thus it is the solemn unction of our Lord by the Holy Ghost which is the ground of St. John's witness to Him as the appointed Messias. 'I have seen, and I gave testimony, that this is the Son of God.' The doctrine of St. John concerning our Lord embraces all His great titles and qualities—He is the Man; the second Adam; the Head of the human race. He is the Lamb of God Who taketh away the sins of the world. He is the Son of God, declared to be such by the great manifestation at His Baptism. He is the Baptizer with the Holy Ghost, the author and source of the new order of grace and regeneration. He is the searcher of hearts, the future Judge, Who will purge His floor and gather the wheat into His barns, and burn up the chaff with unquenchable fire. We shall have yet one more and still more definite witness from St. John as to our Lord, but these are enough to show us that his disciples must have been very well indeed prepared to receive Jesus Christ, and that he not only possessed a most perfect intelligence of the Christian mysteries himself, but most faithfully imparted that knowledge, as far as it depended on him to do so, to those who came to him to be instructed and prepared for the highest work in the future Church of God.

NOTE IV.

On St. John's Knowledge of our Lord.

The sceptical critics of the present day are so fond of fastening upon anything in the narratives of the four Evangelists, on which they consider it possible to build an assertion of discrepancy between the several historians of our Lord, that it may be useful, even in an uncontroversial work, to meet such difficulties as they arise. In the last chapter mention has been made of what appears to be such a difficulty in the statement of St. John Baptist,[1] that he did not know our Lord until he had the sign given to him of the descent of the Spirit, which statement seems at first sight out of keeping with what St. Matthew tells us of the reluctance of the holy Baptist to administer baptism to our Lord.[2] The explanation given above is enough to meet the difficulty, but it may be added here that, when the language of St. John comes to be studied, that explanation is greatly confirmed. It is usual

---

[1] St. John i. 31.   [2] St. Matt. iii. 14.

with that Evangelist to use a direct negative when he means
to deny something only relatively. Thus our Lord says,
'My doctrine is not Mine, but His that sent me;'[3] 'Neither
hath this man sinned nor his parents, but that the works of
God should be manifest in him;'[4] 'No man taketh (My life)
away from Me, but I lay it down of Myself;'[5] 'The word
which you have heard is not Mine, but the Father's Who
sent Me;' and the like. In all such cases the accurate
translation would be a qualified negative, 'My doctrine is not
so much Mine;' 'It is not that the man or his parents have
sinned;' and so on.[6]

CHAPTER IX.

The First Disciples.

St. John i. 35-51; *Vita Vitæ Nostræ*, § 21.

IT was a part of the beautiful character of St. John, a
feature which is very often wanting in those who have
a share of his zeal for souls and who imitate his fervour
in preaching and bringing about conversions to God, to
be always withdrawing himself from notice, disclaiming
credit and refusing praise, and passing on those over
whom God gave him influence for good to the school
and mastership of another. And we may also notice
another feature of his refined sanctity—that even in this
part of his work, which consisted in leading and sending
his disciples on to our Lord, he left almost all to be
done by the grace of God, as if in reference to that
principle which our Lord afterwards expressed in the
words, 'No man can come unto Me, except the Father,

---

[3] St. John vii. 16.   [4] St. John ix. 3.   [5] St. John x. 18.
[6] See Beelen, *Gramm. Græcit. N. T.* in Syntaxi, c. v. § 56, n. 8.

Who hath sent Me, draw him.'[1] St. John had roused
the spirit of penitence in the multitude; he had taught
them to expect and believe in the Son of God, the
Messias, the Baptizer with the Holy Ghost, Who was
to come after him. He had spoken in the most magnificent way about the pre-eminence of Him Who was
to come, and then he had pointed Him out, as soon
as the time had come and the sign which had been
given him had been fulfilled. When our Lord returned
from His temptation, it seems clear that He must have
held some intercourse with St. John, because He was
'coming to him' at the time when he first gave testimony
as to the Lamb of God. According to human and
ordinary ways of proceeding, we might have expected
that St. John would now at once send all his disciples
to our Blessed Lord, and either proclaim to the multitude that his own mission was over, or at least insist
on their at once throwing themselves at the feet of
Jesus Christ to beg pardon and instruction from Him.

Instead of this, we find that St. John simply and
repeatedly pointed our Lord out. The rest was to be
the work of God's grace, pleading with each heart, one
by one. For it is comparatively seldom that great
bodies of men come at once to put themselves under
the yoke of Jesus Christ. Such works of salvation as
conversion to God, submission to the Catholic Church,
the closer following of our Lord in the perfect life,
entrance into religion, and the like, come from individual
acts of God upon single souls, and although personal
influence and direction and the example of others are
not without their proper range of action in bringing
about such results, they still can never play more than
a secondary and accidental part. Thus St. John left
his disciples to take their own course, after having

---

[1] St. John vi. 44.

shown them our Lord, as if to leave them to that action of the Father of which our Lord spoke. Moreover, our Lord Himself had not yet begun His Public Ministry. It seems to have been His plan at the present moment to associate a few chosen souls to Himself, who might be privately instructed and formed, and become the nucleus of the band of the Apostles, to whom He was to intrust the foundation of the Church. We have at present to consider the account which St. John the Evangelist, who is generally thought to have been one of the two first of our Lord's disciples, gives of the quiet and simple manner in which the first members of this little band were gathered together.

There were, then, at least five among the disciples of St. John who were to become at once the friends and companions of Jesus Christ, Who was to be to them their Master or Rabbi, much as St. John himself hitherto had been. One of these five, as has been said, was St. John the Evangelist himself, the younger son of Salome, who seems to have been a cousin of our Blessed Lady. He, with his brother James, of whom no mention is here made, were thus relatives of our Lord, and may have been personally known to Him, for there is no certain proof to the contrary in the fact that He was as yet unrecognised by St. John and others as the Messias, or a prophet or teacher of any grade. Three others were from Bethsaida, a village on the shore of the lake of Gennesareth, Simon and Andrew, two brothers, and Philip. There was also Nathanael, a native of Cana, a town in Galilee, lying not very far from Nazareth—near enough, at all events, for the citizens of each to have had a sort of jealous feeling as to those of the other. There is no mention made of James, the brother of John, but, as he is always placed high in the lists of the Apostles, which lists seem yet to be based in great measure upon the order of time as to the knowledge which each Apostle had of our Lord, it is difficult to suppose that he was far off at the moment when the small knot of St. John's disciples came to follow our Lord.

We know nothing at all of the previous history of any of these first Apostles, except that they had been prepared for our Lord by St. John, and must probably therefore have spent some time in the school of the latter. All except Nathanael seem to have been fishermen, but this does not of necessity imply that they were of quite the lowest class in society, or altogether illiterate and uneducated. The manner in which they severally joined our Lord is recorded with loving minuteness by St. John the Evangelist, and we see that the Providence of God dealt differently in each case, according to the character of the person concerned. The two first, Andrew and his companion, who is supposed to have been St. John himself, followed our Lord's footsteps in consequence of the Baptist's intimation, 'Behold the Lamb of God!' It seems as if our Lord kept silence and did not mingle with others, and that those to whom St. John had pointed Him out were afraid to accost Him of themselves. Our Lord then turned to these two, who were following Him, and not waiting for them to speak, asked them, 'What seek ye?'—words which seemed to imply that He knew them already, and was willing to welcome them and put Himself at their service. They said to Him, 'Rabbi, where bidest Thou?'— acknowledging Him already as their Master, and asking Him for an opportunity to put themselves under Him, and hearing Him discourse and teach at leisure. 'He said to them, Come and see. They came and saw where He dwelt'—perhaps some hut or booth out of the numbers which had been hastily erected in the place of so great a concourse of people, 'and remained with Him that day.   It was about the tenth hour.'[2]

The Evangelist tells us nothing of what passed between our Lord and His two new disciples in that memorable conversation, which may have lasted many hours.   But the effect was that they left Him with their hearts full of joy and fervent faith, eager to communicate to others the blessing which had been revealed to themselves. It was like 'one of those long intimate and secret communings with our Lord in prayer, adoration, or thanksgiving after Communion, from which men go forth filled with a new strength, with new eyes for all things around them, and with an ineffable peace and fulness of soul, a tranquil and immovable conviction that they have been with God.   This 'remaining' with our Lord, the foundation of so much future intercourse, was the treasure of their own hearts, not to be spoken of to others.   St. John tells us of what St. Andrew did immediately afterwards, following the dictates of his tender brotherly love, and we can hardly doubt that St. John did the same as to St. James as his friend as to St. Peter. It was a memorable act, because it was the introduction to our Lord of him who was to be the foundation-stone of the Church.   St. Andrew was the first to find 'his brother Simon, and saith to him, We have found the

---

[2] There is some uncertainty as to the method of computation of hour which is followed by St. John in his Gospel, and we are therefore uncertain whether the time of day was in the forenoon, as our ten o'clock, or late in the afternoon, not very long before sunset.   The other Evangelists generally keep to the Jewish divisions of the day, the third, the sixth, and the ninth hour, answering to our nine, twelve, and three in the day, and there is nowhere any mention of the intermediate hours, seven, ten, and the like, except in St. John and in our Lord's parable of the Labourers in the Vineyard, in which, however, the mention of the eleventh hour may be an intentional deviation from the common Jewish way of speaking.   St. John is thought by some writers to have found in Asia Minor a method of reckoning like our own, and to have used it in his Gospel.

Messias!' It was not a principle, or a truth, or a doctrine, or a method, or a system, which could be conveyed by word of mouth from one to the other—what they had found was a Person Who must be known and seen by each one for himself. So he led him to Jesus, and Jesus looking upon him said, 'Thou art Simon, the son of Jona, thou shalt be called Cephas' (that is, Peter).

It may be gathered from the few words of St. Andrew and of our Blessed Lord to Simon, that the conversation which had occupied the time spent by the two disciples with Him had been on the subject of the approaching kingdom and of our Lord's office and prerogatives, as declared at the Baptism and by the teaching of St. John to his disciples. Throughout the whole narrative of these first interviews between our Lord and the future Apostles, He is spoken of as the Messias, the Person in Whom the prophecies of Moses and the other prophets are fulfilled, the Son of God, the King of Israel. Afterwards there was always the difficulty, Who was He? and opinions concerning Him varied, even among those who were inclined to trust themselves to Him, as Nicodemus, who could not doubt that He was a Teacher come from God, on account of His miracles at the feast. The ready faith of the early Apostles, even though it may not have mounted up as yet to the full height which it reached when St. Peter made his confession of our Lord's Divinity, shows the influence of St. John, whose teaching had been so definite and personal as to Him. And our Lord dealt with them as a Master and a King. His words to Simon convey the promise of a new name, such a promise as in the mouth of the Anointed Son of God implied a great office and dignity, a work which was symbolised by the name given, and a large gift of graces proportionate to the work. For in the kingdom of God there are absolutely no empty titles, merely of honour, nor are there any offices or functions the giving of which is not accompanied with abundant grace and power to enable those on whom they are bestowed to discharge them adequately. Our Lord then speaks as One Who can give this or that office as He chooses, and the name which He confers or promises to confer upon Simon, the son of Jona, expresses the office to which he is to be called and the grace which belongs to it. We cannot be sure whether the name Cephas was ever used by anticipation before it was actually conferred upon Simon by our Lord, as seems to have been the case when the Apostles were solemnly called and inaugurated in their office. But the meaning of the name in his case, and consequently of the office which was to be conferred upon him, is explained in the memorable words of our Lord after his great confession, 'Thou art Peter, and upon this rock I will build My Church.' Thus we see that the Church, the dearest thought of our Lord's Heart, after His Eternal Father, was in His mind at this time, and that it was the presence of Simon Peter that, if we may so say, called it up, the two being inseparable in the love of our Lord as in the Providence of God, Peter and the Church that is built upon him, as in the Incarnation itself there are two persons never to be separated, Jesus Christ and His Mother, through whom He became Man.

The next of the first disciples to be brought in contact with our Lord was Philip, a fellow-townsman of Peter and Andrew. There may have been something timid and shrinking in his character, which made it a matter of difficulty for him to approach our Lord of himself, and the mention of his acquaintance with Andrew and Peter may suggest that they either mentioned him to our Lord or even endeavoured to bring him to their new Master. However this may have been, our Lord dealt with him in a manner quite different from that which He used in the cases already mentioned. 'The next day He wished to go forth into Galilee, and He findeth Philip. And Jesus saith to him, Follow Me! Now Philip was of Bethsaida, the city of Andrew and Peter.' For the ways of God in drawing souls to Himself are as various as they are wonderful, nor does He always use the same way at different times with the same soul. To some it is a suggestion implied in a disclosure of His beneficence, mercy, or greatness, some external incident, or visitation, or personal deliverance or mercy, or something which strikes the soul almost into the dust with the conviction of its danger and need of help, speaks to it in the words of St. John, 'Behold the Lamb of God!' or forces upon it the necessity of looking into the truths which concern salvation, as if He said, 'Come and see; come, make trial of what is here offered you if you will accept it.' Others are led by example, or personal testimony of those whom they love and respect, as when Andrew said to Simon, 'We have found the Messias!' For others God almost takes the whole burthen on Himself, and moves their heart so powerfully, perhaps at the same time giving them some powerful outward call, as to St. Matthew or St. Paul, that they are almost unable to resist it, and with some it is as if He sought them, and found them, and said to them, 'Follow Me!' The vocation is the same to all, though the method be different and in all God does no violence to the human will, which may yet turn away, if it so chooses, from all these gracious ways which God has contrived for its salvation.

If Philip had before hung back timidly, he was after

his first interview with our Lord as zealous as Andrew had been for the extending to others of the benefit which he had himself received. He at once sought out Nathanael, and the method of the conquest of this last to Jesus Christ is told more circumstantially than in the former cases. Philip findeth Nathanael, and saith to him, 'Whom Moses wrote of in the Law, and the Prophets, we have found! Jesus, the Son of Joseph of Nazareth. And Nathanael said to him, Can any good thing come from Nazareth? Philip saith unto him, Come and see!' Philip spoke like a man whose soul and heart have been set free from a great weight and restraint: our Lord has called him, and He has more to say about him to Nathanael than Andrew to Peter. He is He of Whom Moses wrote in the Law, He Who was the subject of the prediction of the prophets. All types are fulfilled in Him, all prophecies are verified in Him. The types of the law, and the prophecies, the two great heads of teaching concerning our Lord, had no doubt been the subject of continual discourse, instruction, and meditation to the disciples of the Baptist, as well as to all the devout few who were at the time 'looking for redemption.' What must have been the power of our Lord's presence on souls that were yearning for Him, what must have been the charm and force and divine unction of His words and whole conversation—for it can hardly be imagined that Philip had not some considerable intercourse with Him before he set out to look for his friend Nathanael —if without miracle or any other argument but what was derived from His looks or His words, Philip could so soon come to the conclusion that He was the One in Whom all the marks by which God had decreed that the Messias should be known were to be found at once! We cannot suppose that either in the case of Philip or in that of Andrew there was any rashness or foolishness or overcredulity, and yet we find them in the space of perhaps a few hours as rooted and fervent in their faith as if they had known our Lord for years.

Nathanael, however, was not to be won at once. The mention of his birthplace can hardly be quite accidental, and it may perhaps be meant to show us how a personal or local or national prejudice may sometimes hang like a blind before the eyes of good men, and make them unwilling to discern God in the action of His Providence or in the person of some one on whom He has conferred great gifts and an important mission in the Church. One of our Lord's proverbial sayings, which He illustrated in His own Person, was that a prophet had no honour in his own country, and the meaning of this saying may certainly be extended so as to embrace the jealousies and narrowness of mind with which we often regard our near neighbours, and remain obstinately incredulous as to the possibility of any wonderful manifestation of grace or power in them. This is one of the littlenesses of human nature which are sometimes found to survive in the souls which have long conquered their passions, and the secret selfishness or jealousy which is the root of our reluctance to believe in the great goodness of God to those with whom we have near external connection shows itself sometimes in its most mischievous form in national or class antipathies. Nathanael's case is a picture of what frequently meets us, when men on the eve of some noble act of faith or devotion are kept back by what is in truth a mere cobweb, generally the result of some prejudice against others, which, personal or even local though it be, is enough to hinder the ordinary action of God's grace. But our Lord, in His goodness and loving ingenuity in winning souls to Himself, condescends to wind Himself round the heart, to find just the opening by which it seems to insist on being approached, and so He meets Nathanael in a way which even he, with all his prejudices, could not resist, taking more pains, as it were, to win him in proportion to the greater difficulties which he opposed to the attraction.

Nathanael said to him, 'Can any good come out of Nazareth?' Philip said to him, 'Come and see.' Jesus saw Nathanael coming to Him, and said of him, 'Behold an Israelite indeed, in whom is no guile!' They were words of great commendation, meant for Nathanael to hear as he was drawing nigh. The particular commendation of being a true Israelite, a man without guile, would seem to have had some relation to those secret thoughts and desires of Nathanael of which our Lord presently showed Himself to have the knowledge, for the words fell upon Nathanael as revealing such a knowledge. Nathanael said to Him, 'Whence knowest Thou me?' as if he had been suddenly struck by finding himself in the presence of One Whose eyes read his heart. If this be so, we must suppose that he had been thinking or praying or desiring some boon to which our Lord's words would refer in a way that was intelligible to him, while at the same time they conveyed only an ordinary meaning to others who may have heard the words. Jesus answered and said, 'Before Philip called thee, whilst thou wast under the fig-tree, I saw thee.'

These words would confirm and deepen the impression which had already been made by the former words of our Lord, because they would fix the time and place at which the thoughts or prayers already referred to were in Nathanael's mind. We cannot, of course, conjecture with any certainty what these thoughts or aspirations were. Nor is it necessary that we should know them, as the important point in the whole scene is simply that by a sign which revealed to Nathanael that He was the reader of hearts, our Lord at once swept him out of the difficulties and hesitations which were besetting him on the score of the insignificance and unhonoured character of Nazareth. Many a man lingers over the decision to take some step in advance in the service of God, to break off a dangerous habit or to lead a higher or more perfect life, to take up the Evangelical Councils or to consecrate himself to our Lord in religion, and his hesitation is often best brushed away by some such revelation of God's nearness, of which it matters not what the details may be. Nathanael may have prayed to be as simple or obedient to God's calls as the Patriarch Jacob, the first Israel, or his prayer may have had reference to the spiritual privileges of the true Israel of God—the favourite title, as it seems, for the devout persons among the Jews, when the external independence and national splendour of the race were well-nigh gone, a title which finds a place in the three Evangelical canticles, the *Magnificat*, the *Benedictus*, and the *Nunc Dimittis*, of our Lady, Zachary, and holy Simeon. But this, as has been said, is only conjecture. It is certain that our Lord's words touched the inmost conscience of Nathanael, and brought him at once to His feet. 'Nathanael answered Him, and said, Rabbi, Thou art the Son of God, Thou art the King of Israel!' going beyond, in some measure, the confession of Philip, as Philip had enlarged upon and unfolded the confession of Andrew, even though he may not yet have believed all that was contained in the title of the Son of God, but thought that it belonged to our Lord in some secondary way, as the angels and holy men are called the sons of God.

Our Lord's answer to Nathanael seems to express surprise at the readiness of his faith. A single sign which had shown him that he was in the presence of One Who could read his thoughts, was enough to change his doubts, or even his prejudices, into enthusiastic conviction and confession. Not unreasonably surely, for every such revelation of God, whether it be by outward miracle or by something which makes us feel close to Him and that He is acting on us and addressing Himself to us, ought to command our faith in whatever person or doctrine in confirmation of whose claims such a manifestation can be truly said to be made, because God cannot lie and cannot manifest Himself in any way in support of what is false. In truth, one of the characteristics of the Christian evidences is their overwhelming superabundance, or, at least, what would be such but for the perverseness and unreasonableness of the world to which they are addressed. Our Lord has a promise for Nathanael as well as for Simon Peter. It is not a personal gift, but one of the great features of the Gospel dispensation which are to be apprehended by all, and perhaps the form in which it is put in our Lord's words, as well as His first speech to Nathanael, may have had some reference to the secret thoughts of which He showed His knowledge. 'Because I said to thee that I saw thee under the fig-tree believest thou? Thou shalt see a thing greater than that.' And He said to him, 'Amen, amen, I say to you,' turning, thereupon, to the other disciples, as well as to Nathanael, 'you shall see the heaven opened, and the angels of God ascending and descending upon the Son of Man.'

These words contain many very notable points. In the first place, we have now for the first time that solemn form of speech of our Lord's which He constantly used when He was asserting something very strongly, and on His own authority. It is the form in which the Truth speaks, claiming belief because He is the Truth, sometimes dogmatically, sometimes judicially, sometimes prophetically, always divinely and with power. St. John always duplicates the affirmatory form, and we may gather from this practice of his who hung so lovingly upon our Lord's words, that it was the habit of our Lord to use the double ' Amen.' And it may be remarked that when our Lord was withstanding Satan in His temptation, He uses reasoning, and cites authority as the foundation of His reasoning, but now He simply makes promises and affirms truth on His own word, expecting that to be received as sufficient warrant for what He asserts. In His dealings with His friends and disciples, in His ordinary teaching, as the Sermon on the Mount, in His disputes with the Jews, as after the miracle at the pool,[3] and the feeding of the five thousand,[4] as well as in His conversations with such people as Nicodemus, He uses the language of authority, and this was the characteristic of His teaching as distinguished from that of the Scribes, as His hearers noted. And as He has said, ' He that heareth you, heareth Me, and he that despiseth you, despiseth Me,' it follows that there is nothing for which the Church has greater authority in His example than for this very habit of witnessing authoritatively to the truth, from which all other Christian bodies shrink, and which it is one of her great offences in the eyes of the world that she never will abandon. It is in the use of this authority of the Church, that her children have the inestimable blessing of her infallible guidance, and the exercise of that virtue of faith which is the condition of every grace.

In the second place, we have the great promise of the

[3] St. John v.　　　　[4] St. John vi.

vision of 'heaven opened, and the angels of God ascending and descending upon the Son of Man.' The promise is addressed to all the disciples, and is therefore to be understood of something general, belonging to the whole economy of the Incarnation. The 'heaven opened' had already been seen at the time of our Lord's Baptism, and His words here may therefore refer to that mystery. What had been then seen for a moment by outward eyes, was to be a permanent spiritual effect of the Incarnation, a continual element in the new dispensation founded upon it. Heaven had been opened, and open it was to remain, and the Apostles were to be the witnesses of the multitude of blessings which were to come to mankind in consequence. The other words, 'The angels of God ascending and descending,' are quoted from the description given in Genesis[5] of the mysterious vision seen by the Patriarch Jacob (Israel) when he was leaving the Holy Land after having received from Isaac the blessing of the first-born, to go to seek a wife from his mother's family in Haran, the vision in which the great promise was made to him which had before been made to Abraham, that in his seed all the tribes of the earth should be blessed, that is, that from his seed the Incarnate Son of God should be born. 'He saw in his sleep a ladder, standing upon the earth, and the top thereof touching heaven, and the angels also of God ascending and descending by it.' This, then, is the vision to which our Lord refers, the fulfilment of which He promises the Apostles that they shall see. It is remarkable that both in the account in Genesis and in our Lord's words the angels are said to be ascending first and descending afterwards, and this seems to signify that the promise

[5] Gen. xxviii. 12.

has some special reference to the economy of prayer and sacrifice and religious works in general, in which the prayers or offerings or good deeds of men are borne up to the throne of God by the Angels, who then return to earth laden with gifts and blessings. Thus the Angel says to Tobias,[6] 'When thou didst pray with tears, and didst bury the dead, and didst leave thy dinner, and hide the dead by day in thy house, and bury them by night, I offered thy prayer to the Lord, . . . and now the Lord hath sent me to heal thee.' So it is said even of Cornelius the Roman centurion,[7] that an angel came to him, and said, 'Thy prayers and thy alms are ascended for a memorial in the sight of God, and now send men to Joppa and call hither one Simon who is surnamed Peter.' These instances will suffice to fix the reference of the vision, and the promise to that intercourse between heaven and earth by means of the angels, in which the dispensation of prayer and of God's blessings in answer to it, and to everything that has the same character, consists.

But it still remains further to explain the last part of our Lord's promise, that the angels of God should be seen 'ascending and descending upon the Son of Man.' This is the first time, as far as we know, that our Lord uses for Himself this name which all through the Gospel history is usual with Him; and which may therefore be properly explained in this place. It must first, however, be remembered that the Son of Man in the promise of our Lord does not fill a place analogous to that of the Patriarch Jacob in the vision at Bethel. Jacob was the person who saw the vision there, as the Apostles are to witness its counterpart and fulfilment in the new kingdom of the Incarnation. In the vision of Jacob the angels of God ascend and

[6] Tobias xii. 12.   [7] Acts x. 4, 5.

descend upon the ladder; in the promise of our Lord they ascend and descend upon the Son of Man. The Son of Man, then, is the ladder, the means of passage and communication between earth and heaven, heaven and earth. That is, the Sacred Humanity of our Lord, as has already been said, unites heaven and earth, it gives to the prayers and worship of man a merit and a right of access to God which they had not before, and secures for them a ready acceptance and a rich reward to which before they had no title, while the angels of God are the ministers who pass to and fro, by means of that Sacred Humanity, bearing the prayers of man to God and returning with the favours of God to man. This it is that the Apostles are to witness, a greater thing even than the revelation of our Lord to a single person by means of His knowledge of the heart and secret thoughts. A greater thing, because it involves a power and a right in human prayer which nothing but God become man can give to it, whereas the knowledge of the heart in particular cases might always be imparted to man according to the will of God. A greater thing, because it covers a larger sphere, it extends to a whole system and economy and not to a particular manifestation of God's power, because it gives a new character to those ministrations of angels which have been from the beginning, and unlocks new treasures of the bounty of God which would have been closed to anything but the merits of His Incarnate Son. And our Lord's words in their reference to the vision of Jacob imply that what the Apostles shall witness is the fulfilment of all that was foretold in that vision, and thus of the whole range of prophecies connected with it, and of the promises of God concerning the blessing of all nations.

We have only further to remark on the meaning of

the title the Son of Man, which our Lord here gives to Himself, and which throughout the history of His Life we find Him so constantly using, while, on the other hand, it is seldom said of Him except by Himself. In the first place, the title is taken from the prophecy of Daniel, who uses it of our Lord in a manner which denotes the union of His Divine and Human Natures in One Person, his language being too magnificent to apply to a mere man. 'Lo, one like the Son of Man came in the clouds of heaven, and He came even to the Ancient of days, and they presented Him before Him, and He gave Him power and glory and a kingdom, and all peoples, tribes, and tongues shall serve Him; His power is an everlasting power that shall not be taken away, and His kingdom that shall not be destroyed.'[8] And these last words are echoed by the Archangel Gabriel in the Annunciation to our Blessed Lady, in words which have passed into the Christian Creed, 'Of His Kingdom there shall be no end.'[9] The Son of Man, therefore, means properly the Incarnate Son of God in His Human Nature, and thus it is the appropriate title by which our Lord should call Himself in His promise to the Apostles concerning the fulfilment of the vision of Jacob, in which the Incarnation was foreshown. Nathanael had confessed Him to be the King of Israel, and our Lord's words send him back to the title used by Daniel in the prophecy which spoke of a far mightier and more enduring kingdom.

Again there are several other reasons given by theologians for the use of this title, which apply universally as well as to the case before us. Thus it signifies not only the Incarnation, but also the manner in which the Incarnation was carried out, that is, by means of the birth of our Lord from a human mother, like other

<hr>

[8] Daniel vii. 13, 14.　　　　[9] St. Luke i. 33.

men, instead of by simple creation, as Adam or Eve. And it follows from the same truth that the title contains a reference to the one promised seed, the one Child Who was to be born of the woman between whom and the serpent there was eternal enmity set by God. The title 'Son of Man,' if used of our Lord in a sense common to Him and to all others, would have no signification in the present context, and we may therefore infer that it is meant to convey the idea of what is special to our Lord, that He is the new Adam, the Head of the Human Race. It expresses on the same account our brotherhood with Christ, as we have a common father with Him, which would not have been the case if He had become Man in another way. And thus also, if indirectly, it turns our thoughts to our Lord's one human parent, of whom He became Man, and points to our relation to her as her children, being one with Him. It expresses also the fulfilment in Him of all the promises and prophecies made to the ancient Fathers about the blessing of all the earth in their seed. And on the other hand it expresses the fruit of the Incarnation to us, which is, that we are made sons of God by adoption, God having become the Son of Man that He might give us power to become the sons of God. Lastly, it expresses the humiliation of the Son of God, who emptied Himself, and took on Him the nature of Man, and in His humiliation delighted in no name more than in that which reminded Him of the low condition in His creation which He had assumed.

NOTE V.

On St. Nathanael.

It is well known that, although there is some difference of opinion on the point, there is very great authority for the identification of the Nathanael spoken of in the last chapter and St. Bartholomew the Apostle. The two, Philip and Bartholomew, are put side by side in the Gospel catalogues of the Apostles, and, as has been said above with reference to St. James, there is some reason for thinking that those catalogues are drawn up mainly on the principle of priority of knowledge of our Lord as His followers, though St. Peter is, of course, always put first. St. John's account of Philip bringing Nathanael to our Lord would account for this juxta-position of the two. The name Bartholomew is evidently a patronymic, not a personal name, Bar-Tolmai. Nathanael, moreover, reappears in St. John's Gospel as present in the last miracle of our Lord after the Resurrection, when all the others named in his company are Apostles. The other arguments will be found in an elaborate dissertation on the subject in the Bollandist Collection,[1] where the evidence from the traditions of the countries in which St. Bartholomew preached is adduced. It will be assumed in this work that Nathanael is the same as Bartholomew.

The contrary opinion seems mainly to rest upon some almost chance words of St. Augustine, who supposes that the language used by Nathanael to Philip shows that he was a learned man, and elsewhere uses his supposed exclusion from the Apostolic band as an instance of the want of learning among the Apostles. There are many such instances in which moral reflections of the Fathers on assumed facts of this kind have been taken as statements of those facts resting upon the authority of this or that great saint, and it is worth while for Christian critics to be alive to the hollowness of such reasoning.

[1] August 25.

CHAPTER X.

The Return to Galilee.

St. John ii. 1-10 ; *Vita Vitæ Nostræ*, § 22.

ONE of the highly-privileged souls of latter times, who
had from her very infancy a marvellous gift of contemplation as to the incidents of the Life of our Lord and other
kindred subjects, mentions here and there in the narrative of her 'visions' which has come down to us her
constant surprise at the shortness of the Gospel records.
It is not necessary to consider here the whole subject of
such contemplations as those of Sister Anne Catharine
Emmerich, the holy person to whom allusion has just
been made, nor can use be made of them in a work like
the present further than as very important and very
beautiful aids in the training and use of the Christian
imagination.   But the remark which has just been
quoted may serve to remind us of what might otherwise be practically forgotten, that is, that there must
have been a whole range of incidents, as well as a
large number of persons and places, through which
the path of our Lord, if we may so speak, passed, of
which no mention is made in the Gospel, and which
must necessarily in some degree and manner, as far as
it may be possible, be supplied in the picture which we
strive to draw for ourselves of what our Lord's Life truly
was.   None of the Evangelists indulge us with descrip-
tions or enumerations, though their simple and short
narratives often leave upon our minds a very distinct

picture indeed, of which the central figure is always our Blessed Lord, but in which the minor details are suggested to our imaginations. The first object of the Gospels, considered as literary works, was, as is explained elsewhere, not so much history as doctrine, the collection of the facts about our Blessed Lord on which Christian instruction and doctrine had been founded. No doubt there were other divine purposes which guided the hands of the sacred writers, but this was the first and the chief, and it has left its mark, so to say, upon the form and method which they have adopted. The use of the Gospels for prayer and contemplation suggests that Christian exercise of the imagination of which mention has already been made, and thus far, at all events, we may safely, if sparingly, avail ourselves of the beautiful pictures which have been drawn for us in contemplations like those to which reference has been made, just as we should of an actual picture drawn for us by Fra Angelico, or any other painter whose inspirations might be as pure, as holy, and as theological as his. Nor should we shrink, even in a narrative which aims at being historical, from helping ourselves now and then by the consideration of what we know must either have been, or be like what actually was, although there may be no distinct assertion to that effect from the pen of an Evangelist. For there are facts in our Lord's life which are generally assumed as certain in the Church; as, for instance, that He ordained some at least of the Apostles priests or bishops at the Last Supper, or that He showed Himself after the Resurrection first of all to our Blessed Lady, assumptions as to which the saints not only use words of sanction and toleration, but language which implies some censure on those who do not see that it could not have been otherwise.

The banks of the Jordan, at the time when St. John

was there preaching and baptizing, must have been crowded with people coming and going, and it is very likely that even the appearance of our Lord once more on the spot, after His long fast and temptation, may have been lost to many who were there amid the press and movement of the multitude. Very quietly and almost silently did our Lord make up His little band of followers, five of whom have been named in the foregoing chapter, and to whom we can hardly be wrong in supposing that St. James, the elder brother of the Evangelist St. John, was soon added, either there or immediately after our Lord's return to Galilee. They were all disciples of St. John Baptist, and there must have been affectionate and solemn leave-takings between them and the holy guide who had led them so far on the path of salvation. St. John himself had all his life been devoted, in one way or other, to the contemplation of the mystery of the Incarnation and to the service and worship of the Eternal Son made man, Whose presence in the womb of His Blessed Mother had caused him to leap for joy before his birth, and had conferred upon his soul the singular favours and graces which have been already spoken of. For all these long years the herald of Jesus Christ had lived in the desert, and can have had but little intercourse with our Blessed Lord; and now that his work seemed to be accomplished, now that he had performed his office of preacher of penitence and baptizer with water for the remission of sins, now that he had seen the promised sign of the descent of the Holy Ghost upon our Lord Himself, and heard the witness of the Father to Him, now that he had borne his official witness to the Person and Mission of Jesus Christ and had pointed Him out as the Lamb of God to His own future Apostles, it might seem that he would have been allowed to fulfil the desire of his heart, and become indeed a servant and a follower of Him the latchet of Whose shoes he had declared himself unworthy to loosen Who could be a better Apostle, who could work more successfully in the preaching of the Gospel, who could have borne a more authoritative and perfect witness than he? But it was not so ordered in the counsels of God. St. John had his work, and it was not that of an Apostle; indeed, great as it was, there was a sense in which our Lord could say of him in regard of that office, 'he that is least in the kingdom of heaven is greater than he.' And like the other great saints and servants of God, like the angels who minister before the throne in heaven, he was not to go beyond the limits of the office for which he had been sent, as even our Lord Himself said that He was not sent save to the lost sheep of the house of Israel, made a difficulty about healing the daughter of the Syrophœnician woman, and left the founding of the Church and the opening of her gates to the Gentiles, to the Apostles after Him.

As far as we are told, this was the last occasion on which the Blessed Forerunner of our Lord could have seen Him to Whom he was so devoted. The months of his life were already numbered, his ministry was soon to be violently closed by an arbitrary act of authority on the part of Herod, and then, after some months spent in prison, his soul was to be set free from his body at the bidding of a dancing-girl, and sent among the holy souls of the patriarchs, prophets, and saints of the Old Testament, to await our Lord's coming at the moment after He had expired on the Cross. Throughout the Gospel history there runs a spirit of sacrifice, not merely of earthly and fleshly ties, but even of spiritual companionship and the holy enjoyment of mutual society and the open communication of heart with heart on the part of those who are dearest to God, our Lord, our Blessed

Lady, St. John Baptist, and others. As if we were to be warned that this life is so short and fleeting, and so entirely to be given up to work, toil, and conflict, that, as the dearest friends on a battlefield must defer their enjoyment one of the other until the fight is won, so the time for such spiritual intercourse, almost the highest delight of holy souls, is to come hereafter. If it was a great sacrifice to St. John not to be allowed to follow our Lord now that He had at last been manifested, if he even knew, as St. Paul afterwards with regard to the clergy of Ephesus, that he was not to see His face any more in this world, still the parting blessing of our Lord must have consoled and strengthened him to fulfil the remainder of his short career with the utmost fervour, boldness, and faithfulness, considering the fewness of the days that remained and the immense work for heaven that might be done in them.

Our Lord's course since He had left Nazareth for the place where St. John was baptizing, had already been a series of wonderful manifestations, partly, indeed, to men, but still more to the angels of heaven, and to the children of His Church who were to live in the generations after His sojourn on earth, and whose minds and hearts were to be constantly fed upon the consideration of these great mysteries, the full comprehension of which, as far as such comprehension is possible to our limited faculties, is to be one of the great sources of their enjoyment in His future kingdom. The silence and obscurity of the Hidden Life had suddenly changed for the marvellous scene which took place at the Baptism in which His unction and mission had been solemnly declared. Then had come the supernatural impulse of the Holy Ghost, guiding Him, according to the will of His Eternal Father, into the barren inhospitable desert, there to fast and pray and suffer temptation for forty days and forty nights,

at the end of which time Satan, who had been so successful in his assaults upon the faithfulness to God of the
first Adam, had measured his strength and used all his
wiles to prevail with the second Adam, and had been at
last obliged to withdraw in shame, confusion, and fury, at
his own utter defeat. Each of these great manifestations
of our Lord had been a step in advance towards the
foundation of His future kingdom and power, for the
great initiatory sacrament of Baptism had been instituted
and endowed with all its rich treasuries of grace in the
first, and in the second a victory had been won in which
our Lord had, as it were, put His foot upon the neck of
the tempter, 'Walking upon the asp and basilisk, and
trampling under foot the lion and the dragon,'[1] who was
henceforth to acknowledge the power of his conqueror
in others as well as in himself, to be weakened and
shackled, more than ever, in his assaults upon them, and
to tremble before the faith, confidence, humility, prayer,
and mortification, with which they would meet him, after
the example and in the might of Him Who had fasted,
prayed, and been tempted in the wilderness. And our
Lord's return to the Jordan valley had come just after
the solemn testimony given concerning Him by His
faithful servant the Baptist, and was immediately succeeded by the great declaration made by the same
St. John, that He was the Lamb of God Who taketh
away the sin of the world, a declaration which summed
up the whole doctrine of the Atoning Sacrifice of Jesus
Christ, and its effects in time and in eternity. And now
our Lord, outwardly simple and avoiding parade or the
assumption of dignity and authority, had still begun
to work as the Master and Teacher of souls, calling to
Him whom He would, one in one way, another in another,
promising high positions in His Church and the fulfilment

<hr>

[1] Psalm xc. 13.

of all the prophecies, speaking with the most majestic authority and showing that He knew the characters of men and the secrets of the heart. We are now to follow the next stage in the great unfolding of the character and prerogatives of our Lord, but for this it was the will of the Father that He should leave the banks of the Jordan, and the crowds prepared for His teaching by the Baptist, out of which He might have selected, if He had so chosen, more followers to be gradually trained for the office of the Apostolate, as well as the Blessed John himself, so willing and so eager to do the part that belonged to him in sending disciples to his and their Master.

'The next day,' St. John tells us, at the beginning of his account of the reception of Philip and Nathanael by our Lord, 'He would go forth into Galilee, and He findeth Philip.' It was, therefore, to Galilee that our Lord's steps were now to be bent, and this, as we gather from later statements of the Evangelist, not in order that He might there at once begin His public preaching, which was not to be until after the approaching festival of the Pasch, and also after the imprisonment of St. John. It seems, therefore, clear that we must suppose that our Lord's intention was to rejoin His Mother. 'The third day there was a marriage in Cana of Galilee, and the Mother of Jesus was there.' As our Lord was not as yet before the world in the character of a public teacher, with a special mission committed to Him such as even in the eyes of the world would explain His absence from His Mother, who was now altogether dependent upon His care, it may well have been that now that the immediate object for which He had left Nazareth had been obtained, it was best for Him to return to her side, that He might show before the world His careful and loving discharge of all filial duty. He was about, as we gather from what St. John tells us a ilttle further on, to remove her, with those who were now dwelling with her, from Nazareth to Capharnaum, the place which was soon to become the centre of His missionary action, and to have the distinction, which Nazareth was to forfeit, of being called 'His own city.' It appears also very probable that the couple who were about to be married at Cana were either both relations of our Blessed Lady, or that at least one of them was allied to her, and they may have earnestly desired that the Blessed Son of Mary, of Whom so many wonderful things had been and were now said, should be present to bless the marriage. And our Lord, Who afterwards was so condescending in accepting invitations and obeying the sort of pressure which people put upon Him to come and partake of their feasts, would now, with all His sweetness and humility, listen to the entreaties which were made to Him either by His Mother or by the family in which the marriage was to take place.

Such, we may suppose, were the ordinary and human motives for our Lord's return. But we may also be sure that neither these, nor the overwhelming love for His Mother which burnt in the Sacred Heart of our Lord, could have turned His footsteps homeward at such a time, if it had not been the will of His Father that now He should go to that particular spot, and that, moreover, the counsels of God in this return looked above all things to that further great manifestation which it was decreed should take place at this marriage-feast. For the Providence of God, especially in the guidance of His saints and chosen instruments, is ever wont to take occasion from simple, humble, and ordinary matters to bring about great effects and great displays of grace or of works to the glory of God. Nothing earthly is truly great in the sight of

God, and even what seem to be the most insignificant actions of our Blessed Lord are often fraught with the greatest issues, and unfold the most magnificent glories of His kingdom. But in truth, if the occasion of the marriage at Cana was ordinary, not rising above the level of other domestic incidents, it still was great and magnificent on account of the Persons Who were engaged in it, for where the Mother of Jesus is, and where Jesus Himself is invited with His Apostles, there whatever is most great and sublime in the order of grace or of the glory of God may naturally find its home.

———

CHAPTER XI.

The Marriage at Cana.

St. John ii. 1-12 ; *Vita Vitæ Nostræ*, § 22.

THE journey from the Jordan valley where St. John was baptizing and where our Lord had now made His first selection of the future Apostles from among the disciples of His Forerunner, to Nazareth or Cana, was enough to occupy three days, and it seems that on the evening of the third the little band arrived at Cana, where our Blessed Lady was awaiting her Son. The marriage festivities among the Jews usually took place in the evening, and thus our Lord would arrive in time for the banquet, before the close of the third day. And instead of at once retiring with His Blessed Mother to converse with and console her after His absence, He and His companions joined the wedding guests of the humble couple who had just been united in the synagogue of the place. We have nothing to guide us as to the rank or station of the bridegroom and bride, except the fact of the wine running short, which seems to indicate comparative poverty, unless it were a mere accident, occasioned in part by the arrival of a larger number of guests than had been expected. But the position of our Lord and His Blessed Mother in the feast seems to have been one of a certain pre-eminence or authority, and this would not have been naturally the case if the families which were now being allied had been of the highest rank.

The marriage festivals sometimes lasted a week, sometimes a couple of days, according to the rank or means of the entertainers. In this case the feast does not seem to have been prolonged, and this is another reason for thinking that the families were not above the middle rank. It was no doubt a scene of much innocent mirth and simple rejoicing, such as our Blessed Lord liked to gladden with His presence, and which gave Him many opportunities of holy and gracious teaching in His familiar, proverbial, and parabolic manner, without taking away from the happy gaiety of the occasion. Some contemplatives have imagined the various games or trials of skill or of chance with which the guests were amused, and have pictured to themselves our Lord as acknowledged by all as the Master and Guide of all, though He was not formally installed or called the 'master of the feast,' and turning the games into simple lessons of piety, explaining the symbolical character of the gifts and prizes, speaking of the sanctity and mystical signification of marriage, or blessing the newly married youth and maiden in a way which purified their affection and delivered them from the lower impulses of earthly passion. Our Lord may often have taken a part in other scenes of domestic happiness and homely rejoicing during the long years of His Hidden Life at Nazareth, but His presence at this feast, immediately after He had taken upon Himself the great office of the Messias, the new Adam, the Lamb of God, shows still more forcibly than any earlier incident in His Life might have shown, how the whole sphere of family life, with all its seasons and occasions of sorrow and joy, labour and rest, prosperity and adversity, has been laid hold of and touched by Him with that touch of His which transforms everything natural and earthly, making it glow with charity and all the kindred virtues, so as to be worthy of the heirs of the heavenly kingdom, and capable of exercising them in the use of His grace and in the acquiring of the merits which belong to their future destinies in glory.

Moreover, it must not be supposed that this action of our Lord, so simple and natural in its outward aspect, was a mere condescension on His part, as it may have been afterwards when He accepted the invitations of persons who did not understand Him, but who pressed their hospitality upon Him in a rude ordinary manner, perhaps half out of curiosity, or thinking that they were doing Him an honour, or, as it were, patronising Him. On the contrary, this feast was to mark another onward step in the great revelation of Him and in that unfolding of His work which was the object of the Providence of His Eternal Father, a solemn occasion in which He was to do a part of that work of the Anointed Son of God which was to last on for all ages after Him in the Church. A part of that work which He came to do had reference to the holy tie of marriage which God had instituted in Paradise when He gave Eve to Adam for his helpmate and companion. That primitive institution of God had been in many ways corrupted and debased on account of the extraordinary force and wide dominion of the lower passions of men, and though among the Jews, and some other nations in a lesser degree, marriage still retained some vestiges of its original sanctity, still even to the chosen people Moses had been allowed to make that concession about divorce of which our Lord afterwards spoke as having been granted on account of the hardness of their hearts, and in practice there was but little left of that reverence for marriage which is still one of the elementary conditions of true social happiness and well-being. It was, as has been said, a part of our Lord's mission to set right this fundamental mischief, and, in so doing, He acted as the restorer and regenerator of the natural human society as well as the founder of the new society of His Church. His action and teaching with regard to marriage is one of the most demonstrative proofs that He has come to transform and ennoble and elevate human life even in the world, and that the far-reaching grace of the redemption of the Lamb of God is intended to penetrate society to the very roots. Marriage was to be restored to its original dignity and purity, and made into a Christian sacrament, representing the union between the two natures, divine and human, in the Person of our Lord, and that further mystical union which He was to consummate between Himself and His Church, which is His Bride. The grace of the Christian sacrament of marriage, like that of all the other sacraments, was to flow from the Sacred Humanity in which He was now present at the simple wedding-feast at Cana. Thus the Fathers tell us that our Lord went to the marriage-feast, not only out of kindness and condescension, not only that He might be an example of perfect holiness and modesty on such occasions, and furnish an argument against any who, as certain heretics in the early days, denied the lawfulness of wedlock, but also that He might, as the Anointed of God, ratify and sanctify marriage, and leave His blessing and His grace upon it for ever. And thus, even if there were no further reason for the mention of this feast by St. John in the miracle which was to mark out this occasion as so great an epoch in our Lord's earthly career, it would still naturally have a place in this fourth sacramental Gospel.

But there was, as we know, a further reason in the counsels of God for our Lord's presence at this homely festival. The time was now at hand for another great display of the power and authority which had so long been hidden in our Lord, and all the circumstances of this fresh manifestation were arranged and chosen beforehand by the will of His Eternal Father. These circumstances are told with the utmost simplicity by the Evangelist. At a certain time in the feast there was a lack of wine. Our Blessed Lady may have had some share in the preparation and arrangement of the supper, if, as seems likely, the family were related to her by blood. At all events, in her careful tender watchfulness for the wants and conveniences of others, she came to know of the deficiency before it was publicly observed. She turned to our Lord and said, 'They have no wine!' 'And Jesus saith to her, Woman,' or Lady, 'what is to Me and to thee?' words which, in the idiom in which they were spoken, as in other parts of Scripture, are equivalent to the other translation—'What have I to do with thee? Mine hour hath not yet come. His Mother saith to the servants, Whatsoever He shall say to you, do it. Now there were there six stone water-pots set, according to the purification of the Jews'— as was the custom with the Jews for purposes of purification, which required the washing of the feet after a journey or a walk, the washing of the hands before meals, and the like. 'Jesus saith to them, Fill the water-pots with water. And they filled them up to the brim. And Jesus said, Draw now,' take water in smaller cups from these large vessels, 'and take it to the ruler of the feast. And they took it. Now when the ruler of the feast had tasted the water that was made wine (and he did not know whence it was, but the servants knew, who had drawn the water), the ruler of the feast calleth the bridegroom, and saith to him, Every one' else ' puts' on the feast-table 'good wine first, and when men have well drunk, then he puts what is not so good ; but thou hast kept the good wine till now.'

It ought not to be a matter of astonishment if the manner in which many parts of this simple narrative are understood varies in various minds and according to the ideas which they have already formed concerning the persons who bear a part in the scene which is here described. In a strictly controversial work it might be necessary to enumerate, or even to confute, the several interpretations which have been put on the words and acts of our Lord and His Blessed Mother, more or less derogatory to the latter, but a discussion of that kind would hardly be altogether in place in the present volume. To those who understand the prevalent Catholic belief as to the wonderful sanctity and fulness of grace of our Blessed Lady, there is no difficulty in seeing in her first address to our Lord an exercise of those gifts of the Holy Ghost which perfect the understanding. It is not necessary to inquire whether our Lord had before this time, in His Holy Infancy, or in the course of the years of His Hidden Life, exercised the miraculous power which was inherent in Him, even in His Human Nature, by virtue of the Divine Union. Our Lady's knowledge of His power and prerogatives would not rest upon experience, and if He had never before wrought a miracle in her sight, she would have understood that it was only because such was not then the will of His Father, and not on account of any absence of power in Him. We can hardly imagine our Lady ignorant of what had taken place concerning Him on the banks of the Jordan, nor, if she had witnessed that manifestation with her own eyes, would she then have learnt for the first time Who He was. Nor could she be ignorant that there was a large display of the most wonderful miracles to be looked for whenever He took upon Himself the office and the mission which was peculiarly His own, or that He had now to some extent, at least, begun to do so. There is, therefore, no reason to look far for that intelligence in our Blessed Lady which would enable her to see that the prayer which she made to our Lord could and might be heard, and that it might be for the glory of God that He should listen to it. It was her characteristic grace to meditate on and ponder the works and acts of God, especially on the history of our Lord and the economy of the Incarnation, to compare them together, to muse over them, and thus to attain to an intelligence of them which was in some sort her own work, as well as the result of a wonderful and special illumination granted to her by God and enhanced by that continual intercourse with her Son, which had now been the occupation of her soul and heart since the moment at which He became Man in her womb. It would hardly require a light and a faith so specially great as the light and the faith of our Blessed Lady, to understand that the time might now have come, if it had never come before, for the manifestation of His glory by a miraculous sign.

Such intelligence and such faith would not, however, of necessity have made our Blessed Lady take upon herself the office of pleading on this occasion with our Blessed Lord, Who must have known, as she was quite aware, the needs of His hosts, and Who was the best judge as to the moment at which the manifestation of His glory by means of miracles should be begun. Our Lady did not act on impulse, but always 'chose the best part,' according to the words of our Lord which are applied to her by the Church in the Mass of her Assumption. The more solemn the occasion, the more decided her own action on it, the more we may be sure that she did and said what she was especially guided to do and to say by the Holy Ghost. Thus when she left Nazareth for the purpose of visiting St. Elisabeth, taking the long journey, the issue of which was to be the sanctification of St. John Baptist in the womb of his mother, she had indeed an intimation that such might be the will of God from the words of the angel concerning St. Elisabeth, but must also have had some special impulse bidding her at that moment go to her cousin. So now she must have chosen to speak on some similar ground. And the two occasions may most fitly be compared together, because the sanctification of St. John in the womb of St. Elisabeth was the first internal miracle of grace that was wrought by our Lord after His Incarnation, and the miracle at Cana was the first external and material miracle which our Lord wrought of which we have any account, and is spoken of by the Evangelist as the beginning of 'signs,' so that it was in any case the beginning of a new sort of manifestation. And both in the one miracle and in the other, our Blessed Lady is instrumental. Her voice sounding in the ears of Elisabeth woke up the soul of St. John to full consciousness and to an intelligence of the near presence of our Blessed Lord, so that he leaped in the womb for joy; and now it is her prayer that unlocks the door, as it were, for a long and most glorious procession of miracles of power and beneficence, which honoured our Lord during His earthly sojourn, and which have continued since His time and in virtue of His power in the Catholic Church. This is the prerogative of Mary in the kingdom of her Son, that good of all kinds, spiritual and material, begins in this way from her, not as if she were its cause and source, but because, as St. Bernard says, such is His will, Who hath chosen that we should have all things through her. Her intervention was His chosen means for the sanctification of St. John by the grace of Him Who is the source of all grace, to her as well as to us, and her prudent and gentle prayer was the appointed condition which was to set in motion the bountiful streams of miraculous benefits which were to gladden the whole world as they flowed from the Sacred Humanity of her Divine Son.

Our Blessed Lady's petition has often been considered by the Fathers and other holy writers as a perfect model of prayer, in that it simply states the need, and leaves everything else to the wisdom and goodness of our Lord, much as that touching prayer about Lazarus, sent to our Lord by the sisters Martha and Mary, 'Lord, he whom Thou lovest is sick.' For the whole economy and system of prayer rests upon our putting before God, as children before a Father in Whom they have perfect confidence, the needs which we feel and all the desires of our heart; not that God does not know them already, and is not already disposed to grant what is asked or desired, for if that were necessary for prayer, we should never pray at all; but that God desires us to exercise the right of children, and to show by such exercise the love of children, because He loves to be asked, and it is a different thing with Him to give un-asked, as He often does, and to give in answer to prayer, which is an exercise of love on our part, and to answer which is a fresh act of love on His part. For He gives abundantly to all His creatures, inanimate as well as animate, material as well as rational, but only to those who have the power and the right to pray does He give in that particularly loving manner in which His answers to prayer are made. Thus our Lady's petition to her Son was as much a petition as if she had thrown herself at His feet and begged Him with tears to hear her, while at the same time it most perfectly expressed her submission to His will, her confidence in His superior wisdom, and, even by its very form, left it open to Him to do as seemed best to Him, without any appearance of refusing His Mother.

Our Lord's answer to His Blessed Mother is most naturally understood in the light of what has already been said of her petition to Him. If it be true that it was a part of the providence of His Father that He should on this occasion begin the manifestation of His glory by means of miraculous signs, and that His beginning of the great series of such signs was to be immediately connected with our Blessed Lady's intercession, we have little need of further answer to the many interpretations of our Lord's own words which regard them as involving something of reprehension. 'Lady, or woman, what is to Me and to thee? What have I to do with thee? Mine hour has not yet come.' The name by which He calls our Blessed Lady is the name which He used to Her when He was hanging on the Cross, and when she, in her incomparable constancy, faithfulness, love, and resignation, was standing beneath, giving to Him the consolation and homage of her compassion, and sharing, as far as any heart could share, in all the pains and sorrows and agonies of His own. At such a time it is certainly not likely that her most loving Son would have addressed her in any way that implied coldness, but rather that He would choose the name most honourable and most tender of all. It is commonly said, that the name woman is used in the language of that time as a title of honour, equivalent to our English word lady; and this is undoubtedly true, so that on that ground our Lord's words are to be understood as implying great honour and reverence. It may also be added that there is no trace in the language of Scripture which even hints at any dishonour or disrespect as contained in the common name woman. But in truth the reason why our Lord used this word to His Blessed Mother would seem to be kindred to that for which He called Himself so constantly the Son of Man, and this would have especial force when it is used on occasions of deep mysterious importance in our Lord's course, as in this scene at Cana and again at the scene of His Passion and Death. At such times it would especially become our Lady to be addressed as Woman in this theological sense, in reference to the mystery of the Incarnation, for she is the 'Woman' of whom our Lord was born, she is the Woman of whom God spake to our first parents when He made them the promise of a Redeemer after the Fall, she is the Woman to whom the whole range of types look forward, who was to conceive and 'compass a man,'[1] she is the Woman, the second Eve, as our Lord is the Man and the Son of Man, the second Adam. And so on these great and solemn occasions, which marked stages and epochs in the unfolding of the mysteries of the Incarnation, our Blessed Lady was addressed by our Lord by what we almost call her official and theological title, whereas on the only other occasion on which we have record of His addressing her, when He was found at the age of twelve years in the Temple, He did not use it.

[1] Jer. xxxi. 22.

The next words of our Lord, 'What is to Me and to thee?' are Scriptural expressions, which it cannot be unsafe to interpret according to their usual sense. David uses them to Abisai, the son of Sarvia, and they are recorded by the Evangelist as the words of the demoniac, or rather of the legion of devils, to our Lord. In each case they express a kindred meaning; they are an expression of wonder or even of complaint at some one who puts pressure or exercises influence upon the speaker. In each case it is practically equivalent to such words as, Leave me to myself, or, Leave me alone; and it may be compared to what God said to Moses, after the sin of the people in worshipping the golden calf, 'Leave Me alone, that My wrath may be kindled against them,'[2] words which did not signify to Moses what they literally implied, but were an intimation to him that he was to pray very earnestly indeed to hinder by his intercession that very kindling of the wrath of God against the people which would have led to their destruction. Here again we see an acknowledgment of power, not that the will of Moses could constrain the will of God, but that it was the will of God that the prayer of Moses should win pardon for the people when but for that prayer pardon would not have been granted. We must therefore understand that here also the proverbial expression, What is to Me and to thee? conveys an acknowledgment of the power and influence of our Blessed Lady, and this meaning would be the same, even if we could bring ourselves to suppose that she exercised her influence imprudently, and that our Lord meant to chide her for so doing; for in neither case would there be any alteration implied in the meaning of the words before us.

<hr>

[2] Exod. xxxii. 10.

No one can doubt that, as has so often been said, the will of our Lord in working miracles and in all that related, not only to His mission as the Christ and the Redeemer, but to the arrangement of His whole life and of every action of it, was guided by the will of the Eternal Father signified to Him by the Holy Ghost, and not by the will of our Blessed Lady. As to this, there is little difference between one set of actions of our Lord and another, and He was doing His Father's business as much when He was obedient to her and to St. Joseph at Nazareth as when He stayed behind for three days in the Temple. But then the rule of His actions was signified to Him by the mouths of Joseph and Mary, and in all that regarded His Ministry and Mediatorial Office it was not so. This is certainly true. But it does not exclude the influence of our Blessed Lady in cases like the present, because it is one thing for our Lord to be obedient to her as His parent, as was the case in the actions of His Hidden Life, and quite another for Him to listen and defer to her prayer, as is the case here. Flesh and blood had nothing to do with the miracle which was about to be performed, but all through the series of our Lord's miracles the power of prayer is continually prominent, though there are some miracles which our Lord performed simply, as it seems, to glorify His Father and to prove His own mission. But in the great number of cases it is the prayer of faith that wins the benefit. And thus there is every reason for supposing that such was the fact in this great opening and typical miracle, and that our Lady's intercession is here shown to have been but the first instance of the prevalence of that influence with God and with our Blessed Lord, as to which it was His will that it should prevail even when exercised by persons of sanctity and faith far inferior to hers.

Our Lord's words to His Blessed Mother therefore seem to mean an acknowledgment of her power over His Heart, as well as an expression of wonder at her great charity and mercifulness in intervening in such a case. It was as if He had told her that her power was great, and that He would not refuse her what she asked, but then He added, ' Mine hour is not yet come.' There have been various ways of interpreting these last words in accordance with the interpretations of the former part of the sentence—such, for instance, as that of St. Augustine, who tells us that the hour when He would acknowledge her as His Mother was not yet come, and would come by-and-by, when He was on the Cross, when He would show Himself her Son by addressing her and giving to her His beloved disciple in His own place. There are many beautiful thoughts connected with such interpretations, but it seems more natural either to understand simply that the moment for supplying the want of wine had not yet arrived, or that but for her intercession the beginning of miracles would not have taken place at that moment. Whichever be the meaning adopted, it was clear that our Blessed Lady at least understood that her prayer was heard, and that in His own time He would provide for the need which she had pointed out, in a way of His own, for He had said nothing as yet to determine in what way He would remedy the deficiency. For she turned to the waiters and said, ' Whatsoever He shall say to you, do ye.' Again did our Blessed Lady display her wonderful gift of counsel and of understanding of the ways of our Lord, inasmuch, as has been remarked by Toletus, she understood from the study of the Old Testament miracles that it was a sort of rule with God to require in the performance of His miracles of beneficence certain conditions imposed by Himself

which had often been apparently unlikely to produce
the results which were to follow, or even such as to seem
rather to hinder it, such conditions being insisted on
as a mark of faith and submission. Thus when Eliseus
was to cure the waters of Jericho, salt was poured into
them, when the head of an axe was to be raised out of
the water, a bit of wood was to be thrown into it,[3] the
wound of Ezechias was to be healed with a plaster of
figs,[4] Naaman the Syrian was to go and bathe seven
times in the Jordan,[5] and the like. Our Lady seems
to have understood that the servants at the table would
be in some way or other the instruments of the miracle,
and as they might not know our Blessed Lord, they
might fail in that strict obedience to Him which is one
of the conditions on which great favours are to be
received. 'Whatsoever He shall say to you, do ye.'

There is no action recorded of our Blessed Lady
in which her quick, decisive energy is more conspicuous
than in this deed of merciful consideration, so full of
charity and of the highest spiritual prudence. Holy
writers dwell on it in connection with the exercise of
her intercessory power as the channel of grace, and
draw out from each particular some trait of her character
and some theme for admiration at its great and tender
mercifulness. They remark on her watchfulness over
the interests of her hosts, for she must have noticed the
failure of the wine before it became evident to the
company generally, and, as it seems, to the very end it
was not known to the ruler of the feast. They remark
that no one made any petition to her, as indeed there
were, perhaps, few there besides herself who thought
that our Lord could provide for such necessities in
such a manner. They notice her exceeding compassion,

---

[3] 4 Kings ii. 21 ; vi. 6.   [4] Isaias xxviii. 31.
[5] 4 Kings v. 10.

because after all it was not so great an occasion, as it might seem, for the setting in motion of the miraculous power of the Incarnate Son of God, in order that wine might be supplied to a wedding banquet, and a newly married couple spared the confusion which a confession of their poverty might have entailed upon them, and the pain of beginning their new life with the sort of stigma which such a failure in the provision of their hospitality might have occasioned. Yet she thought it worth while to leave her place among the women, and go straight to where our Lord was reclining at table, or teaching, in order to plead for them unasked. We need not dwell again upon the faith which her request showed, or the refined prudence of her prayer, or the spiritual intelligence with which she saw the mind of our Lord in His answer, which might have seemed a rebuff to another; nor, again, her careful thoughtfulness in preparing the servants for the part which they were to play in this great manifestation. All through her conduct is that of a most careful and loving mother, who provides for her children while they are without thought for themselves, who knows how to plead for them, and how to guard them against all possible dangers.

It is clear how aptly the display of these features in the character of the Blessed Mother of God is made in connection with this mystery, which, as has been said, was full of deep spiritual meaning, especially with reference to the office of our Blessed Lady in the kingdom of her Son as the watchful Mother of all the faithful, as the powerful Intercessor who represents all their needs to our Lord, as the channel through which all graces are to flow. No doubt there are other things also in the conduct of our Lady here, especially her faith and her earnest desire to see our Blessed

Lord glorified and honoured. But in these features which have been specially mentioned we seem to see an intimation of the immensity of the blessing which God has bestowed upon us in giving her to us as a Mother, whose prayer is all-powerful with Him, who is at the same time more ready to plead for us than we are to invoke her, and whose beneficence and open-handed charity anticipate the wants of our temporal well-being as well as the slightest necessities of our souls.

CHAPTER XII.

Water made Wine.

St. John ii. 1-11 ; *Vita Vitæ Nostræ*, § 22.

IF our Lord had been an ordinary person, who had been asked by his mother or by a friend to grant an alms to the poor, or to do some other act of kindness or of mercy, and who had answered the request in some such words as 'Leave it to me, you need not urge me, but it is not yet time,' and then had immediately proceeded to do what he had been asked to do, it would hardly have been thought that there could have been reasonable ground for doubt that the petition made to him had so far influenced him as to lead him to perform that work of mercy sooner than might otherwise have been the case. It is only because our Blessed Lady is the petitioner in the case of the miracle at Cana, because our Lord is the Person Who performs the merciful work, and because that merciful work is so great a miracle and the beginning of His miracles in the office of the Christ, that certain people feel so much reluctance to admit the plain and natural meaning of the words of our Lord and of His Evangelist. If, indeed, our Blessed Lady's action in the matter was the action of authority, if she is supposed to have commanded her Son, as His Mother, to perform a work which belonged to Him in His character of the Messias, it would then be natural to see in the words of His answer to her something like reprehension, or warning, or, at the least, an explanation that there were certain spheres in which it was not her place to use any such authority. But even this would not alter the subsequent circumstances of the history, as they are related by St. John, though it would make it less easily intelligible why, after having been forced to speak in a tone almost of rebuke, our Lord had gone on to do exactly what He was requested to do, or rather—inasmuch as our Lady's request contained nothing at all as to the manner in which the want of wine was to be supplied—to do what He was requested to do in the most wonderful and supernatural manner possible.

We have seen, however, that there is nothing at all in our Blessed Lady's request to her Divine Son which goes beyond the range of prayer—prayer which might conceivably have been made to Him by any one present, if such a person had had as lively a faith in His power and as perfect a reliance on His mercifulness and considerateness as she had. This being the case, what might otherwise be a difficulty becomes a source of wonderful and most consoling instruction. For, in some way and in some degree, though we are not distinctly told how far, our Blessed Lord did certainly hasten on the time of this great manifestation at the prayer of His Mother. And in this He only acted as God has always acted from the first, as He Himself acted all through the time of His Public Life, and as He has acted continually in the history of the Church from that time to this. That is, certain things have been done and granted by God in His providence and by our Blessed Lord in His Life and in His kingdom, which would not have been done but for prayer, or they have been done sooner or in a more magnificent way than would otherwise have been the case, on account of prayer. Prayer, intercession, the merits and pleadings and sufferings of the saints on earth and the petitions of the saints in heaven, are a recognised force and power in the ordering of the history of the world and of each particular soul, though they are a force and a power the exercise and influence of which depend upon the will of man. And thus there is a strict and natural fitness in the circumstances of this miracle at Cana, which being the first of our Lord's great manifestations of this kind, may well be considered as a typical instance, in which all the influences which ordinarily guide the results in such cases must have their lawful place. We are thus pointedly and plainly told that prayer has the power of modifying, influencing, hastening on to their execution, the decrees of God in relation to human affairs, and that, in particular, with regard to the whole system of miracles and preternatural graces which was now about to be inaugurated, prayer, if it is not always to be the moving power, is at least in ordinary cases to be the required condition as well as the occasion of the great bounties of God. Thus, the lesson which we learn from this incident in the miracle before us is the same as that which is taught us by the case of the Syrophœnician woman who pleaded so urgently and with so much ultimate success for her daughter.[1] Hers was a case beyond the range of the direct mission of

[1] St. Matt. xv. 21-28.

our Blessed Lord, and yet His mercifulness went beyond the bounds which were set to it in order to obey, as we may say, her faith and her prayer. In this case it is the time that is anticipated, in hers it is the limit that is enlarged. And in each case we have the same encouragement and the same beautiful lesson about what seem to be unfavourable answers that we receive when we pray, namely, that they are in truth invitations from God to pray more earnestly and more faithfully, to act as our Blessed Lady acted, as if we had received a promise that what we ask should be granted, in the same spirit as David of old, the man after God's own Heart in this and other respects, who, though he had been told from God that the child of his sin was to die, nevertheless fasted and prayed as long as the child's life lasted, saying, 'Who knoweth whether the Lord may not give him to me, and the child may live?'[2]

The details of the miracle now performed have already been quoted from St. John. The servants received their instructions from our Blessed Lady, to obey our Lord in everything; and then He turned to the largest vessels that could have been within reach, as if to make the miracle more splendid by the abundance with which the deficiency of wine was to be supplied. There were six large stone jars or vessels, placed probably near the entrance of the house to furnish that plentiful store of water which was needed for the daily life of the Jews. The measure which St. John gives of the contents of each would, at the lowest computation, amount to from ten to fifteen of our gallons. They were empty,[3] and our Lord bade the servants set up and fill them with water. When this was done, He bade them draw from them, and take the liquor to the ruler of the feast, probably a friend who had the charge

<hr>

[2] 2 Kings xii. 22.   [3] κείμεναι.

of the arrangements and who presided at the banquet. He tasted it, and it was wine of the choicest flavour, so that in his delight he sent for the bridegroom and complimented him upon its quality. He had done a strange thing, he told him. It was usual to give good wine first, and then inferior; but he had done just the reverse, he had kept the good wine for the last. At the time at which he spoke he was ignorant of what had passed, our Lord, as it seems, being at another part of the table; perhaps, as Ludolph suggests, He had practised on this occasion what He afterwards recommended to others, to go and sit in the lowest place, or perhaps He was quietly conversing or teaching apart from the chief body of the guests.

When it is remembered that our Lord, according to the constant teaching of the Fathers and the uniform belief of devout Christians, teaches us by His acts as well as by His words, and that every circumstance of His actions is full of significance, it cannot seem wonderful that the various parts of this great action of His which we are now contemplating should have been considered by Christian contemplatives as having each their own moral or spiritual meaning. For instance, the circumstance of which notice has already been taken, the largeness and munificence of the gift which was now bestowed upon the entertainers of our Lord, His Mother, and His Apostles, has been dwelt upon as showing how abundantly God repays any who give Him something or do something for Him. Again, it is characteristic of the gifts of God that they should be most choice and perfect in their kind, and that they should be bestowed in overflowing copiousness, as the oil which was multiplied for the widow at the prayer of Eliseus, or again, as when the five loaves and the fishes were multiplied by our Lord for the people in the wilderness, and there remained basketsful of fragments of what had been bestowed in this miraculous manner. There has been the same characteristic to be noted, whenever the saints of God, in fulfilment of our Lord's promise, have had the gift of imitating Him in His miracles of this kind, as well as that of following Him in His virtues. God loves a cheerful large-handed giver, and He is Himself the model and pattern of magnificence in giving. He loves those who are not content with good works or services to Him which are just such as to pass muster and attain the end at which they are named, but who strive by purity of intention and exactness and perseverance to the very end to make what they do for Him and offer to Him as perfectly beautiful and precious as by the help of His grace they may. And so, when He goes out of His ordinary manner in dealing with His children, showering upon them preternatural gifts and favours, everything that comes from Him at such times has a celestial perfection and completeness and a priceless excellence.

It is also noted that now, as on other occasions in the course of His Life, our Blessed Lord took something common and ready to His hand to bring out of it the great wonder which He intended to perform. He might have created the wine in the vessels instead of using water. He might have called bread in abundance into being when He fed the multitudes in the wilderness; but He did not do so. Some holy writers think that in this He paid a kind of reverence and homage to the creative power of His Father, not taking it into His own hands, though His power is the same with that of His Father, leaving it to Him to be the Creator of all as He is the First Person in that Ever-Blessed Godhead, the source and origin of all being. Or, we may add, our Lord chose in this also to be dependent upon His Father, taking the creatures which He had made and making them, as it were, the seeds and germs out of which He wrought what He desired. There may also have been other reasons, indeed, for, great as would have been the miracle if, in the cases of which we are speaking, He had created what He had need of out of nothing, it might still have seemed more like a magical illusion than it could when the water which the servants knew that they had drawn from the well or fountain was turned into wine, or when the five loaves and two fishes of the lad were taken from his basket and multiplied so as to feed the crowds.

Another circumstance, which is certainly unusual in our Lord's miracles, and therefore may be thought all the more significant, is the change of one substance into another, and this so perfectly, that the ruler of the feast and others like him could bear witness to the excellence of the wine which had before been water. Holy writers see in this the symbolical character of the miracle, inasmuch as our Lord came not to destroy but to fulfil, to take up what had already been taught and revealed and practised, and transform it into something more noble and more worthy of Himself. This He did with the Law, changing it into the Gospel, with the whole of the Old Testament institutions, making all things new and more sublime, full of grace and overflowing with spiritual riches. Instead of circumcision, He was to give baptism, instead of external purification, interior cleansing, instead of temporal rewards, an eternal kingdom, instead of carnal sacrifices, the pure oblation of the Immaculate Lamb, instead of legal rites, Christian sacraments. Some authors also dwell on the manifold use made of the element of water in the Old Testament for the wonderful works of God, as in Egypt, the Red Sea, and the Jordan, and suppose that it was now chosen to be the subject of a still higher miracle, because our Lord had just sanctified it by His own touch in His Baptism. Others see in it an image of the weakness and instability of our human nature, which is to be transformed by grace into something noble and divine through His Incarnation. And, inasmuch as our Lord's miracles looked, as it were, forwards as well as backwards, and were preparations and foreshadowings of His great permanent wonders in the Christian sacraments, we can hardly help seeing in this change of the water into wine an anticipation of the great wonder of the change of bread and wine into the Precious Body and Blood of our Lord in the Blessed Sacrament, as the later miracle of the feeding of the five thousand was an anticipation of other features of the same sublime mystery.

The words of the ruler of the feast to the bridegroom were probably uttered in all simplicity, and may have been recorded by St. John to attest the completeness of the miracle. Still, they sound to us as if they had a parabolic meaning, as if the speaker unconsciously prophesied of the characteristic feature of our Lord's dealing with us as the Spouse and Master of our souls. It is the distinguishing mark of earthly joys and goods, that they are soon exhausted, that the first taste of them is the sweetest, that they pall upon the appetite, that however highly valued they may be at first, they soon become insipid by use, and at last, if they are forced upon us beyond satiety, they become disgusting. The world begins well, and ends badly, nothing which has not the transforming touch of divine grace can really please and hold the soul or the heart. On the other hand, God begins by what seems hard and stern, by commandments and rules, limitations on our liberty and restraints upon our nature. 'The fear of the Lord is the beginning of wisdom,' and He first of all trains us in holy discipline. But He raises us higher and higher, He gives us new tastes and perceptions, and when we come to be able to enjoy spiritual delights they are like the good wine which was kept to the last. At first the Cross is hard to bear, the doctrine of humility is difficult, it is a pain to conquer and subdue ourselves; but when once these things find the palate of the soul capable of tasting their sweetness, there is no longer any room left for any sweetness but theirs. And if it is so in this life, if the yoke and burthen of our Lord even here are easy and light to those who take them up courageously, much more is the parable true in the next world, which is the last thing which our merciful God has in store for us, the last and the best.

NOTE VI.

The Bridegroom in the Marriage of Cana.

There are some legendary opinions as to the bridegroom and bride at the marriage of Cana which illustrate the tendency in contemplative souls of all ages to fill up the details of the pictures which are half drawn by the Evangelists, out of their own imagination. It is tolerably clear that the Evangelist St. John was present at the marriage in question, as all the events related by him in the early part of his Gospel rest either on his own testimony, or on that of the persons from whom he may have had what could not otherwise have been known, such as the dialogues of our Lord with Nicodemus and the Samaritan woman. He never mentions himself unless it is absolutely necessary, and as it is clear that he must have known what passed between the ruler of the feast and the bridegroom, conjecture at once fastened upon the possibility that he was the bridegroom himself. This, however, had to be reconciled with the tradition that he was always a virgin, and that on account of his virginal purity he was specially loved by our

Lord, and chosen as the disciple to whom our Blessed Lady was intrusted at the time of His Passion. The idea then grew up that although he was the bridegroom, he was called by our Lord to a more perfect state immediately after the miracle. 'When the feast was over,' says Ludolph the Carthusian, 'Jesus called John aside and said to him, " Leave this thy wife, and follow Me :" and John, having seen the miracle wrought at his own marriage, at once left his bride, and followed our Lord ; and this was the first call of John, who thus came to be familiar and acquainted with Christ. And his bride, whose name was Anachita, or, according to others, Mary Magdalene, of her own accord followed our Lord with other holy women. For the works of God are perfect, and therefore, inasmuch as He called one of the married pair, it was fitting that He should call the other.'

This call of the bridegroom and bride to a higher state than that of matrimony, after the miracle of the water made wine, is a favourite idea with the contemplatives. Sister Anne Catharine Emmerich tells us, 'At the end of the repast, the bridegroom came and found our Lord in private, and declared to Him in a humble tone that he felt himself dead to all fleshly appetite, and that he wished to live in continence with his wife, if she consented. The bride also came to Jesus and made the same disclosure. Jesus then made them both come to Him, and spoke to them about marriage and about purity which is so pleasing to God, and which produces a hundredfold in spiritual fruits. He mentioned many prophets and holy persons who had kept continence, and sacrificed their flesh to the Heavenly Father. He said that they had had for spiritual children a multitude of men who had gone astray, and whom they had brought back to what was good, and that thus they had left behind them a numerous and holy posterity. The pair made a vow of continence for three years, promising one another to live like brother and sister. Then they knelt down before Jesus, Who blessed them.'

There seems to be no authority for the statement that St. Mary Magdalene was the bride, and it is probably a mere conjecture, though it is mentioned by St. Antoninus as well as by Ludolph, and is found in some of the beautiful old *Vite de' Padri* of the middle ages. It may have been founded on the care which St. John has taken to make St. Mary Magdalene prominent in his Gospel, or it may have been a simple conjecture to give some reason for the dissipated and luxurious life which she led before her conversion. Thus St. Antoninus and others mention the legend that she was angered at the loss of her bridegroom after the marriage, and threw herself upon the pleasures of the world in consequence.

Another statement about the bridegroom is that he was the Apostle Simon Cananæus, or Zelotes; but this is evidently founded upon the name Cana. The same reason might make Nathanael himself the bridegroom, as St. John calls him Nathanael of Cana.

———

CHAPTER XIII.

The Beginning of Signs.

St. John ii. 11 ; Vita Vitæ Nostræ, § 22.

THERE are few among the marvellous works which our Lord wrought in the course of His ministry which have so markedly and simply the character of being done as manifestations of His glory as the miracle at Cana. This, indeed, is the feature in the incident on which the Blessed Evangelist, who was present, fastens, as he says, 'This beginning of miracles (or signs) did Jesus in Cana of Galilee, and manifested His glory, and His disciples believed on Him.' In the first place, it was a miracle of unusual splendour, inasmuch as the quantity of wine produced was very large and altogether beyond the immediate needs of the marriage-feast, and it involved an exertion of almost creative power, in that one substance was changed miraculously into another. It was done in the midst of a large company, and must have become public in the neighbourhood and famous over all Galilee. It was done under circumstances of no crying necessity, such as existed when our Lord raised the widow's only son to life, or stilled the tempest, or fed the thousands of men and women in the wilderness. It had, indeed, the character of mercy and pity which distinguishes all our Lord's miracles, except the one which was a sign and parable, the blasting of the fig-tree. But this character is almost lost to sight in the blaze of glory which surrounds the great display of power involved in the miracle, especially when it is considered as a new revelation concerning our Lord, a fresh manifestation of His inherent prerogative as the Lord of the new creation.

This miracle is, as it were, an answer to the challenge of Satan, which our Lord would not take up when it was made, that His power might not seem to be set in motion by a taunt from the enemy of God and man. ' If Thou be the Son of God, command that these stones be made bread !' And now, He commands water to become wine, and so He manifests His glory, ' the glory,' as St. John says, 'as of the only Begotten of the Father,' and ' His disciples believe on Him.' This is the character, then, which belongs to this miracle in the Gospel of St. John ; a character, it need not be said, not peculiar to it, except that it belongs to it in a greater and more special degree. For all through the Gospel history there runs this thread of the glory of God, of men glorifying God, Who had visited His people, Who had given such power unto men, and the like : and this was the end to which our Lord Himself looked, as He said more than once, as when He declared that the man whom He cured had been born blind, that the work of God might be made manifest in him ; or again, of the sickness of Lazarus, who was to die and be raised again, ' This sickness is not unto death, but for the glory of God, that the Son of God may be glorified in it.'[1]　But the miracle of Cana leads the van, as it were, in this series of manifestations, and it expresses with singular clearness as well as unusual splendour this great object of God in the whole dispensation of the miracles of our Lord, both those which He wrought in His Life, and those which have since been wrought by Him through His saints, generation after generation, in His Church.　And the end of the glory of God in all these miracles is combined with that other end, so inseparably united to it as far as men are concerned, the arousing and strengthening of faith. 'His disciples believed on Him.'　And thus St. John almost closes his Gospel with words which echo the same thought. 'Many other signs also did Jesus in the sight of His disciples, which are not written in this book.　But these are written that you may believe that Jesus is the Christ, the Son of God, and that believing, you may have life in His name.'[2]

It is indeed a thing which is sometimes forgotten, that believers and unbelievers are alike agreed as to the cogency of the argument from miracles, which are acknowledged by the common feelings of mankind to be the evidence of the hand and presence of God.　The adversaries of revelation and of the Church do not, in general, deny the force of the argument, they limit themselves to endeavours to explain away the facts, either denying their possibility, questioning their historical truth, or attributing them to fraud. And this is the true reason why men are so determinedly incredulous as to all modern miracles, because if they are admitted as true, they are evidences of the truth of a system which men do not wish to believe.　They can bear them at a distance, as they can

---

[1] St. John ix. 3 ; xi. 4.　　[2] St. John xx. 30, 31.

bear an infallible guide or teacher who never speaks, or whose voice only sounds through the avenue of past centuries in such a way that they can interpret it as they choose without fear of correction. But men like themselves and of their own time working or experiencing miracles, and a man like themselves or an assembly of such men speaking as with authority in the words of the first Council of the Church, 'It seemeth good to the Holy Ghost and to us'—these are things which frighten the mental lawlessness and rebellious independence of the unregenerate with an authority and a power from on high which are far too close and too real for them to tolerate. The whole anti-Christian and anti-Catholic position is full of inconsistencies and of gross faults against logic and reason, but in no part of it has there been a more wilful disregard of evidence and of reasoning than in the controversial works of those writers who have questioned either the Christian miracles in general, or those of the Catholic Church in particular. These miracles are universally characterised by the qualities of beneficence, charity, mercy, and compassion, which are seen so conspicuously in their first cycle, the miracles of our Lord. They are not prodigies of destructive power, scattering calamity, ruin, desolation, over the face of the earth. On the contrary, they are uniformly remedial of the miseries of human nature, breathing consolation, peace, and hope, as it were with the very fragrance of the Gospel message as it first came from the lips of Jesus Christ Himself. Men are ready enough on ordinary occasions to do justice and honour to the discoverers of anything which alleviates the hardness of life or provides them with a safeguard against its dangers —but when it is noised abroad that a servant of God has received the gift of healing diseases, or when some healing spring gushes from a mountain side which has been touched in vision by the feet of the blessed Mother of God, and the news flies over the world that thousands of cures are there continually wrought by her intercession, then the world rises up against the rumour as if it were the herald of a plague or of an invasion of barbarians.   For the world feels that such wonders reveal a new and present action of God the Creator and Master of the universe, Whose voice and eye in the Catholic Church, even though manifested in mercy and loving-kindness, are a most piercing reproach to its own infidelity and perverseness of will.

The children of the Church, who meditate devoutly day by day on the successive stages of the great manifestation of our Lord by the Providence of His Father which may be said to guide the course of His Public Life, can hardly hope to do so without finding themselves from time to time brought across thoughts which seem to have especial reference to the prevalent errors and forms of evil of the days in which they live.   And there are few of us but must be aware of the tendency of our own times to set aside all that rises above the natural order, and, in particular, all phenomena that seem to go beyond or even against the usual uniformity of the laws of nature. Some writers, who still consider themselves Christians, would abandon all that has a miraculous character in the Life and actions of our Lord, thinking that they can still retain His own perfectly beautiful and divine character as the light of their lives and the anchor of their hopes : as if the veracity of our Blessed Lord had not been over and over again pledged to what they would agree with their adversaries in acknowledging to be false.   Others, again, who defend the Christian revelation from a standing point outside the pale of the Catholic Church, in which evident miracles are continually claimed, are obliged either to abandon the argument from miracles on which, as we have seen, the faith of the Apostles and of their converts was rested, as something, at all events, not of the first importance or cogency, or to draw imaginary lines of distinction between Evangelical and Ecclesiastical miracles, which put into the hand of those who deny both, arguments quite as cogent in the one case as in the other. In the face of these common errors it may be well, now that we have reached this great beginning of 'signs,' a period of such immeasurable importance in the unfolding of the knowledge of our Lord vouchsafed to men by the Father, to remind ourselves of some chief great truths on the subject which can never be abandoned without danger to faith, or indeed, without contradicting the simplest conclusions of reason.

The belief in the possibility of miracles, in the Christian sense, rests upon and requires the belief in a Personal God, Who is All Powerful, All Holy, True, and Good, the Creator and Ruler of the universe. No one can believe in such a Being, without also attributing to Him the original establishment and maintenance of the system of the world, which we call nature, and without supposing that He is of necessity perfectly free both as to the original establishment of that system, as to the particular character which he has impressed upon it, the details of all its parts and all its laws and forces, and also as to the maintenance of the whole as far, as long, and under whatever circumstances it may please Him. The question as to whether there are to be occasional interferences of one law of a higher kind with another law of a lower kind, or occasional interferences with this or that part of the system, which can be reduced to no law except to that of the free will and choice of the power that may cause such interferences, is a question entirely of fact, and not of possibility. If God were identical with the world, or rather, to speak more accurately, if there were no God, and if all the forces of nature—what is called, in this hypothesis falsely called, man's free will included—moved on according to the mechanical laws of a blind necessity, then, indeed, what are called miracles would be impossible. But it is instructive to remark that the same arguments which would make miracles impossible, ought also to tend to the destruction of human free will. For man's free will is continually and momentarily interfering with the otherwise regular order of the universe. And if there is nothing unreasonable in man's exercise of his free will to make a stone fly into the air, or to prevent its falling on the earth by the use of a power which is above that of the stone itself, there can be nothing unreasonable in the use by God of the power, which He, the author and the sole source of all natural forces, possesses beyond and above the ordinary laws of the nature which He has made, if He thinks fit to do so.

The belief in God the Creator of the world is a belief either in the greatest of miracles, or, if such a term implies the existence of natural laws already established, in something, as we may say, more miraculous than any miracle itself. Every miracle may be considered as consisting in the production or evolution from something natural of an effect which belongs to a nature higher than and different from its own. To heal a disease by a word or by a touch, by the same means to give sight to the blind, to still a storm at sea, or to raise the dead, is not to go beyond the range of all natures. For it is natural to God to have the power of life and healing, and of controlling the elements, and some of the results mentioned may not transcend the natural forces of the angels. But the things named are beyond nature, because they are altogether out of proportion to the means used, to the power of a human word or a human touch. The creation of the world by an act of His will or a word belongs to the nature of God, but it is a result for which we have to rise to no less a height than to the footstool of His throne, for no power short of His could have accomplished it. For no miracle in the world can we have to rise higher, and for many miracles, or seeming miracles, we have not to rise so high. For there are many effects which can be produced from natural forces by intelligences and powers like those possessed by the angels, which transcend all that can be accomplished by any inferior nature. This truth is of great importance in the consideration of what we call false miracles and lying wonders, but for the present we may put it aside. From what has been said before it follows that in the creation of the world we have an use of the only power that is required to account for the most wonderful miracles, so that when that truth is received, they become not only possible but antecedently probable. For if God has made so great an innovation, so to speak, as to create the whole universe by a mere act of His will, bound by no law whatsoever, but only by the free bountifulness and communicativeness of good which is a part of His nature, it must be thought in all reason that He is more likely than not to continue such innovations from time to time, out of the same bountifulness and with the same freedom, within the range of the universe which He has created. And the force of this argument is acknowledged by the adversaries of religion, for it is obvious and notorious, that many of those who are the strongest opponents of a belief in miracles, are also practical disbelievers in the doctrine of Creation.

There is another part of the Christian, and, it may be said, of all reasonable, belief concerning God and His relation to the world which He has created, which is intimately connected with the doctrine of miracles, and which prepares the way for its reception. This is the truth of God's perpetual action in the universe, His concurrence and presence in ¸all natural causes, giving them the power to produce their effects and actually producing those effects in them and through them. The further 'nature' is separated from God the more strange does His personal action upon it become, but when we understand, as Salmeron expresses it, that what we call 'nature' is God acting according to His usual and habitual manner, and that a miracle is nothing but God acting beyond or above His ordinary manner in nature, the question of the possibility and probability of miracles is put on its right footing. No one can doubt that the fact, that God usually observes ordinary and fixed laws in His action in what we call 'nature,' is a certain presumption that those laws which He observes are good in themselves, and such as it would not be according to His character to make if they were to be constantly and capriciously set at nought. For God always shows a certain reverence for His creatures; He has never yet destroyed a nature that He has made, nor done violence to it. But at the same time we cannot conceive of God as otherwise than free in all things that are not involved as unchangeable in His own perfections, such as His goodness, justice, truth, faithfulness. He cannot therefore be conceived as not free to dispense with or supersede the ordinary modes of His action in nature. For thus to conceive of Him would be to deny Him the power of acting, except in one determined and uniform groove, in the course of nature, the lowest sphere of His action, while in the other higher ranges, in His dealing with and government of spiritual beings, nothing is more obvious than the absolute liberty and entire independence of choice which He exercises in the distribution of His gifts, in the limits within which

He fixes the probation of free intelligent beings, and the like. It is a common error which is corrected more than once by our Lord in His Parables, which contain a description of the heavenly government of His Father, to suppose that God is bound to give to all the same gifts, the same opportunities, the same length of probation, the same amount of forbearance and of mercy, whereas from the beginning to the end of Scripture He asserts Himself as absolutely free in all these respects, though He is bound by His own nature and attributes, if we may speak of Him as bound, to be just and merciful and good to all. This error as to the limitation of the freedom of God in the moral world, is analogous to that with which we are dealing with relation to miracles, and which denies His freedom to supersede a lower law by a higher law, or to break a course of uniform action by some special act of power in regard to the material universe.

If the possibility and probability of miracles cannot be consistently questioned by any who believe in the existence of a Personal God, Who is the Creator and Maintainer and Ruler of the universe, much less can they be questioned by any who believe in a Revelation by God to His creatures concerning Himself. Miracles, in relation to a Revelation, assume the character which is noted by the word used concerning them in the passage on which we are commenting. They are ' signs '—marks of the presence of God, indicating that He is speaking and acting with a particular intention. The end of the whole universe, and of all that we commonly call ' nature ' is, in the Christian view, the glory of God, and it is not difficult to understand how this glory is promoted and, as it were, preached by the heavens and earth and all the variety of natures which make up the universe, which testify, by their observance of the laws which He has stamped upon them, and by the silent witness which they bear to His character, to manifold truths concerning Him, and His eternal power and Divinity, as St. Paul has said.[3] We need by no means limit the witness of nature to that which she thus bears by the unbroken uniformity of her course, nor is there anything, as is clear from what has been said, to make miracles impossible or improbable, in the case of there being no revelation of Himself given by God. But in the case of such a revelation, they become natural even if they are not necessary. A Revelation, in the sense in which the word is commonly used, means a further declaration concerning himself made by God : something which contains truths or promises not before made known. No one can limit the power of God so as to say that He is bound to render such a revelation its own evidence by acting in some all-powerful way upon the hearts and minds of those to whom it is made, or to say that He may not choose as His instruments in the promulgation of His new message men who by nature are in no way raised above the level of those to whom they address themselves. Here comes in the necessity, under such circumstances, of evidence to accredit such messengers, and what we may call the natural evidences in such a case certainly include miracles, which would thus stand in the same relation to the revelation as the ordinary witness of nature to the truths concerning God known without such revelation, each attesting the glory of God in their several sphere. In His ordinary government, He leaves not Himself, as St. Paul says to the people of Lystra, without testimony, doing good from heaven, giving rains and fruitful seasons, filling our hearts with joy and gladness.[4] What then

[3] Rom. i. 20.   [4] Acts xiv. 16.

can be more natural than that, when he so far innovates upon His ordinary government as to reveal Himself more fully and give a new law or a new hope or a new life to the world, He should also innovate upon the ordinary witness of nature to His glory by some more transcendant works of goodness, which may at once prepare men to receive the new truths which He reveals and be the appointed credentials of those who have to declare them? Thus, it is natural for God, in the case of a revelation, to use His power of foreknowledge, which belongs to no one but Himself, and by means of prophecy both prepare men for what He is about to do, and attest that when it comes it comes from Him. So too it is natural that a revelation should be accompanied, when it is given, by some marks of His power over and beyond nature which may accredit the messengers to whom it is committed as well as the message itself. We have thus prophecy beforehand and miracles at the time as the two natural witnesses which might be expected in the case of a revelation, and no one, who considers such a revelation as possible, can find any fault with the presence of such witnesses, especially when they are combined, the miracles themselves being the subject of prophecy. Their evidence really amounts to this, that God, as has been said, is present, has 'visited His people,' that His Power is there, His Promise has come, His messengers have been sent, and that their message is to be received as His.

CHAPTER XIV.

Miracles in Scripture and in the Church.

St. John ii. 11 ; *Vita Vitæ Nostræ*, § 22.

IF we pass on now to the statements of Scripture concerning the miracles with which God has from time to time attested the messengers whom He has sent to mankind, the laws and truths which He has revealed to them, or the special favour with which He may regard this or that person, or institution, or community, we shall find that, from the beginning of time, as the stream of prophecy rose up and flowed onward in ever-increasing volume, so also has God used the evidence of miracles for the purposes here indicated. The greatest displays of the miraculous action of God in the Old Testament are connected with the Law and the Prophets, with the deliverance of the chosen people from Egypt by Moses, and the whole history of the wanderings in the desert, the lawgiving on Mount Sinai, and the entrance into the promised land; and again, with the preaching of the great typical prophets, Elias and Eliseus. Although there is much, especially in the series of miracles of the last-named servants of God, which bears an almost Evangelical character of mercy and compassion, as the raising of the widow's son to life and the cleansing of Naaman, or again, in the earlier cycles, the passage of the Red Sea and the miraculous feeding of the people in the wilderness, still it cannot but be observed that many of the miracles of the Older Dispensation have a character of fearfulness and destruction which belongs more naturally to the sterner dealings of God in chastising His enemies, and in making even His own people serve Him out of fear. The Deluge, the destruction of the Cities of the Plain, the Plagues of Egypt, and the destruction of the Egyptians in the Red Sea, the chastisement of the people in the desert, the death of so many thousands of the army of Sennacherib in one night, and other wonders like these, have all the character of which we speak. And when God made His presence on Mount Sinai to give the Old Law known by visible manifestations, it was by signs of terrific majesty, as St. Paul says "a burning fire, and a whirlwind, and darkness and storm, and the sound of a trumpet, and the voice of words, which they that heard excused themselves, that the word might not be spoken to them, . . . and so terrible was that which was seen, Moses said, I am frighted and tremble.'[1] These are the characteristic signs of a dispensation in which fear held so large a part as in the Mosaic Law.

We have in this another beautiful confirmation of His own message on the part of God. When the new Revelation was given by Jesus Christ, the character of the signs changed with the character of the Revelation. The Revelation was a disclosure, such as could never have been imagined, of God's goodness, mercy, bounty, and ineffable tenderness of love, as well as of His truthfulness and faithfulness to the Promises which He had made. Its witnesses, as the miracles of our Lord may be called, were naturally enough displays of wonderful power over physical causes, as great in that respect as the miracles of the Old Covenant, but having about them a character of love and mercy and condescension

---

[1] Heb. xii. 18–21.

in harmony with the prevailing tone of the Gospel dispensation, and therefore displaying in their way the same qualities in God as the dispensation itself, mercy, love, condescension. There had been some anticipation of this, as has been said, especially in the miracles of Eliseus, but now the full stream seemed to flow of pity and compassion, in the healing of diseases, the relieving of sorrows, the comforting of the bereaved, deliverance from the power of the devil, the cleansing of the lepers, the feeding of the hungry, the raising of the dead. Of the Gospel miracles it may be said, in the words of St. Paul of the dispensation itself, that in them 'the goodness and kindness of God our Saviour appeared,'[2] and that in them God delighted to 'manifest His omnipotence chiefly by showing mercy and pity.'

This leads us on to another feature in the Gospel miracles which has been dwelt upon by holy writers, in virtue of which they are not only the natural witnesses of such a Revelation as that of Jesus Christ, as works of power which have the character of love stamped upon them, but fit witnesses also in another way, inasmuch as they actually represent in figure the dispensation which they attest. That dispensation was the healing of the diseases of the human race, and its deliverance from all spiritual evils. In it God acted the part which our Lord Himself described in His Parable of the Good Samaritan, taking the half-dead, half-murdered and plundered victim from the roadside, tending his wounds, pouring in oil and wine, bearing him home to a place of shelter and rest and safety, and providing for his future, as well as remedying his present ills. There is, of course, an intimate connection between the spiritual evils and the physical evils of man. Diseases, infirmities, afflictions, are in a general way the

<hr>

[2] Titus iii. 4.

consequences of sin. They came into the world as the results of the loss of original innocence. They represent in figure the maladies of the soul, of which in many cases they are even the direct fruit and punishment, and they lead on to death, which is the natural image of mortal sin. There was thus a peculiar natural fitness in the arrangement, that the manifestations of physical power which were to attest the mission of the Healer of all the woes of humanity, should take the particular form of the preternatural relief of those maladies of the body which are so intimately connected with the evils of the soul, both as figures and as consequences. In truth, very few indeed of the Christian miracles are without this parabolic character, and there are often incidents and details in our Lord's performance of them which would be seemingly meaningless unless this feature in His system were taken into account.

From this follows yet another consideration concerning our Lord's miracles, which is illustrated by what has already been said of the part borne by His Blessed Mother in the great 'beginning of signs.' There are, no doubt, some of our Lord's miracles which have more of the character of simple 'signs' than others. Such are His walking on the waters, the miracle at Cana, and the withering of the barren fig-tree. In regard of the first and last of these three, the feature which we are about to notice, that of previous prayer and faith, is entirely absent. There is the same absence of prayer in the persons benefited or affected in many of the Old Testament miracles, as in those of Moses as distinguished from those of Eliseus, which approach more nearly in this and other respects to the miracles of the Gospel. As a general rule it may be said that the miracles of the Gospel bring out very forcibly indeed the power of prayer. Prayer is shown by them to be one of the elementary forces in the kingdom of God, a force as much to be taken account of in any description of the system of God's providence, as electricity or gravitation in an account of the physical universe. What our Lord promised to Nathanael and the other disciples before He left the Jordan for Cana, is fulfilled very signally indeed in the general dispensation of miraculous graces which illustrated His subsequent preaching. We have understood that promise to refer, very mainly, to the new power allotted to everything that can come under the name of prayer in the Gospel dispensation. And we thus see how it may almost be said that our Lady's part in the first great typical miracle at Cana was, in a certain sense, necessary, in order to make that miracle a complete representation of the arrangements of God in regard to this method of communicating His blessings and advancing the glory of His Son. For, if our Lady had not spoken, the part of prayer in that great mystery would not have been expressed.

This element in the system of miracles has its importance as to a further question. In truth, the more we consider our Lord's whole teaching on the subject of prayer, His teaching by practice and example as well as by precept, the more unnatural and impossible will it appear to set any limit except that of God's good pleasure to the influence of this power. And if it be true, as it certainly is true, that our Lord has insisted upon nothing more forcibly than upon the practice of prayer, of faith and confidence in prayer, of importunity in prayer, until He has used words about its power which seem almost to tax our belief too far, while on the other hand He has made it a sort of rule to refuse nothing, not even a miracle, to prayer of the kind on which He so much insists, it seems that something very strong and plain must be needed in order to make it appear possible to a Christian mind that this connection between prayer and the granting of the greatest favours was not to continue. It is contrary to the analogy of the faith to suppose that while prayer was to remain throughout all ages one of the chief duties and most efficacious weapons of His children, while the whole of Christian life and of the life of the Church was, in a certain manner, to rest upon prayer, still, on the other hand, the answers to prayer and the graces which might be obtained and the deliverances won thereby were to be strictly limited to things which might otherwise be in the ordinary course of nature. It is contrary to the same analogy of the faith to think that, though heaven has been peopled with saints, whose intercession is most powerful, and though no generation of the Church on earth is wanting in great servants of God, who are after their death to become saints in heaven, and who have often to perform in their lifetime the most sublime services to the Church at the cost of the most heroic sacrifices, still neither on earth nor in heaven is the prayer of the saints to avail for anything that we can call miraculous. The New Testament would be inferior to the Old, if the prayers of its conspicuous saints were not to be as powerful as those of the ancient prophets. God would be the God of the dead, not of the living, as our Lord said to the Sadducees, if the saints reigning in heaven could never win from Him by their prayers the favours which we call miracles. A deep gulf of mis-belief as to the goodness or the power of God is opened beneath their own feet by those who question the universal belief of Catholics in all ages in this regard.

We are thus led to see how many strong presumptions combine their forces in favour of the expectation that the economy of 'signs' and miracles, which was now for the first time unfolded by our Lord at the marriage feast at Cana, was intended by Him to continue ever afterwards in His Church. This, indeed, is to be noticed all through the manifestations of our Lord, that as they succeed one by one we find that there is always a foundation laid for something new which is to last on in the Church, built and grounded upon that which our Lord has said or done or established. This, which is a general rule in the mysteries of our Lord's Life, is a presumption in favour of any particular feature as to which the special reasons for such permanence are not so prominent as in other cases. In the present case, as we shall see immediately, there are the strongest possible arguments in favour of the continuance. We have just been dwelling on two features in the Gospel system of miracles, namely, the perfect correspondence between the spiritual benefits which are conferred with unceasing bountifulness upon souls, and their figures and images in the external miracles of mercy, and the almost irresistible and unlimited power of Christian prayer, which certainly is encouraged by our Lord not to stop short in its demands even of the most wonderful boons. It cannot fairly be denied that the force of each, and much more the force of both combined, tends strongly in favour of an anticipation of the permanence of miracles in that Life of our Lord in the Church which is the continuation of His Life in the flesh.

Before proceeding to the direct and positive evidence on the subject, it may be well to recall to mind the place assigned by our Lord Himself to the evidence from miracles, even although we must for this purpose anticipate what belongs to incidents in the Gospel history later than the marriage-feast at Cana. It has already been mentioned, that our Lord, in His arguments with the Jews, more than once appealed to the witness which had been borne to Him by St. John Baptist. On one occasion of this kind, which is mentioned by St. John the Evangelist, and which occurred at a comparatively early period of our Lord's Ministry, He added that He had a greater testimony than that of St. John, even the works which the Father had given Him to perfect: 'The works which I do, give testimony of Me that the Father hath sent Me.'[3] Here we have the miraculous signs placed first by our Lord Himself among the legitimate and appointed heads of evidence to His mission—for in the passage from which these words are taken there is a sort of enumeration of such heads of evidence. And in another passage, at the close of His Ministry, our Lord repeated the same thing in another and more terrible way, when He said that the fact that He had done works among them which no one else had done, and that they had rejected Him notwithstanding, made the Jews guilty of sin which under other circumstances they would have escaped.[4] These sayings of our Lord are enough to show how high was the importance which He attached to this evidence of miracles, and they may be confirmed by the still more clear inference which it is natural to draw from the answer which He made to the disciples of St. John Baptist, when they came in the name of their master to ask Him whether He was the Messias or not—'Art Thou He that art to come, or look we for another?' St. Luke tells us that when this question was put, our Lord answered it by deed before He answered it by word. 'In that same hour He cured many of their diseases and hurts, and evil spirits, and to many that were blind He gave sight. And answering He said to them, Go and relate to John what you have heard and seen. The blind see, the lame walk, the lepers are made clean, the deaf hear, the dead rise again, to the poor the

[3] St. John v. 36. [4] St. John xv. 24.

Gospel is preached '[5]—the greater part of the words being a quotation from the prophecy of Isaias. Here then we have a still more clear appeal of our Lord to His miracles as the evidences of His mission. And as the question put to Him by the disciples of St. John took the form of an implicit reference to prophecy and the promises of God—for they did not say, Art Thou a teacher sent from God? but, Art Thou He that art to come, the One for Whom we have been taught to look?—so in His answer our Lord brings in the evidence of prophecy also, pointing to His miracles not in themselves alone, but as having been specially predicted as the signs which were to belong to Him Who was to come.

It is in perfect keeping with this, that when our Lord sent His Apostles, and after the Apostles, His seventy-two disciples, to preach in His name during His lifetime, He conferred on them the gift of miracles and bade them use it freely, as they had freely received, and also that when He sent the same Apostles to preach to the whole world after His Resurrection, He gave them the same power, and specified the signs which were to follow those who believed, with which signs, as St. Mark tells us in the last words of his Gospel, He did in fact confirm the Word which was preached in His name.[6] There is no question among Christians, who believe in the miracles of our Lord, as to the miracles of His Apostles, and there has been at times a tendency even to rest the Christian evidence too exclusively upon those miracles. But our Lord's own appeal to His works and the distinct manner in which He provides similar evidence for those who carry on His mission after Him, leave no doubt as to the legitimate character of the argument founded upon that evidence.

---

[5] St. Luke vii. 20–22 ; Isaias xxxv. 5.
[6] St. Mark xvi. 17–20.

It must be further remembered, however, that our Lord's words concerning the wonderful works which He did, in reference to their continuance in the Church after Him, are not exhausted by the texts which have just been quoted. There is another famous passage in the discourse at the Last Supper, after the institution of the Blessed Eucharist, which is more solemn, larger, and more general in its importance, than the sayings which relate immediately to the preaching of the Gospel. 'Amen, amen, I say to you,' our Lord uses that solemn form of promise and prediction which is the mark of His most authoritative and royal announcements, 'He that believeth in Me, the works that I do, he also shall do, and greater works than these shall he do, because I go to My Father ; and whatsoever ye shall ask the Father in My name, that I will do, that the Father may be glorified in the Son.'[7]   These words seem to raise the promise of the continuance of His wonderful works, of which our Lord is speaking, to something far higher than the provision for what may be in some respects a passing need, the evidence which is required to lead men to receive the Gospel in the first instance at the hands of its accredited preachers.   There are no conditions mentioned in this passage but what are permanent, and of the most essential importance.   Faith is the condition required on the part of the disciple of our Lord : 'He that believeth in Me, the works that I do, he also shall do.'   The source of the power conferred upon him is the entrance of our Lord into His kingdom, His sitting down at the right hand of the majesty on high : 'Because I go to My Father.' The means which are, as it were, to set in motion the power which our Lord possesses in His kingdom are the same which we have seen at work in the mouth of our Blessed Lady at the marriage at Cana, that is, the means

[7] St. John xiv. 12, 13.

of prayer. 'Because I go to the Father, and whatsoever you shall ask the Father in My name, that will I do.' And again, the end to which our Lord will look in the performance of these mighty works by the instrumentality of others, is an end which can never for a moment be set aside or superseded, for it is the end of the glorification of the Father in Jesus Christ as He reigns in heaven and in the Church on earth : 'That the Father may be glorified in the Son.'

A comparison of these passages leads us to the conclusion that the great end and object of the manifestation of miracles is the glorification of God, and that whenever it is true that the 'Father may be glorified in the Son,' by such manifestations in answer to the prayer of faith, then there is the sufficient reason of which our Lord speaks for the answering it in that way. It is not contrary to this that miracles should have a peculiar force and a peculiar office as the attestation of a divine mission, and that therefore they should be poured out, as it were, in especial abundance at certain times, as we have seen, as when a new revelation is given by God, when His religion has to be preached all over the world, and, to be confirmed, to use St. Mark's expression, by signs which men universally and naturally recognise as proving the near presence and immediate action of God the Creator of the universe. This is one way out of many ways in which the Father may be glorified in the Son, for the Son is He in Whom and by Whom the new Revelation is made, and when the providence of the Father makes Him or those who represent Him conspicuous with the glory of miracles, it is the Father Who is glorified in Him or in them. It need not in any way be questioned that there is a certain sense in which miracles, considered as the signs of a revelation, belong with particular appropriateness to certain epochs rather than to others. Thus, when the continuance of the gift of miracles is claimed for the Church, it is not meant that they are always displayed in equal splendour and in equal profusion. It may be freely granted, that the age of miracles was especially the age of the first foundation of the Church, though we hear of them, in those earlier centuries, rather as common in a measure to large numbers of the faithful than as adorning the lives and the preaching of a few more conspicuous saints. It must be remembered that the frontiers of the Church are always advancing, and that the time has never yet been known when in many parts of the world her work has not been as completely a beginning as it was in the days of the Apostles. When St. Augustine came to England, or when St. Boniface went to Germany, or when St. Francis Xavier went to Japan, their work in those countries was the foundation of infant Churches among men as simple and untutored as any that had been seen and convinced by the miracles of St. Thomas or St. Matthew. And again, there are epochs of revival in the Church which may be very fairly compared to periods of propagation, as when the great mediæval preachers, St. Vincent Ferrer, St. Bernardine of Siena, and St. John Capistran, succeeded one another as the revivers of faith and religion in a time of affliction, confusion, and decadence. These and other periods of which somewhat the same account may be given, may seem to rank in the providence of God by the side of other periods when the Gospel has for the first time to be preached to barbarous nations, and as such may be illuminated by a more special magnificence in the bestowal of miraculous signs. But they do not exhaust the great promise made by our Lord in the passage quoted from the discourse after the Last Supper, and it would therefore be unreasonable to limit to them the fulfilment of that promise.

Again, it may be remarked that even in other times,

even when the Church is peaceably established as the mother and mistress of Christian nations, when kings and emperors do her homage, and civilisation and knowledge and improvement of every kind take their laws and principles from her, even then it cannot be said that the age for miraculous signs has gone by. It would not be true to say so, even in the sense in which miracles are promised by our Lord as an evidence of her mission. For in such times she is, indeed, as is commonly said, her own evidence and her own witness : the purity of her doctrine, the unity of her faith and discipline, the universal sway which she holds without dispute, her evident Catholicity as to place and as to time, her unbroken existence and her identity with the Church which was founded by the Apostles, all these are her notes by which it pleases God that she should approve herself as His Spouse in the eyes of the whole world. Most of these notes are such as strike the eyes of every thoughtful and well-informed beholder. There can be but little question as to the supernatural unity of the Church. It is not the unity of a mechanical system, in which everything is, as it were, stamped to a certain pattern, in which every motion is regulated by forces which are entirely independent of the agents which they put in motion. It is the law of charity, humility, oneness in faith, reference for authority — the chief centre of which is also the centre of the organisation of unity—working upon free minds and hearts, which differ in almost everything else except that they have the nature of man and the supernatural adoption of the sons of God, and enabling them to triumph over personal, domestic, local, and national differences in a manner which at once reveals the hand of God. For, in order that the unity of the Church may be a note of the presence of God with her, it is enough that it should be such in kind and in degree as can be the work of no one but Him. The other notes, of Apostolicity and Catholicity, are intimately bound up in her Unity, and they are, like that, evident marks which are written upon the brow of the Bride of Christ in letters of light.

So it is with those three great notes. But the note of sanctity, if it be looked for in the heavenly purity and sublimity of doctrine, in the end and aim and tendency of Christian institutions, especially in those which embody the Evangelical counsels and our Lord's own peculiar precept of charity, is indeed beautifully conspicuous to eyes that are capable of seeing clearly in so much heavenly light. But it is from the very nature of the case less obvious to the mass of mankind than the other three, save that God has provided certain external marks and prerogatives of sanctity which belong to the Church alone. The chief of these marks is the range of graces which are called *gratis datæ*, and among them, in particular, the gift of miracles. It is not the Catholic doctrine that these gifts can be possessed by no one who is not rich in sanctifying grace. But, as a matter of fact and as a general rule, they are so far connected with sanctity as to furnish, in a community in which they prevail, a note of its existence which men cannot well mistake. Here, then, is a reason why this gift should be continued in the Church to the end of time, a reason which is but a development of that for which it is agreed on all sides that miraculous signs are in their proper place as the evidence of a divine mission at the beginning of the preaching of a new revelation. For, in truth, the Church is always making her way and asserting her claims in the face of successive generations of men, and as the forces of evil which are always howling around her put on new forms century after century in making their never-ending attacks upon her, so she in like manner is ever, as it were, coming forth from the Cenacle to make a road to empire for herself, she is ever presenting herself to the disturbed and faithless world in all the radiance and power of a new Pentecost.

CHAPTER XV.

True and False Miracles.

St. John ii. 11; *Vita Vitæ Nostræ,* § 22.

WE cannot limit, as has been said, the mighty and munificent promise made by our Lord to those who believe in Him, to periods or states in which this note of miracles may be absolutely necessary, any more than we limit to such states the action of our Blessed Lord in His eternal kingdom for the glorification of the Father in Himself. But the consideration of the necessity of some such preternatural authentication of the claims of the Church from age to age may be useful as proving that among the many prerogatives of our Lord's Sacred Humanity which we know to have been handed on to the Catholic Church after Him, this at least cannot reasonably be omitted. There is another reflection to be added to the foregoing, which perhaps it may be best to put in the first instance in the form of an objection, or difficulty, the solution of which will lead us still nearer to the fundamental truths which sustain the whole subject. The difficulty, then, in question is this—our Lord has forewarned us, in His last great prophecy upon the Mount of Olives, that there are to be at times great trials of faith in the Church, and that these trials will come with especial intensity and force in the latter days. These trials to faith are to be the severest of all, because they will appear to put other teachers and other religions on a level with our Lord Jesus Christ and the religion of which He is the Author. There are to be false Christs, and false prophets, who are to show great signs and wonders, insomuch as to deceive, if possible, even the elect.[1] And our Lord goes on, 'Behold, I have told it to you beforehand. Therefore, if they shall say to you, Behold He is in the desert, go you not forth; behold He is in the closets, believe it not. For as lightning cometh out of the east, and shineth unto the west, so shall also the coming of the Son of Man be.' Here we have a warning from our Blessed Lord Himself that there are to be at certain times, but chiefly at the end, pretenders to the character of Christ and prophet, who shall confirm, or seem to confirm, their mission by means of signs and wonders more or less analogous to those which have been the evidence of the mission of the Christian Church, and these signs shall be so great and miraculous, that if it were possible even the elect of God might be deceived by them. And our Lord's word seems to place the safeguard of the elect, if not solely, at least chiefly, in the fact that these things have been fore-told. 'Behold I have told it to you beforehand.' And in the same way the future coming of Antichrist, who is to found his own claims on lying wonders and prodigies, is spoken of in similar words by St. Paul, as of him 'whose coming is according to the working of Satan, in all power and signs, and lying wonders, and in all seduction of iniquity to them that perish, because they receive not the love of the truth that they may be saved.'[2] We see, then, that St. Paul's witness is to the same effect as that

---

[1] St. Matt. xxiv. 24.   [2] 2 Thess. ii. 10.

of our Blessed Lord, and the carefulness with which he has drawn the prophetic picture of Antichrist seems to imply that it will be prophecy which will form, in great measure at least, the safeguard of the faithful children of the Church at that time.

It is easy to see that the words of our Lord and of the Apostle imply that there is to be a false witness as well as a true witness borne by miraculous signs and wonders, and this has sometimes been made an objection against the Christian claim to credence on the authority of miracles. There are to be miracles—St. Paul speaks of them as false marvels, pretended and lying miracles— which are to seem to ape and, in the eyes of many, to rival the miracles by which Jesus Christ confirmed His divine mission, and which have remained after Him as among the notes and characteristic prerogatives of the Catholic Church. This, then, is the difficulty which has now to be met, if possible, in such a way that its solution may throw still greater light upon the position which miracles occupy in the Christian kingdom of the Incarnation. We may begin by explaining what the Apostle may mean by false wonders and lying miracles. Under certain circumstances such false prodigies, which are not in truth what they seem to be, may happen among men. Many things may seem miraculous which are not truly miraculous, because they do not surpass the ordinary powers and course of nature. We hear a good deal from time to time about the wonders and miracles of physical science ; results, that is, which can now be obtained by the use of natural means which were before entirely or partially unknown. An astronomer may seem a prophet to an unlearned man, because he foretells an eclipse, and our use of the electric telegraph or of the lucifer match may make us seem magicians to a savage. In this way there may be miracles, falsely so called, even among men ; and we may be certain that we have as yet by no means exhausted that discovery of natural powers and secrets of which our own age is so proud, and which God permits, not that we may be proud, but that we may learn daily more of His goodness and power. Much as we boast ourselves of our knowledge of nature and of the skill which God has given us to use and make servants of the natural forces which we have discovered, we are still but as children beginning our lesson, when compared to the higher orders of intelligent beings, whom God made for the same end with ourselves, that is, for His own glory, and especially that they might read Him and glorify Him in His works, hereafter to enjoy the higher knowledge of Him as He is. It follows from this that there are many things which may seem to be miracles of the highest order to us, which may yet be strictly within the range of natural effects, and that if the angels, either good or bad, the blessed citizens of heaven or the miserable tenants of hell, are directed or permitted by God to interfere in what concerns us, they may produce by their own natural powers, which are so far greater than ours, or by means of their knowledge of the forces of nature and of material things, which so far surpasses our knowledge, results which may appear to us, and be relatively to us, supernatural. But such results are only truly supernatural in an equivocal sense, because the word nature is a relative term, and what is supernatural to an agent like man, is not supernatural to an agent of a higher order.

These considerations explain to us the possibility of false miracles. There are forces in nature out of which they may be elicited, and there are spiritual agents by whom they may be brought about. But are they not only possible, but in harmony with the general principles of the government of God?   Here again we come to truths, which, strange as they may seem to thoughtless persons at first sight, are yet pregnant with grounds for the glory of God.   It has already been said that God reverences, as we may say, the creatures which He has made, inasmuch as they one and all come from Him, and as being made by Him are good and beautiful in their kind, reflecting something, more or less, of His own qualities and perfections.   Even when God punishes them, as in the case of the rebel angels and wicked men, He does not destroy the nature which He has made, nor does He take away from them their natural powers. The fallen angels have lost grace and the superadded gifts which they enjoyed while in His presence, but not those which are constituent parts of the being which they possess.   Another law of His providence is that He permits them to tempt and assail and seduce, if they may, the children of God who are on their way to that same blessed country which those, His enemies, have lost for ever, and in this they serve a certain purpose which tends to the glory of God.   Here, then, is one element in what is required for the permission of false signs and wonders.   It would not be contrary to the principles of God's government to allow the fallen angels, in the use of their natural knowledge and power, which as far surpass ours as the knowledge and power of the most skilful of mankind surpass those of the savage or of the child, to work what might seem to us even great miracles for the seduction and destruction of many, though in truth those seeming miracles might be what St. Paul calls those of Antichrist, lying wonders, that is, either appearances of effects which do not really take place, as a phantom in the air may be supposed to be a man, or not truly miracles, because they do not really exceed the ordinary .course and powers of nature, although they seem to exceed those powers. For it is to the glory of God to have made the universe so full of powers and forces as it is, and to have given so much intelligence and so much power over nature to man and to beings superior to man. It is to His glory that He has, as we have seen, not destroyed the natures which He has created, even though they have rebelled against Him. It is to His glory to permit evil and bring good out of it, rather than to prohibit that exercise of the will of His creatures which produces it; to make its children serve Him and do His work, rather than at once put an end to them, or force their liberty in violently making them good. It is to His glory to permit man, His feeble and dependent child, to be tempted and assailed by beings so much more naturally powerful than himself, in order that, as the Psalm says, 'out of the mouths of infants and sucklings He may perfect praise, because of His enemies,' whom He defeats by creatures far weaker than themselves, and may so destroy 'the enemy and the avenger.'[3] And it is to His glory that these enemies of ours and of His, in all the strength of their natural gifts, in all the intensity of their hatred to Him and to us, should yet be entirely in His hand, not allowed to tempt us or to hurt us, to tax us beyond the strength which He gives to us, or to lead us astray against our own will.

In regard, then, of seeming miracles and wonders, it is as it is in the matter of temptations. The evil spirits are allowed to do just as much, within the limits of their nature, as God permits, and no more. We cannot doubt that they have immense powers of seduction, illusion, and deception, but the use which they make of these powers is exactly limited by God's providence.

[3] Psalm viii. 3.

So also, no doubt, they have great powers of destruction, and considering how great must be their hatred against the race of men whom God has created, and who are destined to supply the vacant places which their own defection has left in heaven, it is easy to imagine that they would long ago have destroyed the world if God had allowed them.   But as to destruction, illusion, and temptation, the evil spirits are chained up by God.   As to that particular work of deception to which the present subject refers, their power of illusion and false miracles, it is surely by no means against reason to suppose that, inasmuch as they are ever burning with the desire to ape God and cast discredit upon Jesus Christ and the Church, they would gladly adorn with all the powers of deceptiveness which their natural gifts put within their reach, the false teachers who do their work upon earth, the founders of heresies, the authors of schisms and of sects, the infidels and scoffers against religion, the prophets and high priests of intellectual error and moral licentiousness and turpitude, who are allowed from time to time to scourge the world.   But here, too, they are held back by God's hand, not indeed entirely, not always to the same extent, but still they are always under control, and are let loose, more or less, according to the decrees of His providence and His justice.

If we now turn to examine how it has actually been in the history of the world as to the permission of the deceptions of the evil spirits, we are certainly startled by the immense extent to which moral and spiritual darkness, superstition, false religions and philosophies of life, have been allowed to spread over the face of the earth, and gradually to obliterate, more or less entirely, the primitive traditions of truth with which our race set forth on its long wanderings after the fall of Adam or the Deluge.   After a few centuries from the latter epoch, we find what appears almost like the domination of evil spirits everywhere. We can see only the surface of the history of humanity, and if we cannot but fear that our eyes never sound all the depths of degradation which have been permitted, we are also certain from what we know of God that there are other depths of His mercy and of His tender provision for the wants of human souls which baffle, not only human perception and imagination, but the exercised intelligence of the highest of His angels. And even from what we know of heathenism, we can see that the light of reason and of conscience was never extinguished. And we know also that that light was always assisted by God's grace, under whatsoever dispensation, to lead men to serve Him and obey Him and so to save their souls. The case of ancient heathenism is almost exactly parallel to that of the many parts of the world in which even now the religion of Jesus Christ is unknown, and in both cases it is not reasonable to deny the very large extent to which delusions and errors as to God and as to man's relations to Him have been or are supported by false signs and wonders, the work of evil spirits. It is most important to understand that the language of Holy Scripture in reference to this subject leads us to think that the permission which has thus been accorded to the enemies of God and of man has been in a great measure judicial. That is, that the powers of evil have been allowed to deceive men more and more in proportion as men were more and more unfaithful to the light which they had, ungrateful to and rebellious against God, and so less and less deserving that He should shield them from the impostures and lying inventions of their enemies. Thus God is said to allow the evil spirits to deceive in order to punish the wicked, as also He is said to allow them to tempt and afflict in order to prove the virtue of the just and good. The great example of this last permission of God is the case of the Patriarch Job, who lived, as has already been said, under the primitive dispensation, before the Law of Moses was given, and whose religion was that simple faith in God the Creator and the Rewarder of men, which might have been the religion of all the world outside the chosen people. Thus Job is an instance of what may have been, in a degree less than in him, in thousands of cases which are unknown to us, both as to faithfulness to the light possessed under such a dispensation and to the primitive tradition which was its great treasure, as to the grace with which that faithfulness was assisted and rewarded, and also as to the licence given to the enemies of mankind to assail and try to the utmost the virtue of the servants of God. Satan is allowed to afflict Job in many very terrible ways, to bring lightning from heaven to destroy his flocks, to cause a strong wind to blow from the desert and make the house fall on his sons and daughters, and the like, and all this was permitted by God that the faith and patience of His saint might be tried as gold in the furnace and proved to be true. The great example in the Old Testament of the other kind of permission allowed to the evil spirits, in which God uses them to punish His enemies, is thought by many of the Fathers to be the case of the lying spirit who was permitted to deceive the wicked King of Israel, Achab, by making the prophets of whom he inquired promise him success in the war in which he was to lose his life. Such is the case in which God allows wicked men to be led astray by the false lights of the evil one, and so brought to their own destruction. And there is yet a further case, according to many holy writers, in which He allows the devils to execute His temporal punishments when they have to be inflicted, and thus we are told that the plagues of Egypt or the chastisement of Herod, whom the angel smote because he did not give glory to God, were wrought by the instrumentality of evil angels. In such cases as these there might even be true miracles wrought by their agency, miracles which exceeded their own natural power, but still miracles which attested the justice and contributed to the glory of God.

We see, then, that evil spirits may have leave allowed them to deceive and to punish men, to exert their natural powers for their destruction or deception, to inflict temporal calamities upon them, or to lead them away from the truth. There is therefore every reason for thinking that at the last, when Antichrist is revealed in punishment for the extreme wickedness of men in those ages, his great power of deception will be allowed as a part of the chastisement. This indeed is what St. Paul says, that his 'coming shall be according to the working of Satan in all power and signs and lying wonders, and in all seduction of iniquity to those that perish, because they receive not the love of the truth that they may be saved. Therefore God shall send them the operation ' or working ' of error, to believe lying, that all may be judged who have not believed the truth, but have consented unto iniquity.'[4] That will be the last and the worst stage of the world's history, short though it will be, because then, in punishment for the sins of the world, which will not simply have not known our Lord, but will have rejected Him on account of its own love for iniquity, Satan will be let loose to an extent to which he has never been let loose before, and those who have turned away from Jesus Christ will be chastised by being deceived by His arch-enemy, Antichrist. Those who have sealed their

----

[4] 2 Thess. ii. 9, 10.

eyes to all the evidences and notes of His Church, will be deceived by the false miracles of the man of sin.

This, as everything else in the course of Providence, will be for the glory of God. It is for His glory that there should be a time when the elect are to be tested and tried and proved and tempted and assailed, not by any limited or restrained or weakened power of Satan's seductiveness, but by the full force at his disposal, which he will be allowed to use against them as he was allowed to use his powers of affliction against Job, and without success. Satan will serve our Lord's purpose in putting His Church to her last and greatest trial, as a preparation for her last and greatest victory, while, to those who hate the truth and take pleasure in iniquity, he will be the executioner, as he has often been before, of the just sentence of God's anger against them.

We thus at last come to the full answer to that difficulty as to the miracles of our Lord which rests upon the fact that all through the history of mankind, and notably at its close, there have been and may be and are to be false miracles and wonders which are wrought by the enemies of God, and which tend to impugn the truth of the Revelation of Jesus Christ. If we put aside the fact that these things have been the subject of prophecy, they would be to a certain extent difficulties, like other apparent parallels between the religion of our Lord and other religions falsely so called. That is, they would require explanation, and a criterion as to what was true and what was false would have to be found in a comparison between the doctrines which might be supported by the two series of miraculous proofs. But signs and wonders are not the only proofs of our Lord's Divine Mission, although when they are indisputable they are unmistakable authentications of it. When He Himself appealed to them, as has been seen in His answer to the question of the disciples of St. John Baptist, He couched His appeal in words which were taken from the prophecies concerning the times of the Messias. That is, He appealed to His miracles as works showing the presence of God's power with Him in a way which had been pre dicted by an exercise of that foreknowledge of the future which belongs to God alone, Who foresees what shall be because it depends upon His will that it shall be. This foreknowledge of the future is a gift which is communicated to no creature as a part of its nature, although it is 'in part' as St. Paul says, given to those to whom it pleases God to give it. 'We know in part, and we prophesy in part.'[5] In this way, the miracles of our Lord, if they are considered as evidences, fall under the head of the fulfilments of prophecy, and attest God's fidelity and veracity as well as His power. 'As He hath spoken by the mouth of His holy prophets, who have been since the world began,' 'As He spoke unto our forefathers, Abraham and his seed, for ever,'—as Blessed Zachary and our Blessed Lady herself sang. The false miracles of Antichrist, in this light, are no less attestations of God's veracity than the true miracles of our Lord, and when the time comes for them to be displayed, they will be so far from being difficulties to the elect that they will be signs of the approaching deliverance which will follow them, as our Lord Himself says in His great prophecy, 'When these things begin to come to pass, look up and lift up your heads, because your redemption is at hand.'[6] Thus the prophecy of our Lord will be the guarantee to His children against the deceptiveness of the false miracles of His enemies. Those miracles will be signs of the deliverance of the Church, just as much as the wonders in the sun and in the moon and in the stars, or

[5] 1 Cor. xiii. 9.   [6] St. Luke xxi. 28.

the. distress of nations, foretold in the same passage. He has foretold what He will do and what He will permit, and the fulfilment of each prediction is a proof of His truth and faithfulness.

It must also be remembered, that as the false miracles of Antichrist will come at the end of the history of the Church, they will come after she has long been in possession, and after her divine mission has been proved to the world by a long and multifarious chain of evidences of which miracles do not by any means form the whole. Thus, lying wonders, which might seduce men if there had been no Christian Revelation, will have comparatively light weight, even putting aside the argument from prophecy, with those who know the Church and the religion of Jesus Christ. For it will be evident that if they affirm anything, they will affirm something which is contrary to that which is already established as the truth of God, Who cannot contradict Himself. Thus St. Paul says to the Galatians, that if an angel from heaven were to preach another gospel, he should be anathema.[7] The doctrine of the Church will always be the test of miracles, both then and in all previous times, and whatever is contrary to her doctrine will be thereby proved to be false. Again, the time of Antichrist will be very short, and he will be opposed by the two witnesses spoken of in the Apocalypse, who are supposed to be Enoch and Elias, the ancient saints of God who have not yet paid the debt of death, who will then have the power of working very wonderful miracles in defence of the truth. The two witnesses will be slain by the enemy of God, but his triumph will be, as has been said, very short, and the coming of our Lord, by which he will be destroyed,

[7] Gal. i. 8.

will have, as our Lord Himself tells us, circumstances of splendour and glory which no one can possibly mistake.

CHAPTER XVI.

Miracles and Faith.

St. John ii. 11; *Vita Vitæ Nostræ*, § 22.

THE Evangelist St. John, who was, as has been said, one of the followers of our Lord who were present at the time of His first great miracle, makes special mention of the effect which that miracle, by the grace of God, produced in the minds of himself and his companions, and it can hardly be supposed that we are not meant by him to take particular note of this impression. He tells us that our Lord 'manifested His glory, and His disciples believed in Him.' His language means something more than simple belief in what any one says, and perhaps the words might be more accurately rendered, that they put faith or conceived faith in Him,[1] in the same way as is expressed in the *Credo* when we say, 'I believe in God the Father,' and the rest. The disciples had hitherto seen no such proof that God was with our Lord as was now presented by the miracle. They had first of all received Him as their Master on the authority of St. John Baptist, who declared Him to be the Lamb that took away the sin of the world, and the One Who was to baptize with the Holy Ghost, the Son of God. All these high attributes of our Lord may not have been understood

---

[1] ἐπίστευσαν εἰς αὐτόν. This preposition is always used of a person, not of a thing or saying, as in c. iv. 60, ἐπίστευσε τῷ λόγῳ.

as conveying the full truth concerning His Divine Person, but only the truth concerning His Divine Mission. Even the title of the Son of God had its manifold meaning, inasmuch as it was a name which might be given to angels or to saints. And, though Christian theology teaches us that the sacrifice of the Lamb of God, in order to be efficacious for the taking away of the sins of the world, was to be the sacrifice of a Divine Person in a created nature, still this truth required penetration, and was not self-evident in the mere name of the Lamb of God.

After the testimony of St. John to his own disciples had come the evidence of the conversation and character, the wonderful attractiveness and majesty, of our Lord Himself, which, in the case of St. Andrew and the other disciple who were the first to join our Lord, seem to have deepened and perfected the faith which they had at first conceived upon the authority of St. John. Our Lord's words, as we see in more than one instance in the Gospel history, had a marvellous power about them, and this was a second head of evidence concerning Him to these early disciples. Again, with the notions which they had already had concerning Him, both from St. John's witness and their own experience of His conversation, they could not have but been still further struck by the authority with which He spoke, by His taking on Himself to promise a new name, and in that name a high mysterious office to Simon Peter, by His declaring the character of Nathanael in a manner which showed that He assumed such knowledge as His own as a matter of course, and by His making a great promise to them all concerning the fulfilment in Himself of the vision of Jacob. For to do all these things was silently to assert a power and a dignity of a very lofty rank indeed, and yet they had no alternative but either to suppose that the assertion was true, or to withdraw the belief which they had already so much reason for giving to what He said or what He implied.

We have here a transition and a progress in the faith of the disciples which may be said to consist in this, that at first they believed, on St. John's authority, certain things concerning Him, but now they began to believe in Him, to rest their faith upon Him and His word, to be ready to accept on His authority whatever He might tell them concerning Himself or any other. This state of mind was described later on by St. Peter, when he said to our Lord, after the miracle of the five loaves and the great discourse on the doctrine of the Blessed Sacrament which gave offence to so many, 'Lord, to whom shall we go? Thou hast the words of eternal life.' [2] Though at this moment, before the miracle at Cana, it is not certain whether they could have expressed their faith in Him in the words which follow, 'We have believed and have known, that Thou art the Christ, the Son of God,' at least in the full height of their meaning. When then in addition to all the former grounds of faith in Him which they had, the disciples saw Him work so very marvellous a miracle as that of the conversion of the water into wine, and work it, moreover, so easily, and with so much authority, without even a prayer to His Father as to One greater than Himself, their faith in Him was increased in the same proportion as that which the greatness of the power claimed and proved by the miracle bore to anything else which they had before seen or heard from or concerning our Lord. Henceforth, they had a new ground for their faith, a ground which, in the Providence of God, had been reserved for this occasion. If they

[2] St. John vi. 69.

had asked themselves beforehand, whether or not our Lord could perform such a miracle, we may suppose that they would not have thought it impossible that He should do so. But when they had seen Him work it, their knowledge concerning His power was altogether of a different order, and so their faith in His Person was a new faith, inasmuch as it now rested on an unmistakeable proof of the presence of God with Him which they had not before received. Just so we have seen St. John Baptist saying that he did not know our Lord until the sign of the Holy Ghost descending upon Him was vouchsafed. Thus it is not unnatural that the Evangelist should now for the first time declare so solemnly that the disciples believed in our Lord, although in truth they had already had so many other reasons for believing in Him, and although these reasons had all their due weight with them.

There are, no doubt, many stages and degrees of spiritual perception and conviction concerning the truths of God, some of which may be so vivid and over-whelming that it may seem to those to whom they are granted that they have never before believed or known God, or our Lord, or His Presence in the Blessed Sacrament, or His action on their own souls, and the like. Every near and sudden approach to us of what is divine startles and touches the soul as it were with the awakening of a new sense, and this it is which, in its highest form, is the natural effect of a miracle, which seems a personal act on the part of God, an act of His will specially interfering, and, as it were, making us feel His Presence and hear His voice, in a way in which they are not felt and heard in the ordinary course of nature, for the simple reason that it is ordinary, however much He is present always and everywhere. Our Lord more than once implies this doctrine concerning His miracles, as when he said to the Jews of Jerusalem, 'If I do not the works of My Father, believe Me not, but if I do, though you will not believe Me, believe the works, that you may know and believe that the Father is in Me, and I in the Father.'[3] And again, when He speaks of their sin, which was occasioned by the fact of His miracles, which they had rejected, He says, 'They have both seen and hated both Me and My Father.'[4] And the Evangelist, when, before turning to the history of the Last Supper and the Passion, he sums up in sorrowful words the scantiness of the effect which our Lord's Ministry had produced upon the Jews, rests His complaint chiefly upon this want of perception as to the due import of the miracles. 'Whereas He had done so many miracles among them, they believed not in Him.' And he quotes a little further on the passage of Isaias, which our Lord Himself quoted when He explained to His disciples why He adopted the less open method of teaching the people concerning the Father which consisted in the use of parables, about their hearts being blinded, and their hearts hardened 'that they should not see with their eyes nor understand with their hearts, and be converted, and I should heal them.'[5] Our Lord's quotation of this passage is mentioned, with relation to the occasion of the beginning of the parabolic teaching, by the three earlier Evangelists, and the same prophecy is twice quoted by St. Paul, in his Epistle to the Romans and in his speech to the incredulous Jews at Rome, soon after his arrival in that city as a prisoner.[6]

Thus, in the case of the disciples on the one hand, and in that of the blinded and hardened Jews on the other, we seem to have the lesson drawn out for us as

[3] St. John x. 38.   [4] St. John xv. 24.   [5] Isaias vi. 10.
[6] St. Mark iv. 2 ; St. Luke viii. 10 ; Romans xi. 8 ; Acts xxviii. 26.

to the proper effect which miracles are in the divine counsels intended to have, as well as the conditions under which that effect may be either secured or prevented. It is a matter which has been discussed among theologians, whether miracles such as those of our Lord have a necessarily demonstrative effect upon the mind of those who witness them as to the truth of the claims either of the person or of the doctrine with which they are connected.[7]   And the most reasonable conclusion seems to be that the evidence, to reject which convicted the Jews of sin, was the combined evidence of prophecy foretelling miracles as the signs of the Messias, and miracles fulfilling the prophecies, and so forcing on those who witnessed and knew both, the proof that our Lord was to be believed in, together with the teaching and assertions, open and implied, of our Lord concerning Himself. The miracles, apart from the prophecies and all other proof, could not of themselves have demonstrated Him to be the Messias or the Son of God. The miracles, taken together with the prophecies, proved Him to be God, if the miracles were clearly such and the prophecies known and understood. And the same miracles, followed by the assertion of our Lord that He was the Messias and God, were a proof amounting to moral certainty that he was so.

The disciples, as we see, were prepared to believe the testimony of the miracles by more than one element of moral evidence. But this would have been lost to them if their hearts had been hardened by attachment to sin, and their ears and eyes made dull and heavy by worldliness or pride. The case of the people in general was that of persons who were in this way dulled and bowed down to earth : seeing they could not see, so as to feel the force of the evidence of the miracles, hearing

<hr>

[7] See Suarez, *De Mysteriis Vitæ Christi*, Dissert. 44.

they could not hear, so as to understand the fulfilment of the prophecies and the import of our Lord's own teaching. There were some cases worse even than this, cases in which the mind was armed and fortified against conviction by the perverseness of the will, from self-love, jealousy, and other evil motives, and among such persons we find the blasphemy against the Holy Ghost, the resolute attribution to the evil one of wonderful works which they could not deny and would not attribute to God. In general, even with the people, it was the want of faithfulness to the light which they had, the want of consideration of the teaching which God had provided for them, which made them turn away from what seems to us the overwhelming cogency of the splendid miracles of Jesus Christ, especially if such want of consideration and of faithfulness were coupled with attachment to the good things of the world. It was of such that our Lord made Abraham say in the parable, 'If they hear not Moses and the prophets, neither will they believe if one rise again from the dead.'[8] And so indeed it turned out, for our Lord did rise from the dead, and yet great numbers of the people did not believe.

It has already been said that the Catholic Church is, in a great measure, her own evidence, and that in particular she is marked out by the hand of God with the four great notes which are mentioned in the Creed, under one of which the particular evidence of miracles may be classed, as far as it exists in the present day or in any other generation. And it is also evident that if the Church is rejected by the world, if men seem still to have eyes and see not and to have ears and yet hear not, it is only that those same reasons, which dulled and blinded the Jews amidst the glorious

[8] St. Luke xvi. 31.

light which surrounded the Person of the Incarnate Son, are now still working to make them inattentive to the claims of His Spouse. Miracles, in particular, have a certain force when they are vouchsafed to confirm and advance and perfect and comfort the faith of those who have already used faithfully the light of reason, or the witness or nature, or the Christian Revelation, as far as it has been made known to them, and in such persons they promote largely the glory of God by deepening their faith in His Son. They add authority to the words of the servants of God, and quicken the confidence of the faithful in the intercession of the saints and in the power of the Blessed Mother of our Lord. But to the world at large they are almost as if they did not exist, so occupied are the mass of mankind with temporal things and sensual pleasures, like the brethren of the rich glutton.

CHAPTER XVII.

Capharnaum.

IT seems clear from what St. John tells us, that the miracle at Cana in Galilee was wrought at no great distance of time before the Pasch, the festival for which it was the custom of the devout Galilæans to go up to Jerusalem. Our Lord was intending to be present at the feast with the rest, and must have had some special reason, such as has been already supposed, for returning to Galilee for so short a time when He was already so near to Jerusalem as the place where John was baptizing, a place which the caravans of Galilæan pilgrims to the feast would have to pass on their road to Jerusalem. No doubt the cause which guided our Lord's footsteps to Cana was that it was there that His first great miracle was to take place, at the instance of our Blessed Lady ; and the ordinary human motive may have been that our Lord intended at once to provide for her a new home, at a place which He destined to be the seat of much of His most constant preaching, and the centre from which He would issue in those missionary circuits of Galilee which were to occupy a large portion of the three years of His Ministry. It seems to have been in execution of this plan that, as St. John tells us, after the miracle of Cana, ' He went down to Capharnaum, He and His Mother, and His brethren, and His disciples, and they remained there not many days.' We

have thus a deliberate choice made by our Lord of what
was to be for some time more of a place of residence
for Him than any other, and we find Him placing
there His Mother and the family with whom she seems
now to have lived, before there had been any such
reason given Him for quitting Nazareth as was afterwards furnished Him by the savage violence which
His townsfolk offered Him because He would not do
any miracles to please them.

Capharnaum, the place which our Lord thus selected,
which He so highly favoured that He was able to speak
of it as exalted to heaven in consequence of the blessings
bestowed upon it, has fallen so completely under the ban
which He pronounced against it because of its unfaith-
fulness that the very spot on which it stood cannot be
precisely fixed. There is, however, no doubt as to the
neighbourhood in which Capharnaum stood. It was on
the borders of the Lake of Gennesareth, and in the centre
of the region which bore the same name. The land of
Gennesareth was the most populous and fertile part of
the country of Galilee, which was itself superior to other
parts of Palestine for fertility and population. The
passage of Josephus, in which this favoured region is
described, has often been quoted, and yet may well
be inserted here. 'A region of the same name,' he says,
'extends along the Lake of Gennesareth, the natural
beauty of which is admirable. For such is the fertility
of the soil that it rejects no kind of plant, and they who
cultivate it have left no sort unplanted there; and such
is the temperature of the climate, that it suits the most
different wants of nature.' The climate owes its peculiar
softness and richness—not without the drawback of
extreme heat—to the fact that the lake itself around
which it lies is no less than five hundred feet below
the level of the Mediterranean, and the whole region

is in a cavity of the earth's surface, such as is nowhere
else to be found, as far as our information goes, save in
the Holy Land, where the whole valley of the Jordan
and the Dead Sea are at the same low level. 'In addition to palm trees,' Josephus continues, 'which thrive
best by heat, and figs and olives in their vicinity, which
require a milder air, nut trees, the hardiest of plants,
flourish there in the utmost abundance. It might be
said that nature had been purposely ambitious of forcing
herself to collect upon one spot discordant principles,
and that the seasons, with a salutary conflict, each, as
it were, challenged exclusively the possession of the
country; for not merely does it so unaccountably
nourish the different productions at many different
periods of the year, but it also preserves what it
nourishes. The noblest of the kind, such as grapes
and figs, it supplies for ten months without ceasing,
and fruits of every other description, growing old on
the trees round about, are supplied for the whole year.
For besides the temperature of the air, it is watered by
a very fertilising spring, which the natives call Capharnaum.' [1]

Other subsequent writers have enlarged on the picture
thus sketched by the Jewish historian. Myrtles, almond-
trees, apple-trees, pomegranates, oranges, dates, citrons,
and other products of more southern climates abounded
in this terrestrial Paradise. It was, moreover, so situated
as to be a point of meeting for several great roads, and
so a most advantageous spot for our Lord's intended
residence. The road from the south, from Egypt and
Jerusalem to Damascus, passed through it. St. Paul
must have traversed it when he rode on his expedition
against the Christians of Damascus which was to lead to

---

[1] Josephus, *De Bello*, iii. 8. The translation is taken from Greswell,
Harmony, ii. p. 269.

his own conversion. Other roads led down the western side of the lake, at about the centre of which was the land of Gennesareth, to Peræa and the fords of the Jordan near Jericho, or down the same Jordan valley through Samaria, or through the midst of Galilee to Acco. Moreover, Capharnaum was well placed as a spot whence our Lord could easily pass, in case of any pressure of persecution, across the lake to Ituræa, or northwards or to the north-west into Syria or Phœnicia, and we shall find Him, in the course of His Ministry, availing Himself of these facilities. These reasons may have furnished our Lord with the motives of prudence on which He may have acted in making this selection. At all events it is clear that His active Ministry could not so well have been carried on in Nazareth, nestled as it was among the hills around it which give it even now an air of seclusion and retirement, and that, as has often been the case with the saints after Him, He chose now to throw Himself into the centre of the busy hives of population, while at the same time He was fulfilling the prophecy which St. Matthew quotes a little later on in his history, and which fixes this very ' Galilee of the Gentiles ' as the region which had been lying in darkness and in the shadow of death, and which was now to be illuminated by the brightest rays of the Sun of Justice. The very name, Galilee of the Gentiles, points to the comparatively large measure of intercourse which must have existed between persons of various nationalities in a region like that of Gennesareth, a region of traffic and commerce and industry, lying on the very borders of the Holy Land, and in immediate contact with Syria and Phœnicia.

This removal of our Lord to Capharnaum is therefore another onward step in the development of the counsels of God concerning His active Life. It is the leaving a quiet home, a dwelling-place where He might lead a life of prayer and contemplation and interior union with His Father, for a centre of human activity, a place where His time might never be His own from the multitude of calls upon His charity and condescension, for the busy haunts of men, where strangers would be coming and going, where His days would have to be spent in the sight of watchful enemies as well as devoted · friends, where the sick would send for Him, the questioner seek His instruction, the caviller be ready to ply his objections, the Pharisee bid Him to His banquet, the crowds press round Him until He was obliged to take refuge in a boat and teach them as they stood on the shore, and where Scribes and emissaries from Jerusalem would be collected to inspect and catechise Him. Here He was to have no time for prayer, save what He could save from the night, and even then He might sometimes have to steal away in order to be alone. As a rule, though He was to be received with much welcome and even enthusiasm at first, and by the multitude, still He was to be rejected by Capharnaum, though not so savagely as by the Nazarenes. Still here He chose to dwell, as far as He dwelt anywhere, for there were at least in Capharnaum a number of souls whom He was to win to His Father's kingdom, and even to raise to high places in it. Here Magdalene was to come, the first of all to beg for the forgiveness of her sins, and to show that great love which won that forgiveness. Here was the home of Peter, here was the ruler of the synagogue whose daughter He was to raise to life, here was the nobleman whose son was to be restored by a word at a distance, and the good centurion who loved the Jews and built them the synagogue, and who was to show a faith which had not been found in Israel. Here was Matthew, the holy publican, ready to leave his gainful trade at a word and to celebrate his abandonment of the world in a princely banquet in which publicans and sinners came to throng about Him Whose loving historian, as well as Apostle, he was to become. Good and bad, predestined souls as well as souls which were to be wooed in vain by all the attractive condescension and earnest entreaties of our Lord, · were gathered in that bright and prosperous town by the side of the lake, and, as is always the case, for the sake of the good who were to become so dear to Him, our Lord was willing to expose Himself to the coldness, ingratitude, and even the hatred and persecution which He was to experience from the rest. Capharnaum is a picture of any crowded seat of industrial activity, of wealth, prosperity, and worldly enjoyment, in which the missioner who follows in the footsteps of our Lord will seldom fail to find consolation, souls that have been prepared for him by grace, a few of which are enough to compensate for days of toil and nights of prayer, even though they are but few, because the seed that springs up on good soil and brings forth a hundred-fold is more than enough to make up for the waste of that which falls on stony soil, or among thorns, or by the roadside.

It seems that we may conclude from the choice by our Lord of Capharnaum, that it was already determined in His mind that Galilee was to be the earliest and chief scene of His missionary labours. It might have been thought natural that He should have begun at Jerusalem, and that the preaching of the new kingdom, if set forth forcibly and attested by powerful miracles there, might have gone forth from thence with authority to win men all over the Holy Land, and thence to spread over the whole world. Such was, in truth, to be the course of the Gospel preaching, but not in the lifetime of our Lord. He would go up to Jerusalem at the feasts from time to time, He would exercise His authority there in purging the Temple from the profanation of the traffic carried on in its courts, He would work great miracles there, and draw to Himself a few simple souls, such as Nicodemus or Joseph of Arimathæa. Nor need we doubt that a far larger number were prepared for future conversion by His teaching in the Temple, especially in the later months of His Ministry. But our Lord seems to have avoided all through, unto the very end, any challenge to the authorities at Jerusalem, whom even to the last He taught the people to obey though not to imitate, at least any challenge so direct as would precipitate that final conflict between Himself and them which was to issue in His Passion. Thus, from the very first, He preferred, as we see, to make Galilee the scene of His preaching, as it had been the home of His Hidden Life. Before He left the banks of the Jordan, after His Baptism and Temptation, He had already begun to make His selection of future Apostles, and they were all Galilæans, though from the accounts given in the Gospels we should be inclined to think that the majority of St. John's hearers and disciples must have been from Judæa and the other more southern parts of Palestine. Thus, even in the scene of His public labours our Lord still chose what was lowly and unobtrusive, and even as the future Princes of His Kingdom He preferred simple and ignorant fishermen to the prelates and doctors of the holy city.

CHAPTER XVIII.

The Cleansing of the Temple.

St. John ii. 13–22 ; *Vita Vitæ Nostræ*, § 23.

IT was now time for the Galilæan pilgrims to start for
the feast of the Pasch at Jerusalem. The Galilæans
ordinarily travelled in companies, like caravans, friends
and neighbours keeping together, and taking the road
down the Jordan valley on the eastern side, in order to
avoid the hostility of the Samaritans, whose bigotry was
more likely to be aroused by large bodies of travellers
journeying together, their ' faces as if they would go to
Jerusalem,' and especially as the time of the great feasts
drew near. Our Lord and His disciples, now penetrated
with the deepest faith in Him and the most fervent zeal
for the mission which He had begun to undertake, would
thus pass near the place where He had first called them
to His side, up the long ascent which leads from Jericho
and by Bethany over the Mount of Olives to Jerusalem.
Immense multitudes of pilgrims like themselves thronged
the sacred city, or encamped in the open country close
around it, arriving often some days before the feast itself,
in order, as St. John mentions, to purify themselves from
legal defilements.

The Temple, which had been rebuilt at an immense
cost and with great magnificence by Herod, was now
in that perfect beauty which attracted the enthusiastic
admiration of Jews and strangers alike, which is described
in glowing language by Josephus, and made even the

Apostles draw our Lord's attention to it as He sat over against it on the Mount of Olives after His last day of teaching in its courts. Though the final labours of its costly restoration were not accomplished, as it seems, till a later date than this, the Temple was in all substantial respects complete as well as magnificent. There was, however, a great abuse which had crept in of late, and which must have scandalised the pious Jews and the visitors from a distance, who had been accustomed to venerate the Temple as the centre of the worship of the holy people, a sort of antechamber to heaven itself, where God vouchsafed to dwell, Himself 'the praise of Israel.' There were two institutions connected with the Temple which gave occasion to the abuse in question. The first consisted in the numberless sacrifices, partly necessary and obligatory at certain times or for people under certain conditions, partly matters of devotion not prescribed by any law, but imposed by custom and their own zeal upon persons of wealth and piety. For these sacrifices a large number of victims were necessary, and it was a convenience for the devout worshippers to find them ready on the spot, instead of having to bring them from a distance. The Talmudists state that a certain Bava ben Bota had at this time obtained leave from the Government to collect animals for sacrifice in the porticoes of the Temple, oxen, sheep, doves, and the like, . and here he seems to have established a regular market. It is said that the Jews made the synagogues all over the country places of traffic, but nowhere could there have been so brisk a scene of business as in the Temple itself at the time of one of the great feasts. Besides this, shops had been established on each side of the great eastern gate, and had gradually penetrated into the sacred building itself, in which the exchange and sale of money was continually carried on. Each Jew was bound to pay half a shekel annually to the Temple, and the collection of this tax was made just before the Pasch. The Jews arriving from all parts of the world naturally brought with them coin of the countries in which they lived, and these coins were not received in discharge of the tax, many of them being idolatrous. The money-changers were ready in the shops and offices already mentioned, to provide the pilgrims with the half-skekels in which the Temple tax was to be paid, taking ample care of their own interests in the commission which they charged on the exchange. Both in the case of the sale of victims and of the exchange of money, there can be little doubt that the sellers had a great advantage over the buyers, who were, in fact, completely at their mercy.[1]

It was in the midst of this scene of traffic and gain that our Lord now appeared, with His small company of disciples following Him. 'And Jesus went up to Jerusalem. And He found in the Temple them that sold oxen, and sheep, and doves, and the changers of money sitting. And when He had made, as it were, a scourge of little cords, He drove them all out of the Temple, the sheep also, and the oxen, and the money of the changers He poured out, and the tables He overturned, and to them that sold doves He said, Take these things hence, and make not the house of My Father a house of traffic. And His disciples remembered that it was written, The zeal of Thy house hath eaten me up.'[2]

The Fathers and other Christian writers have dwelt upon this action as one of the greatest of our Lord's miracles, as it is called by St. Jerome. We certainly cannot easily account for the entire absence of resistance to our Lord's act on the part of those whom He so summarily dismissed from a place which they could not

---

[1] See Sepp. *Leben Jesu*, p. 2, § iii. ch. iv.
[2] St. John ii. 13–17 ; Psalm lxviii. 10.

have occupied except with at least the tacit license of the priests and rulers of the Temple, and to remain in which was almost necessary for the gains on which they were bent, unless we suppose that there was some preternatural force brought to bear upon them. There is no reason for thinking that the people at large saw anything very scandalous in the presence of the traffickers in the Temple, so that it might have been dangerous to resist our Lord on account of the support He would have been sure to receive from the crowd. And it must also be remembered that, although He was already known to many, chiefly among His Galilæan fellow-countrymen, He had not as yet gained that wonderful influence and ascendancy in the minds of the people in general which afterwards made it so necessary for His enemies to contrive their attacks against Him without irritating the populace. Nor can we suppose that the mere weakness of an evil conscience would have made these vendors of what was necessary for the Temple service cower before any one, whoever it might be, who might attack them. It is rather the characteristic of persons who are acting against light in matters connected with the direct service of God, to have very hard consciences indeed when their own interests and their own personal feelings are concerned. There are usually no more unscrupulous persons in the world than those who have come to use places in the Temple of God for the purpose of their own enrichment or their own aggrandisement. We are therefore led to suppose that the hidden Godhead of our Lord, and the majesty of His Manhood which was united to the Person of the Eternal Son, made themselves felt in some mysterious way, such as was at the command of our Lord at any moment, and that the result was a panic such as that which fell upon the armed multitude which went out in the dark of night to the Garden of Gethsemani to seize Him, and which fell to the ground before Him at the simple words, 'I am He.' Some of the Fathers tell us that our Lord's external appearance varied, if He so chose, to various persons and at various times, and they imagine that on this occasion there was something terrible in His look and voice which made it impossible for the sellers in the Temple to think of resistance or disobedience. It is also within the power of the angels, many of whom were continually in attendance on our Lord, to produce on men's minds an impression of awe and undefined fear at the more sensible presence of the invisible world, and this power also may have been exercised now. Again, few people, unless they are inveterate in wickedness, can altogether divest themselves of the reverence due to holy places, and in the case of the Temple there was a grandeur and majesty about the building, the crowds of worshippers, and the solemn services, and sacrifices, imposing enough to make those to whom our Lord addressed Himself ready to yield, especially as the reverence which they could not help feeling for the holy place must have worked powerfully on their consciences, reproaching them for their act of profanation, hardened as they might be. In this way we may understand that the absence of all resistance to our Lord was partly due to supernatural causes, partly also to what remained of religious and devotional feelings in the hearts of those who were so summarily driven out of the Temple.

The action of our Lord was in itself an act of zeal, as the Evangelist tells us by his quotation from the Psalms, and of no ordinary zeal, but of such as corresponds to the strong expression, 'The zeal of Thy house hath eaten Me up,' taken entire possession of Me, and made Me wholly its own. Our Lord's ordinary manner was one of extreme gentleness and humility, though of course

of wonderful majesty ; and when He came across persecution or arrogant treatment from others, He usually
either retired before it or bore it meekly and in silence.
But it is characteristic of true meekness and true humility,
which take no thought for their own credit or dignity, to
be set on fire when the honour of God or of anything
that belongs to Him is concerned, and then the firm-
ness, vigour, courage, and boldness of action which such
persons show are far stronger and more irresistible in their
effects than the impetuosity and audacity of persons
of less perfect virtue.   Every Christian is bound to be
like a lion in defence of the honour of God, and we
see in the histories of the martyrs many instances in
which the naturally gentlest and weakest of human
beings have either borne incredible tortures with the
most wonderful constancy, or have been as free and
bold in speech and conduct, rebuking the persecutors
or insulting the false divinities to whom they were
commanded to offer sacrifice, as if the whole power
of the world had been at their feet instead of being
arrayed against them.   And we find the same courage in
the meekest saints when they once determine on active
attacks on what is wrong or dishonourable to God.

It is so with all true zeal.   More particularly, of course,
our Lord's action in this cleansing of the Temple
seems to look forward to and sanction the conduct of
His saints and servants when there have been scandals
to be reformed and abuses to be driven out from the
sanctuary of the Church—and the language used by
St. Bernard, or St. Bridget, or St. Catharine of Siena,
rises to the mind as corresponding to this act of zeal
on our Lord's part, and still more the heroic under-
takings of such reformers as St. Gregory VII., who found
the whole world in arms against him, when he began
his war against simony and the degradation of the

clerical order by the violation of the rule of celibacy. The Church of God has the promise that the gates of hell shall not prevail against her, and one of the ways in which that promise is specially fulfilled is in the inherent power which she possesses of shaking off defilement and corruption and spiritual evils which from time to time seize upon parts of her system, and which ere now have invaded the sanctuary itself. There have been times when some among her rulers have been worldly, when the riches and power with which the piety of her children has clothed her have made her high offices objects of earthly ambition, and when in consequence great scandals have arisen, and customs, the tendency of which has been to eat away her spiritual life, have become prevalent. The sanctuary has not been free from buyers and sellers, gain has been made even in the house of the Lord, and sometimes the hierarchy, sometimes the religious orders which have the special mission of embodying the Evangelical counsels in permanent institutions, have been tainted by the breath of covetousness, or even of still lower vices. The fine gold has become dim, and the salt of the earth has lost its savour. At such times our Lord visits His Church, as on this occasion He fulfilled the prophecy of Malachias that He should come suddenly to His Temple and purify the sons of Levi. Such visitations of our Lord often consist in external calamities and persecutions, or in internal rebellion.

But they are seldom unaccompanied by the presence of some great saints or some determined ecclesiastical rulers, who, at the cost of great suffering to themselves, carry out, by the mercy of God, and assisted by the revival of a better spirit in the body of the faithful or in the clergy, or in the religious orders, the reform which is needed to restore the pristine splendours of the Bride of Christ. The action of those who are the instruments of our Lord in work of this kind is the echo and repetition of this great and powerful act of zeal on the part of our Lord Himself.

Holy writers are also accustomed to consider the symbolical character of this action. For the true temple of God is the heart of the faithful, and especially of the faithful worshippers, and all worldly cares and evil imaginations and wishes are the buyers and sellers in the Temple. Our Lord is always burning with zeal to cleanse the hearts of the faithful, to drive out for them all that hinders the perfect worship and service of His Father, to which they ought to be consecrated. 'Every day,' says Alcuin, 'God spiritually enters His Church, and takes note how each one behaves himself ·therein. Let us take care therefore not to occupy ourselves in the church with laughter or idle talk, or with thoughts of hatred or evil desires, lest He should come suddenly and scourge us and drive us forth from His Church.' And Ludolph goes on to explain in the same way who are meant by the various classes which are driven out by our Lord. The innocent sheep, he tells us, that give their wool for the clothing of others, are works of holiness and piety, which are sold when they are performed hypocritically and for the applause of men. The oxen which labour at the plough are preachers, and when these seek their own gain and promotion instead of the love of God they are sellers in the Temple, however hard they may labour. He gives other instances of the same kind of interpretation.

We can hardly think that this great action of our Lord was accomplished with any circumstances of violence or excitement. He drove the sellers and the animals before Him, and every one obeyed Him instinctively. There is a sort of discrimination in the chastisement which is inflicted in the several cases, for the money of the changers was poured out upon the ground, and their tables overturned, so as to render the continuance of their traffic impossible at the time, the sheep and oxen were driven out, while the vendors of doves which were kept in large cages, were simply told to take them away, and not to render the house of His Father a house of traffic. The doves, as we see in the account given by St. Luke of the Purification of our Blessed Lady, were the offerings of the poor, and our Lord seems to have dealt more gently with those who were selling them than with the rest. Thus in a short space of time, and without any resistance, the whole area of the Temple court was purged from the taint of traffic and the infection of covetousness which had hitherto defiled it. The introduction of such practices in the Temple must, as has been said, have been disliked and resented by all the more devout among the Jews, but it was established by custom and ministered to convenience, and it probably had considerable support from people in authority, who, as is often the case in similar circumstances, did not hesitate to derive some personal profit from the custom. In a moment all was swept away at the simple bidding of our Lord. A few strokes of the 'scourge of little cords' had cleared the Temple.

Our Lord, no doubt, looked mainly to the actual purification of the Temple of His Father, in which anything like barter was unbecoming, and for which He always inculcated by word and by example the greatest possible reverence. But we can hardly help seeing that this action of His was symbolical, much in the same way as, at the end of His Ministry, the cursing of the fig-tree, which was an image of the Synagogue which He had striven in vain to purify and to render fruitful. And in this manner we understand how it was that He was now content with this single action, when it would have been within His power, perhaps, to prevent the future defilement of His Temple in the same way; for we find that three years after this the same bad custom had resumed its sway, and He again purged the Temple. The symbolical character of His action explains this in some measure. And it must also be remembered, that it is the method of God in His providence to punish signally one or two instances of a crime or a sin, and then often to leave other instances unpunished, at least in this world. We can hardly doubt that the wickedness of the world before the Deluge, or again the peculiarly abominable profligacy of the Cities of the Plain, have been frequently paralleled and equalled at other times and in other cases ; that the nations which were exterminated in Palestine by means of the Israelites, were not more detestably wicked than others have been since their time. Scripture is full of cases of sins which have been repeated over and over again without the same temporal chastisements falling on them as those recorded in the sacred annals, such as the sin of Onan, or Core, Dathan, and Abiram, and many of the transgressions of the Israelites which were at once and signally punished by God. It is God's way to set His mark on a certain kind of sin by a great punishment which is a warning as well as a punishment, and then to leave men, if they will, to heap up for themselves worse punishments in the next world if they defy His warning. It is not always so, because there are certain sins, notably sins that fall under the head of blasphemy against the Holy Ghost, the persecution of the Church, and other sins which are, as it were, insults to God in the government of the world, which He is in a manner bound to visit at once, and of them it is truly said, in our Lord's words, that they are not without punishment both in this world and the next. But in other cases, after one or two signal instances of punishment, men are allowed without special interference on the part of God to go on in their sin and at last die in it. For, except for some such reason as exists in the cases mentioned above, when it is necessary for the defence of the positive institutions which God has set up that the punishment of offenders should be visible to all the world, it is not in keeping with the method by which the providence of God deals with mankind, that instant and open punishment should fall upon every sin here and now, even upon those of the very kind upon which, in particular instances, such visible punishment has descended. The judgments of God in this respect may be compared to the reproaches of conscience, which are keen, loud, and terrible the first time that a deliberate sin of any kind is committed, but which, when they are not heeded, speak less loudly and less threateningly, until at last their voice is hardly perceived amid the clamour of passion. And then, when the end comes, and the time for attending to them is gone by, they wake up in more than their first power, and become the judicial punishment of the soul which has deserved by its own perversity to have its ears for a time dulled to their warnings.

CHAPTER XIX.

Our Lord at the Feast.

St. John ii. 14–22 ; *Vita Vitæ Nostræ*, § 23.

THE action of our Lord in cleansing the Temple of the money-changers and the victims for sacrifice which were there offered for sale was an action of unquestionable authority. It implied that He was the Lord of the Temple Who, according to the prophecy of Malachias, should suddenly come to it, or at all events that He was a prophet, acting in the name of God, and more than that, One Who spoke of God as His Father. He had acted in a manner quite different from that of a man who had not full and inherent authority, for He had made no remonstrances, nor had He sought in the first instance to bring about what He desired for the glory of God by means of the ordinary authorities of the Temple. For, as they must have tacitly, if not actually, permitted the abuse, which could not have existed but for some kind of sanction on their part, so also must they have been able to put a stop to it if they had chosen. Our Lord had paid no sort of attention or court to them, and had acted on His own authority. The Jews, by whom St. John generally means the authorities at Jerusalem, understood in the action some claim on our Lord's part either to be a prophet or the Messias Himself, and they seem to have taken this so much for granted that they did not ask Him as they had asked

St. John, Who He was, but only for some credentials in virtue of which they might have His authority proved to them. 'The Jews therefore answered and said to Him, What sign dost Thou show us, seeing that Thou dost these things?'

We cannot tell whether at the time at which these words were spoken our Lord had begun to work miracles at Jerusalem, as He certainly did at the feast, for they were the cause alleged by Nicodemus for his faith in Him as a Teacher sent from God. But it seems that the kind of sign which the authorities now required of Him was a miracle of that sort which was a pure 'sign' and nothing more, a portent such as those which are related in the case of Moses, when he required confirmation for his mission to the Israelites, and God bade him cast his 'rod on the ground, and it became a serpent, and put his hand into his bosom, and it came out covered with leprosy.[1] Such also was the sign given to Ezechias, when the line went back on the sun-dial of Achaz.[2] The miracles afterwards wrought by Moses, especially the plagues of Egypt, were punishments, and the miracles of our Lord were benefits. There seems to have been a strange hankering among the Jews for a sign of the kind just mentioned, a hankering which quite accorded with their hardness and perversity of heart, exacting from Almighty God just what they chose themselves to dictate to Him as the evidence of his own work among them, when the character of that work, and the many other ways in which our Blessed Lord's mission was attested, ought to have been more than enough for them. As it was, our Lord never gave them a sign of this kind. There was to be one great sign in the providence of God which was to authenticate His mission and prove His work, to become, as it were, the formal and official attes-

---

[1] Exod. iv. 3, 6, 7.   [2] Isaias xxxviii. 7, 8.

tation on the part of God to the truth of His teaching, and the power which He claimed, and for that it was necessary that He should first die by their means and almost by their own hands. This great sign, the one greatest miracle on which, as St. Paul says, our faith depends, was His Resurrection from the dead, and in order that that sign might be given, it was necessary that they should first slay Him. But this could not be spoken of openly and plainly now, and so our Lord veiled it in a figure taken from that holy thing before Him, as to the sanctity of which they had been so little careful as to admit into it that kind of profanation which He had just driven out of it. The holy thing was the Temple itself in which worship and sacrifice were continually offered to God, in which He dwelt in a special way, and which was in a certain sense the tabernacle of God with men, the link between God and man, the channel of the communications of prayer, adoration, blessing, and pardon between earth and heaven. In these respects, and in others, the Temple was a type and figure of the Sacred Humanity of our Lord, so that He could use it as an image which would convey in a parabolic and figurative manner the truth, which they were not fitted to receive more openly. So He said, 'Destroy this Temple, and in three days I will raise it up.'

It may be remembered that later on in His Ministry our Lord used other words in reference to a similar question put to Him concerning a sign. St. Matthew tells us,[3] 'Some of the Scribes and Pharisees answered Him, saying, Master, we would see a sign from Thee. Who answering said to them, An evil and adulterous generation seeketh a sign, and a sign shall not be given to it, but the sign of Jonas the Prophet. For as Jonas was in the whale's belly three days and three nights, so

[3] St. Matt. xii. 30.

shall the Son of Man be in the heart of the earth three days and three nights.' This is the importance of the prophetic action of Jonas—for he left behind him no prophecy but that—that the marvel which happened in his case was a type of the marvel which was to take place in our Lord ; and this marvel in our Lord was to be the sign given to the men of that generation, inasmuch as our Lord's Resurrection was to be the great sign of the truth of His Mission and of the Power which He claimed. This sign, then, is the same with that of which our Lord here speaks, only that He makes no mention of Jonas, who was thrown into the sea in order that others might be saved, but speaks of that terrible part in the bringing about of the sign which these rulers at Jerusalem were to have, in that they were to be the persons who were to destroy the Temple of His Body, which He was to raise up after three days and nights, as Jonas had been delivered miraculously after the same space of time. They were to be the people who were to take counsel among themselves to put Him to death, and whose chief was to stand up and tell them that it was 'expedient that one man should die for the people, and that the whole nation perish not'[4]—in this, as the Evangelist tells us, prophesying and uttering, in his official capacity, a divine truth the meaning of which he did not understand.

Thus the words which sounded so like a strange boast on the part of our Lord, a challenge to them to do something which was impossible and unreasonable, inasmuch as they could never have thought of putting His power to that test, were in truth a prophecy of the part which these prelates of the Jews were to take against our Lord, as well as a true answer to the demand for a sign to prove His authority. In this last respect the sense is the

<hr>

[4] St. John xi. 50.

same as if He had said, 'My authority to do this will be proved by My Resurrection.' In the prophetic sense it is as if He had distinctly told them that they should themselves be the persons to destroy the true Temple of God, the human body and life in which God dwelt among them. Moreover, we see that already these rulers had taken their part, already their attitude and conduct to our Lord was one of hostility, hostility which had only to be carried out to its full length in order to lead them to put Him to death. And, by a strange arrangement of Providence, when the time came for this hostility of theirs to work itself out fully and finally, they could find no better contrivance for bringing against Him a charge which might seem to convict Him as they desired, than a perversion and distortion of these very words in which their own wickedness was foreshadowed. They were in the act of fulfilling their own part in the sign of Jonas and in this prediction of our Lord, by destroying the Temple of God in His Sacred Humanity, when they put forward false witnesses who said, 'This Man said, I can destroy the Temple of God and after three days build it up again,' and 'I will destroy this Temple made with hands, and after three days I will build another not made with hands.'[5]

It may be noted also, that the sign of the Resurrection given by our Lord was indeed the greatest of miracles, and a sign which proved most conclusively His divine mission, and the dignity of His Person, as St. Paul says, according to the Greek reading, which is cited by St. Chrysostom and other Fathers, that He was 'declared to be the Son of God in power, according to the spirit of sanctification, by His Resurrection from the dead.'[6] Still even this was not a mere sign, nor

---

[5] St. Matt. xxvi. 61 ; St. Mark xiv. 58.

[6] Rom. i. 4. τοῦ ὁρισθέντος υἱοῦ Θεοῦ ἐν δυνάμει. κ. τ. λ.

was the benefit which it conveyed limited to our Blessed Lord Himself, and the glorification of His own Body, but it is the seed and cause of the resurrection of all mankind, and of all the glories and beatitudes which the saints in heaven shall enjoy in their risen bodies. It is the mystery and work of God on which our faith is built, on which all our hopes for the future depend, and its effects are to last on for ever and ever in the glorious kingdom of the children of God. All this is included in the words of our Blessed Lord, for His Resurrection cannot be separated from its effects in us. And thus we have another reason why He should give this sign and no other to the Jews, because it brought to His mind the work which He came to do, the Passion He was to undergo, on which His Heart was occupied from the very first, and the glorious victory and triumph which was to follow, and the kingdom which was to be founded upon the Cross.

To the Jews to whom He spoke all these things were of course hidden. They took His words literally, and He does not seem to have said anything more to enlighten them, while, on the other hand, we are not told that they pressed Him any further at that time. It was just forty-six years since Herod had begun the restoration of the Temple, which had been in fact its rebuilding, and the work was not yet complete. ' The Jews then said, Six-and-forty years has this Temple been building, and wilt Thou raise it up in three days?' But, adds the Evangelist, He spoke of the Temple of His Body, which was to be destroyed, or as His words signify more properly, dissolved, in death, soul and body being separated and loosed one from the other, and then He was to raise it up again by His own power, not, as was the case and is to be the case with other resurrections, to be raised by the power or prayer or merits of another. And this was to be the great sign, as has been said, and thousands even of the Jews were to be converted by it, and to understand that He Who had power to rise from the dead had authority also to cleanse the Temple.

It would seem that St. John's purpose in relating this saying of our Lord's was threefold. The two other Evangelists already quoted had mentioned the charge made by the false witnesses against our Lord, but had omitted any account of the actual words which He had used on this occasion, on which the charge was founded. St. John therefore, as all through his Gospel he supplies such omissions, adds this fact to the history, a fact which occurred in that early part of our Lord's Ministry of which nothing had been said by the three other Evangelists who preceded him. Again, it is his object all through to trace the hostility of the prelates at Jerusalem to our Blessed Lord, and the various occasions on which this hostility was called forth succeed one another almost uninterruptedly through a large part of his Gospel. He here, then, gives the first instance on which that hostility was provoked and manifested, the first occasion on which there was anything like an open breach between our Lord and the Priests and Pharisees. But lastly, he is equally bent upon recording the various steps by which the disciples were led on in their knowledge of our Lord; and as this was so remarkable an exhibition of His power and authority it must have sunk deep into their hearts, a power and authority of a different kind from that shown in the great miracle at Cana. For here He took upon Himself no less a right than that of the Lord of the Temple of God, without any respect or regard to the constituted authorities, setting them aside and superseding them by His own action, and giving them a peremptory answer which they did not understand.　Neither did the Apostles themselves, he tells us, understand it at the time, but 'when therefore He was risen from the dead, His disciples remembered that He had said this'—perhaps even the fact that the words had been made a ground of accusation against Him brought them to their memory—'and they believed the Scripture, and the word that Jesus had said.'　When the Apostles looked back after the Resurrection and Ascension on all that had fallen from our Lord's lips and all that they had seen Him do, we cannot doubt that in numberless cases it was as in this case, that they saw the deep meaning of words and actions which they had not understood at the time.　Before our Lord left them, He gave them, as St. Luke tells us, the gift of understanding of the Scriptures, and all that He had said to them.　'These are the words which I spoke to you while I was yet with you, that all things must needs be fulfilled which are written in the Law of Moses, and in the Prophets, and in the Psalms, concerning Me.　Then He opened their understanding, that they might understand the Scriptures.　And He said to them, Thus it is written, and thus it behoved Christ to suffer, and to rise again from the dead the third day,'[7] and the rest.　And it was to be a part of the office of the Holy Ghost to bring to the remembrance of the Apostles whatever our Lord had said to them.[8]　This saying, then, about the 'dissolving' of the temple of His Body came back to them, at that time, after the fulfilment of the wickedness of the Jews in putting Him to death, and by His own glorious Resurrection, and as St. John tells us, their faith both in the Scriptures which had prophesied concerning Him in so many ways and in the word of our Lord Himself on this occasion, was confirmed.　It is remarkable also that the prophecy concerning the three days and nights was per-

[7] St. Luke xxiv. 44–46.　　　　[8] St. John xiv. 26.

fectly well known to the Chief Priests, who made it the ground of their application to Pilate that the sepulchre of our Lord might be watched by soldiers for that time. This may have come to their knowledge in consequence of our Lord's frequent predictions concerning the Passion and Resurrection, made from the time of St. Peter's confession; but it is not impossible that it may have been connected in their minds with the 'three days' spoken of on this occasion, and that hence, if they had been minded, they might have been able to understand truly the words which they so cruelly perverted in the mouths of their false witnesses.

St. John's words, telling us that after our Lord was risen from the dead, and not before, they remembered this saying of His, and that the effect of that remembrance was that they believed the Scripture and our Lord's own words, may be understood as referring generally to that intelligence of the prophecies, whether contained in the Scripture or uttered by our Lord, which grew upon them in virtue of the gift which our Lord conferred upon them at that time. Then we have a sort of contrast drawn by St. John between the evidence from prophecy and the evidence from miracles. As soon as they saw Him work the great miracle at the marriage-feast the disciples believed in our Lord. For the argument from a miracle when it is once perceived and acknowledged as such, does not require any further confirmation to produce its effect, except, indeed, in the case of miracles which are themselves the subjects of prophecy, in which case there is a fresh force added to them when the prophecy is recognised in its fulfilment. But it is clear that all through the Ministry of our Lord the Apostles were not quick to recognise in Him the fulfilment of all the prophecies, and especially of the prophecies which spoke of His Passion. So much was this the case, that He had

to reproach them with their want of discernment. And
if this was the case with the Apostles and friends of our
Lord, much more must it have been the case with the
Jews in general. They were students of the Scriptures,
and when their learned men were asked by Herod as to
the birthplace of the Messias, they were able to tell him
exactly. But yet the fulfilment of all these prophecies
was going on before their eyes, and they did not know
it. They made difficulties about Nazareth and Galilee,
and of course the humility, poverty, and obscurity of
His Life were stumbling-blocks to them. After the Resurrection and the day of Pentecost, however, we find
the fulfilment of the prophecies continually and most
strongly dwelt on by the Apostles, and it would seem
almost as if this were the chief argument on which they
insisted with the Jews and all those who had any
knowledge of the previous revelation of God to man.
Thus in the Gospel which more particularly represents
to us the teaching of the Apostles to the first Christian
Church at Jerusalem, the Gospel of St. Matthew, we find
the argument from the fulfilment of prophecy continually brought out in one detail after another ; while in
St. Mark, on the other hand, which was written for
the Church of Rome, which was at least largely composed of Gentiles, the miracles of our Lord are more
dwelt on than the fulfilments of prophecy.

The formal Christian proof, of course, embraces both
these elements, or is rather perhaps a combination of
the two into one. The apparent blindness both of the
Apostles and of the Jews in general, to the marvellously accurate fulfilment of the prophecies, which made
up, we may almost say, the visible life of our Lord, is an
instance of what meets us continually in the history of
the Church. It requires a special illumination from
God, and also a certain amount of recollection and

prayer, a life to some extent above the world, to understand the Scriptures, and in particular to understand them in their practical application to daily life. Many points of the Gospel law, the example and precepts and counsels of our Lord, the necessity of faith and obedience, the prerogative of poverty and purity, the duty of forgiveness, the rule not to judge our neighbour, or again, the rights and endowments of the Church and our duties towards her, the sinfulness of schism, and the like, as well as many of the positive doctrines and institutions of the kingdom of God, all are luminously clear to the eye practised in the revelation of our Lord. And yet most of these are matters as to which men are ordinarily as much in the dark, as far from having any practical conviction of their importance, as the Jews were as to the fulfilment of that vast range of 'divine oracles' which God had committed to their especial charge. And so with regard to matters which seem to fall under the head of prophecy, our Lord's promises to His Church, the manner in which in history He permits assaults upon her on the one hand, and allows her to be tried by every kind of calamity without being overwhelmed thereby on the other, and other like lessons of experience, are lost upon the world at large, so that one persecutor succeeds to another without being alarmed by the fate of his predecessor in iniquity. And even the children of the Church are not always alive either to the lessons of history or the promises of prophecy, and so are tempted either to despair amid her calamities or to forget that they have a large part to do in prayer and penance in order to ensure her triumph.

We gather from what is here added by the Evangelist, that our Lord worked many remarkable miracles at this feast in Jerusalem. They are not told us in detail, as St. John seems only to mention them in order to introduce the effect which they had on the minds of many, and our Lord's prudent behaviour towards them. 'Now when He was at Jerusalem, at the Pasch, on the festival day, many believed in His name, seeing the signs which He did.' They were attracted by the display of miraculous power, and probably were ready to hail Him as a Messias after their own mind, One Who would deliver the nation from the Roman yoke, and set up a glorious earthly kingdom in which His followers would find places of power and consideration. The doctrine of the Cross, when it began to be preached, was to shake off from our Lord most of the adherents of this kind, who were forward to join Him as long as His cause seemed likely to prosper and beat down all opposition by means of the power of miracles, and it is quite possible that many of those who had at one time been ready to believe in Him in the sense now spoken of, may afterwards have taken part against Him as His persecutors. St. John here gives another note of the Incarnate Son of God in our Lord. He had been brought up at Nazareth, almost as much in retirement from the world as St. John Baptist in the desert, and He had hitherto had no opportunity of learning the inconstancy, shallowness, and selfishness of men by experience. Others, even good and religious·men, men with their hearts simply set upon advancing the glory of God, are constantly in danger of having their simplicity deceived, and of being used as tools by men who pretend to listen to them and become their disciples. They purchase their knowledge of mankind by sad experience, and find out only by degrees how few men there are who can be trusted. It was not so with our Lord. As to these 'disciples of prosperity' of whom the Evangelist is now speaking, from the very beginning He saw through them, and 'did not trust Himself unto them, for that He knew all men, and because He needed not that any should give testimony of man, for He knew what was in man.'

Our Lord is thus in this instance the example to all those of His servants who have, in particular, the office of teaching or preaching, or in any way advancing the cause of God after Him. For such persons there is hardly any virtue more necessary than prudence to guard their simplicity and to guide their zeal. Our Lord afterwards told the Apostles that He sent them forth as sheep among wolves, and they were to be on that account wise as serpents and simple as doves.[9] We find the saints, such as St. Ignatius and St. Francis Xavier, in their own conduct and in their instructions to others in the same position, insisting most earnestly on this precept of divine wisdom. They made themselves all things to all men, and yet they would never commit themselves to any, or put themselves in the power of any, always keeping their independence, never submitting to any obligation or favour which might compromise their Apostolical liberty, cautious in trusting their plans or their secrets to professed friends, however sincere their professions, living and acting and speaking as if thousands of eyes were upon them, and as if all that they said was to be repeated by a thousand tongues. And there is probably hardly any kind of mischief to the cause of God which has not at some time or other been promoted by means of indiscretion, want of caution, over-confidence in supposed friends, on the part of those who are engaged in the service of God. St. John attributes this wisdom on the part of our Lord to His inherent knowledge of man. 'He knew what was in man.' This may either be referred to His divine knowledge of all things, or, as we find in many theologians, to that gift of the Holy Ghost which is called the dis-

[9] St. Matt. x. 16.

cernment of spirits, and which is one of those gifts called *gratis datæ* which perfect the understanding, and which was bestowed in its plenitude on the blessed human soul of our Lord.[10] It is this gift which is communicated in a larger or smaller measure to the saints and servants of God. Nor can the necessity for some such gift, or for the Christian prudence which guides the soul in ordinary ways to the same effect, be denied in the case of the general mass of Christians, all of whom have to make their way, after the example of our Lord, through a world full of snares and dangers, many of which consist in the wiles and insidious conduct of men like themselves.

CHAPTER XX.

Nicodemus.

St. John iii. 1-21 ; *Vita Vitæ Nostræ,* § 24.

AFTER speaking of the many who were willing in a certain manner to give themselves to our Lord as His disciples, but to whom our Lord would not trust Himself, the Evangelist· goes on to tell us how He dealt with one whose soul was very dear to Him, and who was afterwards to render Him more than one service, to end by confessing Him openly at the very time of His Passion by burying His sacred Body, and to die after persecution and confiscation in His faith and in His grace. The narrative of the Evangelists for the most part clings so closely to the steps of our Blessed Lord, that we may be apt to forget how many there were, whether at Jerusalem or in other parts of the

[10] See Suarez, *De Incarn.* Disp. xxi. sec. 1, n. 7.

country where He had preached, who only saw Him occasionally, and whose faith in Him had to grow up to its perfect stature at a distance and in the midst of an atmosphere hostile to Him. That it should be so, was greatly to His glory, even although not all had at once the courage to make an open profession of allegiance to Him, or the special vocation of the Apostles to leave all things and follow Him. St. John in a later passage speaks of many of the earlier believers in our Lord who were deterred from declaring themselves by human respect, after the time when the authorities at Jerusalem had decreed that any one who professed faith in Him should be excommunicated from the Synagogue, and he says of them, 'that they loved the glory' or good opinion 'of men rather than that of God.'[1] This does not make it untrue that at an earlier time there may have been many whose souls were secretly trained by divine grace, and prepared by slow degrees for a perfect and open faith in our Lord. It is His characteristic, as the prophet tells us, not to break the bruised reed or quench the smoking flax, much more was He and is He always patient with those whose hearts are set in the right direction, although they may move but slowly along the path by which others seem to run. And it often turns out that men in this position, whether they are kept back by the providence of God or by their own unconscious deficiencies, are able, like Nicodemus, to defend the cause of truth when others have not the opportunity, and to minister to God's service in ways to which others have no access. The gradual training of Nicodemus, Joseph of Arimathæa, Gamaliel, and others like them, was a work of God which has its counterpart in His treatment of numberless souls at any time,

---

[1] St. John xii. 43.

not less than the more direct method which He pursued with St. Peter, St. John, or St. Paul.

'But there was a man of the Pharisees named Nicodemus, a ruler of the Jews.' Nicodemus is thus introduced to us as in contrast, as has been said, to others whom our Lord would not trust. He was a Pharisee, a member of the strictest, most religious, and most respected sect among the Jews, and also a man of high birth and office, apparently a chief among the teachers and expounders of the Law. 'This man came to Jesus by night'—out of timidity, as there seems no reason to doubt, though some writers have seen in the fact nothing more than an arrangement for the sake of convenience, as both our Lord and Nicodemus might have been fully occupied in teaching during the day, and it is thought that if St. John meant to imply secrecy, he would have said so without mentioning the time. If fear of men were indeed the motive, still our Lord did not on that account reject Nicodemus, but, on the contrary, received him with the utmost sweetness and condescension, opening to him very freely the treasures of His divine teaching to an extent which makes this dialogue of His with Nicodemus seem as a typical specimen of the doctrines on which He insisted at this stage of His Ministry, as the Sermon on the Mount, which was delivered in the course of the subsequent year, is a typical specimen of His moral and practical teaching during the same period. It is this which makes the summary of the dialogue or discussion which is preserved to us by St. John so wonderfully valuable and interesting. We cannot be sure that we have all the words of our Lord or of Nicodemus on this occasion, for if such were the case the dialogue would have been short indeed, occupying only a few minutes of time, whereas there is nothing to forbid the supposition that Nicodemus had more than one interview granted to him. But we may be sure, not only that the account given by St. John is strictly accurate and true, but also that if there were more interviews than one, and if more passed at that interview which is here spoken of than is related, still, we have that main outline of the instruction which the Holy Ghost desired to be recorded for the benefit of the Church.

We may consider Nicodemus as representing the state of mind and feeling of the learned and pious Jews of Jerusalem, men who had many prejudices and some personal defects, perhaps of pride, to hinder them from acknowledging our Lord, but whose hearts were still touched by the need of salvation, and their minds occupied by the general expectation of the Messias, an expectation, as they well knew, founded upon solid grounds in prophecy and in history. We are not told whether Nicodemus had been one of the Pharisees who had humbled themselves to submit to the baptism of St. John, though our Lord seems to allude in the course of the dialogue to the words of His Forerunner. But he could hardly have been ignorant of the deputation which had lately been sent to St. John by the Sanhedrin, and as he was himself a Pharisee, and a distinguished teacher, it is not unlikely that he may even have been one of that deputation. Since that time, however, there had been new evidence and new witnesses produced, in the order of Providence, in authentication of our Lord's mission, and on this head of proof it is that Nicodemus grounds that kind of belief which he had already conceived concerning Him. 'This man came to Jesus by night, and said to Him, Rabbi, we know that Thou art come a teacher from God, for no man can do these signs which Thou dost, unless

God be with him.' Nicodemus estimates accurately, we may almost say, with theological precision, the force of the evidence of the miracles of our Lord, if they were to be taken apart from other considerations which belonged to the same subject-matter. The miracles in themselves proved exactly that God was with Him; but if they were taken in conjunction with the witness of St. John Baptist, with our Lord's manner of working them, that is, as One Who was using His own power, and with His way of speaking of Himself, and of God as His Father, they might have been enough to form the ground of a still higher faith concerning our Blessed Lord. Our Lord, however, did not point out that He was not only a teacher come from God, but He took the position which Nicodemus assigned to Him, and began at once to instruct him as to that which was the question uppermost in his mind, even although it may not have been as yet mentioned—the kingdom of God.

'Jesus answered and said to him, Amen, Amen, I say to thee, unless a man be born again, he cannot see the kingdom of God.' Our Lord, then, at once speaks with authority. As a teacher come from God He would have the right to deliver the message in His name; but He speaks as in His own, with the solemn form of asseveration which He usually adopted in such cases. He speaks of the kingdom of God, or the kingdom of heaven, which had been notified by St. John Baptist as approaching; and He assumes that this is the subject as to which Nicodemus expects Him to instruct or persuade him. In the Jewish notion the kingdom of heaven or of God was a blessed, prosperous, and glorious continuation or restoration of the empire of the throne of David, extended over the whole earth and adorned with every circumstance of magnificence and temporal well-being. Or, if to men like Nicodemus it was something more connected with the necessities of the soul or the functions of the interior life, still it was something growing out of the existing institutions of Judaism into which men might pass from them with no great violence or radical renovation. Our Lord, however, speaks of it as an entirely new life. 'Except a man be born again, he cannot see the kingdom of God.' The Greek word signifies born from above, as well as anew, and it is not easy to determine which should be its exact sense here. But the one need not exclude the other, and it seems clear that Nicodemus understood our Lord to speak of being born afresh. Men must be born again, or rather, they must be begotten again, and from that new generation are to arise all the faculties, capacities, functions, and exercises of an entirely new life. The kingdom of God is a new creation. The contrast between that kingdom and all outside it is the contrast between the primeval chaos and the beautiful world which was evolved therefrom when the fiat of the first creation was uttered by God. And as in that first creation nothing was made of itself or was the cause of its own existence or of the form or nature in which it came forth, but all was the work of God, so in this new creation all is to be the act of God, for our Lord's words are properly to be understood, as has been said, 'unless a man be begotten again.' There must be a new act of God the Father of all—not indeed destroying man's nature, for that is against the law of His kingdom, so that it is a man remaining a man who is to be begotten anew—but giving to him a higher nature, according to that wonderful expression of St. Peter, that we are 'partakers of the divine nature.' Such, our Lord declares, is the kingdom of God, and therefore no one can enter into it or see it unless he is raised to the nature of its citizens by the new generation of which He speaks.

Though the ideas of Nicodemus concerning the kingdom of God may have been much higher and nobler than those of most even of his colleagues among the Scribes and Pharisees, it is certain that they did not rise to the simple grandeur of the thought which our Lord put forward in these words. But, as is so often the case, instead of attempting to open his mind to the greatness of this truth as a whole, he found a difficulty for himself in the literal and even carnal interpretation of the language used by our Lord. ' Nicodemus saith to Him, How can a man be born when he is old? Can he enter a second time into his mother's womb, and be born again?' As if he had no idea of any birth but that of a carnal order, nor of any means by which such a birth could be brought about except by a repetition of the means by which men are first born into the world. And his words seem to imply that he took our Lord's instruction as applying to himself, for he was probably advanced in life, saying, ' How can one be born again at my age and time of life? If this is the condition, how can I ever hope to see the kingdom of God?' Whereas, in truth, this doctrine of the necessity of a new birth by means of which men are to be elevated to the capacities and conditions of the kingdom of God was not a new doctrine, inasmuch as there had never been a time when such an elevation had not been possible to man, and even necessary, if he were to be made partaker of that supernatural union with God in which citizenship of His kingdom consists. Adam and Eve had been elevated by sanctifying grace before their fall to the supernatural condition which God meant them to hand on as an inheritance to their children, and after the fall of man and the promise of redemption through the seed of the Woman, there had always been means of this new birth within reach. Such, under the law of

Moses, had been faith and circumcision, under the old law of nature, faith alone or faith together with certain ceremonies as to which we are ignorant, inasmuch as they are not expressly mentioned in Scripture. And by these means men were born again and saved by faith in the Messias Who was to come, just as we who believe that He has come.[2] We cannot suppose that Nicodemus was ignorant of this, but his words seem to make a difficulty which this knowledge ought to have obviated.

Our Lord's next answer to him is a more clear precise statement of the same general truth, with an additional and more particular explanation of the means of regeneration under the Gospel, the new dispensation in which the kingdom of God was embodied. 'Jesus answered, Amen, Amen, I say to you,' again repeating the solemn formula of assertion, 'unless a man be born [again] of water and the Holy Ghost,' as the instruments of his regeneration, 'he cannot enter into the kingdom of God.' Thus our Lord insists upon His former statement, only making it more precise, and announcing the new positive law of the kingdom which was to be binding on all as soon as that kingdom was established after the Resurrection, when it was to be proclaimed to all the world by the Apostles whom He sent in His name first to teach and then to baptize all nations, adding this law, 'He that believeth and is baptized shall be saved.' It is here that our Lord certainly alludes to the teaching of St. John Baptist, who had declared that he himself indeed baptized with water, but that One was to come Who was to baptize with the Holy Ghost. The twofold nature of man is to be regenerated by a sacrament containing both a visible and invisible agent, water and the Holy Ghost, and our Lord declares this, not as a message from Him Who sent

---

[2] See Salmeron, *Comm. in Evang.* t. viii. tr. 4, p. 28, from whom the last words are almost translated.

Him, as St. John might have done, but in His own name and as the Giver and Founder of the sacraments, which have their grace through His merits and their place in His kingdom through His institution. Thus He acts as Lawgiver and King in the kingdom of God, and then in His great condescension to the dulness of Nicodemus He explains his difficulty, and at the same time, to instruct him still further in the fundamental mysteries of the kingdom, He gives a reason why the agent of the regeneration of which He speaks must be the Holy Ghost. The reason consists in the spiritual character of the kingdom, and the explanation is founded upon this. No second natural generation is requisite, for the life which is to correspond to the new kingdom is spiritual. A man, it may be said, lives by more than one kind of life, for he combines, as has already been said, the various grades of being in the material creation, the vegetative and the sensitive, of which he partakes as well as lower creatures, and the rational, in which he rises above them. But the rational life does not extinguish the others, and there is nothing unreasonable or impossible in its being superadded to them. In like manner the spiritual life of the kingdom of God is to be bestowed on man, and it must be bestowed by generation. But, as it is a spiritual life, the principle by which it is imparted must be spiritual. 'That which is born of the flesh is flesh, and that which is born of the Spirit is spirit'—it would be strange and impossible indeed, if a carnal generation were necessary for a spiritual existence, but it is nothing strange if man who has his natural life from a natural principle should have to derive a new supernatural life from a supernatural principle. 'Marvel not, therefore, that I said to thee you must be born again.' For if that which is born of the flesh is flesh, certainly you need a new generation to be born to a new life which is so far above the flesh.

But the wondering of Nicodemus extended not only to the thing itself of which our Lord spoke, but also and even chiefly to the manner in which the effect was to be produced, and therefore our Lord goes on, not indeed to explain the manner, but to give a reason why a difficulty as to the manner should be no difficulty as to believing the result. As if He had said, If you marvel as to how this can be done, remember that all the operations of the Holy Spirit are incomprehensible and cannot be traced. 'The Spirit breatheth where He wills.' He is free, and He acts freely in all that He does, bound down to no laws, not obliged to come at one time because He has come at another, not bound to give holy thoughts and illuminations to the mind and movements to the will to-day because He offered them yesterday, nor to treat all alike, nor to distribute His gifts according to any method and order that you can trace, but only according to His own good pleasure. You cannot tell that He is approaching, or when He will come, or how He will work on your soul; but, lo, He is there when you did not expect Him, and at other times when you strove to win Him to you He did not come. You only hear His voice, and you cannot mistake its power, its sweetness, the peace which it breathes, the light which it pours on you, the strength which mantles through your spiritual being when He is there. In a moment all is light and vigour and health, where before was obscurity, weakness, and languor. He comes and He goes, whence and whither you know not; you know His presence and His departure, and that is all. 'So is every one that is born of the Spirit,' that is, in such manner is it that every one is born of the Spirit who is so born. The operation is in silence and in a moment; it is known by its effect, but its stages cannot be traced, nor can an account be given of its beginning, its middle, and its end; its progress cannot be described. The regeneration of man is after all but one of the operations of the Holy Spirit of God, and it is neither more nor less discernible even as to manner than the rest.

The doctrine of the operation of God's Spirit on the souls of men ought not to have been hidden from such a man as Nicodemus, because it is laid down in various parts of the Old Testament, especially in the books of Solomon and in the Psalms. Nor ought one whose life was consecrated to holy learning and the service of God to have been wanting in at least some sort of interior experience which might have enabled him to understand better the teachings of Holy Scripture. Again, inasmuch as the particular working of the Holy Ghost in which our Lord was instructing him was the sanctification and regeneration of the soul which takes place in the Sacrament of Baptism, there were many heads of teaching in the Old Testament which might have prepared him for this also. So when he answered our Lord, still in a kind of bewildered doubt, 'How can these things be done? Jesus answered and said to him, Art thou the master in Israel, and knowest not these things?' The expression, 'the master,' or teacher in Israel, with the definite article, has seemed to some to imply that Nicodemus held the high office in the Sanhedrin which gave to its holder a name almost equivalent to the teacher[3]—but it is perhaps safer to understand our Lord to mean, Art thou the teacher of whom we have heard? or something of that sort. And, inasmuch as by still persisting in his incredulity Nicodemus seemed almost to question the authority with which our Lord spoke, He insisted upon that authority, as He had a right to do even by the confession of

---

[3] Chàkàm, or 'wise man.'

Nicodemus, that the miracles proved His divine mission, and a far greater right than an ordinary prophet or messenger from God, because He bare witness of His own, and was not only a delegate. ' Amen, Amen, I say to thee, that we teach what we know, and we testify what we have seen, and you receive not our testimony.' The words may be understood, as Catholic commentators have explained, in two ways. They may allude to the witness of our Lord and His Eternal Father and the Holy Ghost, of which mention is made more than once in the New Testament, and in that case the saying refers more particularly to the doctrine which our Lord was now urging upon Nicodemus. Or our Lord may speak of what is called the 'created' knowledge of His Blessed Human Soul, which was the source of His testimony to the truth in the discharge of His office of Teacher and Prophet, and then the other person to whom He refers as sharing in His testimony and in its rejection by the Jews must be St. John Baptist, as representing the whole band of authorised witnesses to the truth, whether before our Lord's coming or after, the Prophets and Saints of the Old Testament on the one hand, and the Apostles and the Church throughout all ages on the other. For the words, 'we speak what we know, and testify what we have seen,' seem to echo the saying of St. John Baptist about our Lord, when he had recognised Him by the sign given to him from heaven, 'I saw and I gave testimony that this is the Son of God.' Especially does this seem to be the case, because the doctrine of regeneration in baptism by water and the Holy Ghost is in the dispensation of the Incarnation the natural outcome and issue of the mystery of our Lord's Baptism, in which He was declared to be the Son of God, with a particular reference to that adoption of sons which is communicated to us from Him by means of the Sacrament of Baptism which was then inaugurated and founded. Thus our Lord speaks what He knows, for He needed no sign or illumination, or instruction from above, and St. John testifies what he has seen, and the natural response to such teaching and such witness is the devout reception of and faith in the doctrine of regeneration as to which Nicodemus has difficulties. As the 'master in Israel' he might have been prepared for this doctrine by many features in the Old Dispensation and more than one passage in the Old Testament. And one thus prepared for the doctrine should have readily received its positive affirmation and declaration on the part of One Whom he acknowledged to have a divine mission, all the more, as another divine messenger had been sent before Him who had borne so clear a witness to Him, a witness bearing in its details on the very doctrine now affirmed. But 'you receive not our testimony.' There is nothing wanting on the part of God, short of what He cannot and will not do, that is, force the assent of the creatures whom He has made free. He desires their free willing acceptance of His message and His work, and nothing else, and this they will not give Him. These words of our Lord are echoed, as it were, through all the Christian centuries; it is the continual complaint of His Church, 'You receive not our testimony.' The Apostles and Evangelists are succeeded by the Pontiffs and Doctors and the authorised teachers and witnesses in the Church, and it is true as to them, even in the case of many who are, like Nicodemus, not indisposed to the truth, that their testimony is received but with difficulty, while in the case of others it is rejected altogether.

Our Lord's next words imply a further complaint or fear on account of the difficulty which even good men like Nicodemus made as to believing His witness. Nicodemus had stumbled, as it were, on the very threshold of the palace of truth, and if this were so, how could he be led on and on into its inner chambers? When, in the Epistle to the Hebrews, the Apostle gives a short catalogue of heads of teaching which he considers as elementary and such as may be taught to beginners, he speaks of not laying again the foundation of penance from dead works, and of faith towards God, of the doctrine of baptisms, and imposition of hands (in penance or confirmation), and of the resurrection of the dead, and of eternal judgment.[4] Wonderful as is the mystery and great as is the work of God in the Sacrament of Baptism, it is nevertheless an elementary part of the great scheme of Christian doctrine. It is one of those works of God in the mighty scheme of the Incarnation which are wrought on earth and belong to the earthly stage of the revelation of the sons of God. The sacraments are wonderful, beautiful, mysterious, and they require the exercise of divine power and the operation of no less a worker than the Holy Ghost. Yet there are other parts of the same divine scheme which are more entirely heavenly in their character, as belonging to that stage of its fulfilment which is to be wrought out entirely in heaven, more sublime, more completely above the realms of sense and human comprehension; and if these were proposed to you as matters of faith, how could you receive them if you do not receive what I now declare to you? 'If I have spoken to you earthly things and you believe not, how will you believe if I shall speak to you heavenly things?' The heavenly things which our Lord speaks of may be those divine truths concerning the nature of God, the unity of Essence, the Trinity of Persons, their mutual relations,

<hr>

[4] Heb. vi. 1, 2.

and the like, which are embodied in such documents as the great symbol of the Church which goes by the name of St. Athanasius. These are certainly things which are to be believed as conditions of salvation by all to whom they are lawfully proposed, which are far more difficult in themselves than the doctrine of regeneration. Or perhaps the heavenly things may be the truths concerning His own Divine Person, and the cause of His Incarnation; or again, the fruits of the Incarnation which are to have their development and expansion in the eternal blessedness of the redeemed in heaven, those things which eye hath not seen, nor ear heard, nor heart of man conceived, which are yet the fruits which are to grow up from the seed, so to speak, of that regeneration and renovation in baptism which takes place on earth. In both these cases there are things which in themselves are more difficult to human conception than the doctrine of the new birth; and if you reject My testimony as to the easier, you are in great danger of not being able to accept it as to the more difficult.

The connection of the next words of our Lord with the preceding is not at once obvious, and we must remember that the report of this discussion with Nicodemus may consist rather of the chief heads of doctrine which our Lord set forth at that date, than of a complete narrative of all that passed at the time, much of which may have had particular reference to the personal difficulties of Nicodemus, and so have been less to the purpose of the Evangelist. We may, however, without doing any violence to the text, suppose that there is no break in the argument, and that our Lord's words which follow are meant to insist on the duty of belief in His testimony on account of the dignity of His Person. There would thus be a sort of transition in the grounds on which He claimed the faith of Nicodemus, first on account of His miracles, which proved Him to be sent from God as a teacher, then on account of His solemn affirmation in the character of such a messenger, and lastly on account of His Personal dignity, which rose so far above that of prophet or teacher, who could only have heard what was in heaven, or heavenly things, whereas He is in truth the only-begotten Son of God, Who is in heaven. 'And no man hath ascended into heaven.' That is true, indeed, and if you require such a personal ascension in any man whose word you are to take and whom you are to believe, you will seek for such a ground of faith in vain—unless, indeed, you come to Me, 'Who have descended from heaven,' that is, Who have become Incarnate upon earth of a pure Virgin, and so have become 'the Son of Man, Who is in heaven,' being all the time the only-begotten Son, for ever with His Father in heaven. The form of expression is highly Hebraic, and must be understood according to the same principles of interpretation with the passage lately commented on, in which, 'so is every one who is born of the Spirit,' means in such wise it is that any one is born of the Spirit. It is not that any man has ascended into heaven to be able to bear witness to the things which he has seen and heard and knows, but instead of that God has become Man, descending from heaven for that purpose, and so the witness of the Son of Man is the witness of One Who is in heaven. Thus the sense is the same with that of another passage in the beginning of the Gospel of St. John, where the Evangelist says, 'No man hath seen God at any time.' Our knowledge of God does not rest upon the witness of any man who has been admitted to the vision of God; but we have still a witness concerning God, for 'His only-begotten Son, Who is in the bosom of His Father' and yet is the Son of Man upon earth, 'He hath declared Him.'

We have thus a clear declaration of our Lord to Nicodemus, of the truth as to His own Divine Person, and in the sentences which follow we find the unfolding of the doctrine of the Incarnation carried still further, even to the teaching concerning the Cross and Passion and the object for which He became Incarnate and suffered. Here, again, we are not quite obliged to suppose that the argument with Nicodemus on the necessity of faith in what our Lord laid down at the beginning is carried on, as if the words were to be exclusively considered with reference to that argument; though, as has been said already, it is not difficult to understand them in that connection. The name, the Son of Man, which our Lord here again uses—as far as we know, for the first time in His disputations with the Jews and their rulers—includes, as has been said, the doctrine of the Incarnation and the fulfilment of all the types and prophecies therein. At a later time in our Lord's Ministry we find the Jews making a difficulty as to the name, and saying, 'Who is this Son of Man?' If Nicodemus was unable to understand it, or made any objection to it, we are not told of this by St. John; and, as has been already said, he might have prepared for its use as well as for the meaning conveyed in it by more than one passage in the Old Testament. Its use marks a further onward step in our Lord's disclosure to him concerning Himself, especially when we add the still more clear statements which follow in the same discourse.

Our Lord now proceeds to unfold His teaching in such a manner as to carry it on not only to the necessity of faith but also to the doctrine of redemption and atonement, to the Passion and Cross, which again were to be the meritorious cause of all the graces bestowed upon men in the sacrament of regeneration with which He had begun. He takes one of the most famous types of the Passion in the Jewish history, a type which could hardly have been understood in any other way by the devout and learned among the Jews themselves. When the people, as is related in the Book of Numbers,[5] murmured rebelliously against God, and were punished by a plague of fiery serpents, so that many lost their lives, Moses, on their repentance, was told to make a 'brazen serpent and set it up for a sign, which when they that were bitten looked upon, they were healed.' Our Lord now declares that in like manner, and therefore with a like object, the 'Son of Man' is to 'be lifted up,' using words which He seems to have delighted in in speaking to the Jews, when and with whom He could not speak openly of His Cross and Passion. Thus, later on in the same Gospel, we find Him telling them, 'When ye have lifted up the Son of Man, then shall ye know that I am He'[6]—and again, at a time still nearer His Passion, 'I, if I be lifted up from the earth, will draw all things to myself.'[7] 'For,' He now says, 'as Moses lifted up the serpent in the desert, so must the Son of Man be lifted up.' And, as He when lifted up is to be like the brazen serpent, a means of healing to all who have recourse to Him, so is there to be a correspondence in the manner and condition of such recourse and such healing. For, as the Israelites were saved by looking at the serpent of brass, so are men now to be saved by believing in the Son of Man—'that every one that believeth in Him may not perish but may have everlasting life.' It is no longer a question of the particular difficulty made by Nicodemus as to the doctrine of the new birth. That, like everything else which our

---

[5] Numbers xxi. 4–9.
[6] St. John viii. 28.   [7] St. John x. 32.

Lord taught, was to be received on His authority.   But He is the object of faith as well as the witness and authoritative teacher of the truth, and men must believe in His Person as well as in His words, in ' His name ' as well as in His doctrine.   We may illustrate the greatness of this further claim on faith on the part of our Lord by what passed between Him and St. Martha before the raising of Lazarus.   Our Lord tells her that her brother shall rise again.   She replies, Yes, at the general resurrection.   Then He further puts to her that He is the Resurrection and the Life—' He that believeth in Me, though he were dead, shall live, and every one that liveth and believeth in Me shall not die for ever.'   And He asks her whether she believes this.   And she answers by a declaration of faith in His own Person, which includes and carries with it belief in every head of doctrine connected therewith and flowing therefrom— ' Yes, Lord, I believe that Thou art the Christ, the Son of the living God, Who art come into the world.'

Here, then, is another ground added to those which have been already laid down for the necessity of faith in our Lord's teaching.   Not only has He the testimony of miracles, and of St. John, not only ought He to be believed on His own word, not only is His Person that of the Son of Man Who is in heaven, the Son of God Who is come into the world, but moreover faith in Him is the condition on which men are to receive the benefits intended for them by His Eternal Father.   This very faith, about which Nicodemus made so much difficulty, is actually the condition of salvation and of eternal life.   But now our Lord has come to that which was the thought ever uppermost, if we may say so, in His Sacred Heart, ever rising to His lips—the thought of His Father's love.   There was reason, as the commentators remark, for further explanation here, because the image of the brazen serpent, important as was its place in the series of types of our Blessed Lord in the Old Testament, could not certainly express to Nicodemus the whole doctrine, a part of which it figured. It represented wonderfully many features in the plan of redemption ; as, for instance, the truth that our Lord was to be in the likeness of sinful man, though He was to be Himself without sin ; or again, the mode of His death, which was to be on the Cross, that He might be made, as St. Paul says, a curse for us, and so redeem us from the curse of the Law, as it is written, Cursed be every one that hangeth on a tree.[8] The looking on this serpent was a beautiful image of the faith in our Lord, and in this also the type was full of significance. But the types of the Old Testament, like the burning words of the prophets themselves, are but inadequate when we look for the expression of the personal action of God and the motives of our Redemption by Jesus Christ. And so our Lord, if we may venture to say so, breaks out into words which explain to what original cause that ineffable blessing of salvation and eternal life is to be traced up, at the same time excluding other lower causes which might perhaps have been imagined. The Son of Man was not to be 'lifted up' as the serpent on account of fault of His own, nor by any necessity as of fate, nor because it was not within the power of God to save man in any other way, nor because He was Himself too weak to defend Himself from His enemies. The cause was none of these, but only the immense love of God, Who determined to save the world in a manner so full of love, as well as of wisdom. 'For God so loved the world, as to give His only-begotten Son, that whosoever believeth in Him may not perish, but may have life

---

[8] Gal. iii. 10, 13. See the annotation of Toletus (21), on St. John iii. 14.

everlasting.' This is the purpose for which the Son of God is sent into this world, mercy, pardon, salvation, eternal life; and the condition required on the part of man is faith. 'For God sent not His Son into the world to judge the world, but that the world may be saved by Him.' The time is indeed to come when He will come to judge the world, but now He is come to warn in order that then He may not have to condemn. By-and-by it will be the time for the justice of God, now it is the time of His love and mercy. 'He that believeth in Him is not judged.' Our Lord when He came found the world under condemnation and judgment, the sentence was passed against all sinners, and even original sin, which is not personal, was enough to exclude men from the kingdom of heaven, inasmuch as the entrance to heaven had been forfeited by Adam for himself and all his children. But faith in our Lord was like the looking at the brazen serpent in the wilderness, it delivered those who used it as a means of salvation. Thus 'he who believeth in Him is not judged.' The sentence is reversed, judgment has no hold upon Him. 'He that doth not believe is already judged, because he believeth not in the name of the only-begotten Son of God.' He is already judged, because, as it is said in another place in this same chapter, the wrath of God remaineth upon him; he has had the opportunity of escaping it and averting the judgment to which he is already liable, and he has not availed himself of that opportunity; and moreover he has added another reason for his own condemnation, in that he has refused his belief in the name of the only-begotten Son of God. Thus on two grounds he is already judged, as a sinner for his sins, the punishment of which he might have escaped by faith, and also for the new sin of incredulity, of refusing to believe in the name of the Incarnate Son.

Finally, our Lord points out the reason and ground
and essence of this judgment. It is not ignorance, that
is, a true incapacity to grasp and know the truth, and act
upon it; it is not difficulty in obtaining knowledge, it is
not hardness or severity on the part of God. 'This is
the judgment,' this it is which condemns the incredulous: 'that the light hath come into the world, and men
have loved the darkness rather than the light, because
their deeds were evil.' Here we have the state of the
heart and of the conscience set down as the reason of
faith or unbelief, which depend in a great measure upon
the will. 'For every one that doth evil hateth the light,
and cometh not to the light that his works may not be
reproved.' To any one who is attached to a bad life of
vice and wickedness, the pure light of truth is an object
of terror, and his fear of being forced by an awakened
conscience to give up his sin makes him shrink from the
light as a pestilence. No one loves darkness or wickedness as such, no one but is afraid of the truth if his
works are evil; and so men do not 'come to the light,'
do not inquire into questions of faith and give themselves
the opportunity of believing, because they are afraid of
its effect upon their lives. The purity and holiness of
the law of God prevent men from embracing the truth
of God. On the other hand, men of goodwill and good
lives welcome every additional ray of light as something
congenial and connatural to the state of their hearts and
consciences. 'He that doth truth, cometh to the light,' as
drawn to it by an invincible instinct, 'that His works may
be made manifest that they are done in God.'

This is our Lord's commentary, so to speak, upon the
fact that His testimony is not received. He puts His
finger upon the seat of the moral disease which blinds
the eyes because it corrupts the heart, and at the same
time He points to the source of moral health, which, by

the assistance of God's grace, makes the eye keen to receive the light, because the heart is right and the conscience at peace. These truths shed a fresh light, if any were needed, upon the immense importance of the ministry of St. John in preparing the way for our Lord, and explain the resistance to the light, not only of the Pharisees and priests of Jerusalem, but of thousands of souls in every generation since His time, who have turned away from the claims of His Church upon grounds which perhaps seemed to them intellectual and critical, but which were in truth the repugnance of evil consciences or of hearts set upon self-indulgence, to light which brought with it the obligation of the law of purity. This explains the apparent want of cogency in the Christian evidences to so many minds. It is easy to prove the utter inconsistency of false religions and of imperfect forms of Christianity, and not more difficult to point out the childishness and ignorance of the laws of reasoning which mark the most intellectual or the most popular of the sceptical works against Christianity. Behind these weak defences of unreason there lurk hearts which are afraid of the light, and are happy to find any excuse, however hollow, for not 'coming to' it. This also shows the wonderful importance, in the machinery which Satan employs to keep men from our Lord, of the lies which are so profusely circulated and so shamelessly repeated against the Catholic Church. They are the most useful of all aids to the souls who wish to keep at a distance from her, and they deter from approaching her thousands who would otherwise find nothing in their own hearts to work against her claims.

Thus our Lord's conversation or conversations with Nicodemus ran through a large cycle of holy doctrine. Beginning with the necessity of the new birth, and an explanation of its spiritual character, He went on to ground His doctrine on His own authority as the Son of Man, the Messias promised of old, the Incarnate Son of God, faith in Whom was the necessary condition of salvation in the counsels of the Eternal Father. He spoke in figure and type, not explicitly, and in connection with the necessity of faith, of His Passion and Atonement, and opened the promise of eternal life which was to be won by faith and obedience. He explained the purpose of His own present mission in the world, and the love of His Father for mankind, of which that mission was the issue. On the other hand, He pointed out how it was that the world would turn away from Him, because of its evil deeds, and that this was in truth the substance of the judgment and condemnation of unbelief. And, indeed, it may be said that the final judgment of all sinners may be summed up in the same sentence. No one will be condemned for faults which were not of his own choosing, for ignorances which he could not avoid. But in the case of every sinner there will be these two elements, the existence of which will make the sentence irrefragably just—the light which might have been and was not approached, because of the evil heart which feared to learn that it must abandon the sins to which it was attached.

CHAPTER XXI.

Last Witness of St. John Baptist.

St. John iii. 22–36; *Vitu Vitæ Nostræ*, § 25.

WE have no very definite note of time to fix for us with perfect certainty the length of our Lord's stay in Jerusalem on the occasion of this feast of the Pasch, the first which occurred after His Baptism. But it is most probable that He never remained long in Jerusalem on these occasions, and that at this time, moreover, as He had not begun publicly to preach, though He had already manifested His power by a number of marvellous miracles which must have attracted the notice of many others beside Nicodemus, He would have a special reason for retiring almost at once when the feast was over. He had, indeed, another kind of work to perform for which it was necessary that He should be in a place where there were facilities for administering baptism, and where people could come to Him in crowds without attracting that notice which would have been caused if He had received them at or near Jerusalem. So St. John tells us that 'after these things Jesus and His disciples came into the country of Judæa'—as distinguished from the city of Jerusalem—'and there He abode with them, and baptized.' It has been conjectured by some writers that our Lord now went about from place to place in the country parts of Judæa, which were well populated, and sown, as it were, with cities and towns, though not to the same extent as Galilee. The time was to come, as we shall hereafter see, when our Lord was to make Judæa for a considerable space of time the chief scene of His teaching, but we can hardly understand St. John's words in this place thus, as it seems certain that our Lord was fixed in one place, to which people could come and find Him there. He remained therefore at some spot, probably near the Jordan, in the north-eastern part of Judæa, and baptized, chiefly by the hands of His disciples, as St. John mentions in the next chapter. The object of this baptism was probably to take up and continue that movement to penitence and the confession of sins which had been set on foot by St. John, a movement all-essential to fit people for the reception of the Gospel and of our Lord as the Messias. And, inasmuch as the baptism was evidently to external observers much the same as that of St. John, it would not be absolutely necessary to assume that our Lord now administered, or caused to be administered, Christian baptism, at least universally. Some of the Fathers suppose that at this time, or before, our Lord baptized His Blessed Mother, St. John Baptist, and some of the Apostles; and it seems hardly likely that the Christian Baptism should have been confined to a few only, especially as one object of the statement that our Lord baptized, though it was by the hands of His Apostles, seems to be to show that His own Baptism now began to be administered. The sacrament had been already instituted, as has been said above.

We can understand why for a time our Lord lingered about the scene of the baptism of St. John, in the country of Judæa and not very far from Jerusalem, in the hope, perhaps, that the persons in authority, the prelates and Pharisees at Jerusalem, on whose action so much was to depend as to the external success of His preaching, might be touched by the spirit of penitence which breathed all around them, and come, as well as the rest of the people, to the baptism which was to be the usual preparation for the receiving of the Gospel. St. John Baptist himself, meanwhile, was continuing his work, though he had already borne witness to the advent of the Messias, had pointed Him out, and had sent some of His own disciples to Him. But he had withdrawn, for reasons which are not mentioned, from his former place of baptism, on the eastern side of the Jordan, and was now baptizing at a spot on the other side of the river. The place was Ænon, near Salim, a place which it is difficult to identify. The Evangelist adds, 'because there was much water there;' and from this it would seem that the place was chosen on account of its convenience in this respect, and that we have in this an indication of time, inasmuch as early in the summer, between the Pasch and Pentecost, the rainy season would have been over for some time, and there would be a scarcity of water except in particular spots. 'John also was baptizing at Ænon, near Salim, because there was much water there, and they came and were baptized. For John was not yet cast into prison.'

There were thus for a short time two centres of attraction, if we may so speak, to which devout and burthened hearts were drawn, and where they might confess their sins and make profession of a state of peni-tence, as well of a readiness to receive the new kingdom of God. Both were, no doubt, vigilantly watched by the Jewish authorities, especially those who had already become hostile both to our Lord and St. John, as also by the spiritual enemies of all good, who would be anxious to bring about some collision or rivalry between the friends of either teacher, as a means, such as is so frequently successful in the Church, of injuring the usefulness and fruitfulness of both. Between our Lord and St. John there could be no rivalry, nor, may we suppose, could our Lord's Apostles look with any but the most loving eyes upon him who had been to them the master who had sent them to and prepared them for our Lord. But every religious movement, or body, or constitution, or system, has its less prudent and perfect hangers-on and disciples, and it is usually among such that the elements are to be found out of which the jealousies, which are so fatal in any religious work, can be created. In the case before us, we learn that the disciples of John were moved to a sort of jealousy in behalf of their own master by 'the Jews'—the Judæans, as distinguished from the Galilæans, and other inhabitants of the Holy Land, or even, as has already been said, according to the meaning of the word in St. John's Gospel, the people of Jerusalem. 'There arose a question between some of St. John's disciples and the Jews concerning purification.'[1] From what follows, it seems that the question was as to the relative efficacy of the two baptisms for the purification of the soul. The Jews may have interfered as enemies; or there may have been some among them who had received or witnessed our Lord's Baptism, and so may have raised the question with the disciples of St. John, who were already to some extent aggrieved by the comparative waning of the popularity of their own master.

'And they came to John, and said to him : Rabbi, He that was with thee beyond the Jordan, to Whom thou gavest testimony, behold He baptizeth, and all men come to Him!' Even in the very words of their complaint they were inconsistent, because the witness of St. John to our Lord had been so distinctly the witness to One higher than himself, that it could not be matter of wonder or complaint that all men should

---

[1] Some of the best manuscripts have the singular μετα Ιουδαιου, as if a single unnamed person was the cause of the dispute.

go to that higher Person. Moreover, they must have been blind to the peculiar beauty and distinctive grace of the character of St. John if they could imagine that he would share in their complaints. It is comparatively common to find a great zeal for the glory of God and the salvation of souls, a ready devotion to hard missionary labours, and the fatigues of the Apostolate, while the worker is cheered by success, and sees and feels the reward of his toil and self-sacrifice. It is less common to find those who can labour on under discouragement, with scanty fruit as the only return for their labours, or who can rejoice in the success of others, while they themselves are unsuccessful. But it is a part of St. John's pre-eminent distinction in the kingdom of God, that he gained so completely and fully the crown of disinterestedness and entire freedom even from the most subtle forms of jealousy. And thus he is a special pattern throughout all ages for all the ministers of religion and preachers of the Word of God, who are to rejoice in the success of others as if it were their own, and to be ready always to see themselves surpassed in fruitfulness, neglected, and thrown aside, where there is no fault of their own to account for it. If St. John delighted at all in any success that waited upon his own efforts, it was because it enabled him to prepare more souls for Jesus Christ, and to pass on to Him a large school of disciples. To himself he was absolutely nothing, glad that his light, which at one time was so burning and shining, as our Lord says, should pale and wane, and at last be entirely hidden from sight by the greater glories of the Sun of Justice.

John answered and said, 'A man cannot receive anything except it be given him from heaven.' I can have no gift, no office, no power, no influence, no success, unless it be given to me; if I have this or that, then, it is not my own, it is only a gift; if I have it not, it is not my fault, but only because it has not been given to me. God is free in the distribution of His gifts; they all come from Him, whatever they are, and they do not belong to those who receive them; and those who have them not, have no claim to them, nor can any one without folly expect to find them in such. Each has his office and his gift, and no one can stretch himself beyond the measure which is allotted to him from above. This is the general principle of God's rule in the distribution ·of gifts, and men are gratefully to use what they have, and not to consider themselves entitled to what they have not. But as to himself and our Blessed Lord, St. John goes on to point out the particular working of this rule. First as to himself, he had told them of his own inferiority, 'You yourselves do bear me witness that I said I am not Christ, but that I am sent before Him.' I never claimed to be more than His Forerunner, and how can it grieve me when the Lord before Whose face I was sent has come and entered on His work? Then as to our Lord. 'He that hath the Bride, is the Bridegroom; but the friend of the Bridegroom, who standeth and heareth Him, rejoiceth with joy because of the Bridegroom's voice. This my joy therefore is fulfilled.' Our Lord then, he tells his disciples, is the Bridegroom, and the Bride belongs to Him, and to no other. The crowds which flock to His Baptism are the souls which are His own. He has espoused our nature to His Divine Person in the Incarnation, and has thereby begun the espousals between Himself and His Church, the great earthly object of His love. These espousals are to be accomplished upon the Cross, when she will be born, as it were, from His wounded side, as Eve was taken by God from the side of Adam, and there was to be thenceforth an inseparable union between them lasting throughout all eternity. The news that He has begun to baptize and to gather people around Him is to me the news that the Bridegroom is taking to Himself His Bride. And as the friend of the Bridegroom would be no friend, and a traitor to all truth and honour and loyal friendship, if he were even to wish the Bride to be his own, so it would be a heinous treachery in me to wish to be the Baptizer in the Holy Ghost, or to draw to myself the hearts which belong to Him, for whom He has come down from heaven, for whom He is to pay the price of His Blood. On the other hand, as the true friend of the Bridegroom never rejoices more than when he hears the voice of the Bridegroom speaking to and caressing the Bride, so is my joy now full, because that for which I came to prepare the souls of men is now being accomplished in them, the Lord and Lover of souls is rejoicing over them.

St. John goes on, as one whose heart is full of thoughts which he has long been desirous to pour forth, to add a number of beautiful heads of doctrine concerning our Lord, taking an occasion from the affectionate but narrow jealousy of His own disciples to testify still more fully concerning our Lord, both, as it were, to relieve himself and also to give them, without reproaching them, the strongest grounds for perfect submission and devotion to Jesus Christ. 'He must increase and I must decrease.' It is the counsel and will of God that I should fade away in popularity and fruitfulness, at least external, and that He should gather to Himself the love and obedience of many who have begun with me, and of the people at large. And he goes on to contrast our Lord and himself as to several distinct heads. First, as to nature and origin, 'He that cometh from above is above all.' He is from heaven, I am from earth. He is Lord of all. Then, as to their teaching, 'He that is of the earth, of the earth he is, and of the earth he speaketh.' Of my own self I can speak only earthly things, because I am but of the earth; if I have had higher things to speak, they have not been my own; and the words of one of earth have no power over the hearts of men; the words of One from heaven sink into them, subdue them, and possess them. My teaching is of entering into the conscience and of confessing sins, and of doing penance, and of preparing to believe in the coming Messias, all which things are matters of present experience and of that part of man's existence which is passed here below, but He that is come after me has sublime and eternal truths to teach concerning the nature of God, He has to reveal the Father to mankind, and to raise their hearts and minds to the spiritual verities of heaven and the everlasting reign of the saints. Then again, there is a contrast between our Lord and himself as to the manner of their testimony. St. John could witness what he had been told, could give a message which had been delivered to him, no more and no less; his witness was second-hand, and he knew no more than he taught. 'But He that cometh from heaven is above all, and what He hath seen and heard that He testifieth;' what He knows of His own eternal and divine knowledge, and what as Man He has heard and been taught, what He has received as communicated knowledge to His Human Soul and what He has been commissioned to teach in the discharge of the office which He has taken upon Himself, to carry out the command of His Father.[2]

[2] Compare our Lord's words (St. John viii. 26), 'Many things I have to speak and to judge of you. But He that sent Me is true, and the things that I have heard of Him, these same I speak in the world.' Again, xv. 15, to the Apostles, 'I have called you friends, because all things whatsoever I have heard of My Father I have made known unto you.' See also vii. 16, xiv. 25.

St. John then seems to turn aside for a moment, as if struck by the same thought which had been expressed by our Lord Himself to Nicodemus, the dulness of men to this authentic and authoritative testimony of the Incarnate Son. 'No man receiveth His testimony; he that receiveth His testimony hath set to his seal that God is true.' The form of expression is like that which has been already noted in this Evangelist, and it is remarkable that here, as before, it is in the words of St. John Baptist that the form occurs. There is first a general negative, and then a particular affirmative as to the same thing. No man receives the testimony of Christ, but some do, and by doing so affirm on their own part the truthfulness of God. That is, few receive His testimony; and those who do so, do that, by their assent, which is always done by those who make an act of faith in any divine revelation or attestation, that is, their faith is a sort of seal which, as far as depends upon human assertion, ratifies, confirms, and attests the veracity of God on Whose authority they believe. For as to this there is no difference between faith in the word of God and faith in the word of man : in each case faith is a solemn affirmation that he who speaks is true, just as when we obey God or man for the sake of God we affirm thereby that there is in the person whom we obey the authority of Lord and King. And then St. John goes on to continue his teaching as to our Lord in such a strain as to draw out more and more fully the contrast between Him and any other teacher. No wonder that men should assent to Him as true. For 'He Whom God hath sent' not by any ordinary mission, as prophets and teachers are sent, who, as St. Paul says, know in part and prophesy in part, but as His own Son into the world, to save it and enlighten it, He Whom God hath sent in all that fulness of mission which belongs to a Divine

Person, 'speaketh the words of God.' His words, as our Lord Himself said, are not His, but His that sent Him, with Whom He is One in will and in act, and He has the Spirit of God, not by participation and in measure communicated to Him, as may be the case with prophets and angels, but in fulness, so that everything that comes from Him and is uttered by Him is the word and utterance of God, whereas prophets and apostles may speak of their own spirit as well as of the Spirit of God, and so not all that they may say is of God, nor can they speak all that is of God. In these particulars the Incarnate Son of God differs from all other messengers who have ever been and ever may be sent.

'For God giveth not the Spirit by measure.' These words have sometimes been understood by remembering what has been remarked by more than one commentator, that the testimony here given by the Blessed Baptist runs in many respects parallel to the words of our Lord Himself to Nicodemus in the earlier part of the same chapter in the Gospel of St. John. If this be taken into consideration, it appears that the passage just before this, as to belief in our Lord's words and as to His speaking the words of God, corresponds to what was before said by our Lord about Himself, as the object of faith, as figured by the brazen serpent. The next words of our Lord speak of the immense love of God in giving His only-begotten Son, no prophet, or angel, no one short of the Son Who is in the bosom of His Father. If the words of the Baptist are to be taken as following and echoing those of our Lord, then it would seem that we are to understand what he says about the unmeasured gift of the Spirit, in the same way, of the gift of our Lord; as if St. John had meant to say, God has given to man a spiritual treasure beyond all measure, no less a treasure than His own Son.[3]   In this sense of the words we have a direct declaration on the part of St. John as to the gift of the Son of God.   The other sense which has been attributed to the words by the majority of com· mentators implies the same thing, only the Son is understood as having been sent into the world, and enriched beyond all measure with spiritual gifts in His human soul and for others.   The words are without any qualification as to person; it is not said, 'to Him or to men, God giveth not His Spirit by measure,' and thus the sense is general—it is not the way of God to give the Spirit by measure and weight, as it were, as if the measure that had been given to some merely human messengers and representatives of God was to be the rule in other cases, especially in the case of the Incarnate Son, or as if He could not give larger measure of spiritual gifts even generally in the kingdom of heaven, the Gospel dis· pensation, than ever before.   But perhaps the Person spoken of all through may be considered as supplying the limitation which is wanting in absolute expression, and we are thus to understand that the Spirit of God is imparted beyond all measure to the Incarnate Son in His Humanity.   For our Blessed Lord, as theologians tell us, had as Man a threefold treasure of grace, the grace of union, habitual grace, and the grace which was given to Him as Head of the new Creation.   The grace of union, the root of which is the union of the two natures of God and Man in His Divine Person, is necessarily limited in respect of the finite human nature which is united to the Person of the Divine Word : but in respect of that Person to which it is determined it is infinite, because the Person of the Word is infinite.   And also it is formally infinite, in that on account of the divinity of the Word subsisting in that particular human

[3] See Toletus, in loc.

nature, the Man Jesus Christ was infinitely dear and pleasing to God, and it was also infinite in its effects, in that on account of the Divine Person every action and work of Jesus Christ was of infinite price and merit before God. This is what we are taught concerning the grace of union. The habitual grace possessed by our Lord, which was infused into the soul of Christ, is in itself and simply finite; but still in a certain way it is infinite and unmeasured, in that it was not restricted to any particular kind of grace, or to any particular measure or degree thereof, or to any particular manner in which it was possessed. Our Lord in this sense enjoyed grace of every kind and in every degree, both in extent, inasmuch as His grace contained every kind of grace, and in intensity, inasmuch as He had every kind of grace in every way and in the highest degree under each kind; and lastly, subjectively, in that He was filled with grace to the full capacity of which His nature was capable. Then as to the grace which He has as Head, and which He received from others. In this also there is a certain infinity and absence of all measure, because He could impart every kind of grace to His saints, and He could communicate it to an infinite number of men, if such number there were, and His fulness could never have been exhausted, even by infinite communications from it. This may serve as a brief summing up of what is dwelt on more fully in another part of the present work as to the grace of Christ. In reference to the present text it is enough if we understand the words of the unmeasured grace given to our Lord Himself.

St. John concludes with a clear dogmatic statement as to the Incarnation and mission of the Eternal Son, and the necessity of faith in them. Our Lord had spoken to Nicodemus of the love of God for the world, out of which had come the gift of His Son to the world, that it might be saved by Him. St. John draws out the other side of the same truth, that out of the love of the Father for the Son came the charge which He gave Him for the redemption of the world, and the power with which He has clothed Him for the execution of that purpose. 'The Father loveth the Son, and hath given all things into His hands'—all things, in this connection, especially signifying all that relates to the salvation of the world, as it is said of our Lord on the eve of His Passion, 'Knowing that the Father hath given Him all things into His hands, and that He came from God and goeth to God.'[4] 'He that believeth in the Son hath life everlasting, but He that believeth not the Son, shall not see life, but the wrath of God abideth on him.' Here then we have again the necessity of faith, as to which the Jews were now being tried to the utmost by the presence among them of the Incarnate Son. It need hardly be said that faith is here spoken of as the condition of salvation, as it had been from the beginning, for 'without faith it is impossible to please God,' and faith is the door to and foundation of that union with God in which alone true life consists, including obedience, charity, and all the virtues. But now the Son of God Himself is the witness on Whose word faith is to be grounded, as well as the object of faith. To disbelieve Him is the worst form of unbelief. The wrath of God abiding on those who will not believe is to be understood, as we have already seen in the dialogue with Nicodemus, of that anger of God which rests upon all men as sinners, even for original sin, and much more for actual sin, from which men may be saved by faith in our Lord, but which cannot be removed from them unless they believe.

[4] St. John xiii. 3.

CHAPTER XXII.

The Friend of the Bridegroom.

St. John iii. 29, 30 ; *Vita Vitæ Nostræ*, § 25.

THE beautiful image of the Bridegroom and His Bride, which, like that of the Lamb of God, was introduced, if we may say so, into the common language of the Gospel dispensation by the blessed Forerunner of our Lord, is a figure which not only speaks to the understanding and feelings of every one, but also is connected with a cluster of spiritual associations which it may be well to dwell upon separately. As the doctrine of sacrifice was the foundation of all religion and worship from the very beginning, so the institution of marriage was the foundation of all social and family life, and the corner-stone on which human life in this world is rested. The doctrine of sacrifice was to have its full accomplishment and fulfilment in the sacrifice of the only-begotten Son of God in His Human Nature on the Cross, and it was by virtue of that sacrifice that prayer, whether of homage and adoration, or thanksgiving, petition, or propitiation for offences, had its value and efficacy with God. There was to be something analogous to this with regard to the divine institution of marriage, for it was to be made a sacrament of the New Law, and to have its ratification and sanction, its spiritual foundation and meritorious pattern, in the union between the two natures in the

One Person of Jesus Christ, and in the further union between Him and His Church, which is the end and consummation of the new dispensation.   And thus it is significant of the position which St. John occupies in relation to our Lord, that it should be from his mouth that Jesus Christ should receive both these great titles, the Lamb of God and the Bridegroom.

When our Lord spoke of the original institution of marriage, He repeated the solemn words in which that institution was announced.   And when we consider that He is Himself the second Adam, and that the Church is taken from His side, as so many of the Fathers tell us in their contemplations on the Passion, we see in the words of that original institution a significant reference to Him and the Church, which raises other incidents and expressions in Sacred Scripture to a higher spiritual meaning than we might otherwise discern in them.   Thus, there are two most graceful and poetical stories in the Book of Genesis which at first sight appear pre-eminent among such early narratives, only for their singular purity and simplicity—the story of the mission of Eliezer by Abraham to bring a wife for his son Isaac from among his own kindred, and the story of the long love borne by Jacob for his beautiful cousin Rachel, and the hard service he so joyfully underwent for the sake of winning her as his wife.   Seen by the light of later pages of Sacred Scripture, these idylls, if we may so speak, of Patriarchal history, glow with fresh and spiritual beauty, without losing their natural grace and simplicity.   They express the long search and desire of Christ for His Church, the love with which He regards her, the labour He has undergone for her sake, the rich treasures with which He endows her, the perfect union which He forms between her and Himself.   They are another mystical version of the truths embodied in the Parable of the Good Shepherd. The same may be said of portions of other similar stories in the Old Testament, as the histories of Ruth, the ancestress of our Lord, and Esther the Queen of Assuerus.

There are several passages in the Psalms in which the same image is used, and it is drawn out in full detail in the great Psalm which is more directly to be understood of the Incarnation and of the Espousals of Christ, the forty-fourth, *Eructavit cor meum.* The doctrine is again drawn out still more fully in the Canticle of Canticles, the book which has been the delight of mystical souls from the earliest ages of the Church, and which has called forth so many beautiful spiritual commentaries. The image, again, is found in the prophecy of Isaias,[1] and as we have said, it was first uttered in the New Testament by St. John Baptist in this place, and from his mouth, as it were, adopted by our. Lord Himself, Who, in answer to the question put to Him by the disciples of the Baptist about fasting, spoke of the children of the bride-chamber as being unable to mourn as long as the Bridegroom is with them.[2] Our Lord uses the same figure in His parables, as when He speaks of the King who made a wedding feast for his son, and also in the wise and foolish virgins. Thus we trace the figure from the Gospels into the Epistles, in which the words and mysteries of our Lord meet us in the form of dogmas and sacraments. St. Paul speaks of the union between Christ and His Church as the model of all true and loving marriages, and connects the sacrament of marriage itself with that union as its mystical and spiritual consecration : and then, as the volume of Holy Scripture had begun with the union of Adam and Eve in the holy tie which God made for them, the last page

---

[1] Isaias lxii. 8.   [2] St. Matt. ix. 16.

of the same sacred writings tells us of the marriage supper of the Lamb, and how His Bride has made herself ready for Him.[3]

It would not be easy to exhaust, or even to give an outline of, all the wide range of spiritual truths, especially regarding the interior dealings of our Lord with the souls which are most entirely His, which have been founded by holy writers on this title of Spouse as belonging to Him, and the various passages of Holy Scripture which refer to Him under this title.   A few words have already been said as to His relation to the Church as His Spouse. The union between them is fruitful, and will be fruitful unto the end of time on earth and in heaven, for the spread of the Church is nothing but this fruitfulness, the generation of souls to our Lord by the sacraments, their conversion and perfection and consummation in sanctity, and their final union with Him in eternal blessedness. A great deal more has been said about the immense love of our Lord for single souls, each one of which is the object of His special affection, and for each one of which He became Man and suffered on the Cross, according to that saying of St. Paul, 'He loved me and gave Himself for me.'   Holy writers have thus applied the expressions of love in the Canticles, such as 'Thou hast wounded my heart, my sister, my spouse,' and the like, and have explained how our Lord seeks them out in the low abject condition which is theirs by nature, how He cleanses them and adorns them and makes them exceedingly beautiful, and then makes them His own.   They trace out the obligation which rests on such souls to behave to our Lord as to a spouse Who has thus dealt with them,

---

[3] Apoc. xxi.   Much of what follows in the present chapter is taken in an abridged form from the treatise of Father Arias on our Lord's title of Spouse, *Thesaurus Inexhaustus Bonorum quæ in Christo Habemus*, t. i. tr. 4.

in such acts as the perpetual remembrance of Him, as
a thing always with them which makes Him present to
them, the continual occupation of their thoughts about
Him, His goodness, power, beauty, sweetness, liberality,
the particular benefits which He has bestowed on them,
the price which He has paid to be enabled thus to enrich
and ennoble them, and the whole course of His particular
Providence in regard of each. Their hearts are to follow
their minds by frequent aspirations of love, ardent desires
and prayer to be able to serve Him perfectly, to give
Him their whole lives in true purity, and to fulfil in
everything the desires and wishes which He may form
concerning them. And they are to be always longing for
the time when their union with Him shall be more perfect
than it can be here on earth, when they may see His
beauty in heaven, enter into the possession of His glory,
enjoy to the full the sweetness of His conversation, and
be never more separated from Him.

Such souls as these are bound to be severe with themselves in all cases of negligence, or coldness, or weariness
in His service, as so many acts of disloyalty and treachery,
and they are not to be easy in pardoning themselves
without much self-reproach and self-chastisement for such
infidelities. Again, they are to depend upon Him and
His guidance in everything, according to that saying in
the Psalm, 'As the eyes of servants are in the hands of
their masters, and as the eyes of a maiden are in the
hands of her mistress.'[4] Thus, they are to consult our
Lord in everything that they say or do, and in all their
dealings with others, not only because it is most prudent
and indeed the only safe way so to do, but also out of a
loving faithfulness and obedience, that they may do His
will and be pleasing to Him in all these things. And
one of the chief proofs of this same loving fidelity of

[4] Psalm cxxii. 2.

theirs is to be in the manner in which they take all adversities and sufferings of whatever kind with the utmost patience and even willingness, as coming from His love, and as the most desirable portion of all for them, simply because they do so come from Him to them. And in the same way it is a part of their faithfulness to be very constant and persevering in His service under temptations, dryness, desolation, or external persecution, because it is just at times like these that faithfulness is the most tried, and shown in its most perfect purity.

The office of our Lord to the souls which belong to Him has also been drawn out by Christian writers in many details in connection with the title of Spouse or Bridegroom. In the first place, as to instruction and guidance, the divine precepts and laws of the Church which apply to all the faithful are brought home to those whom He loves with peculiar force, they understand them, value them, love them and honour them in their hearts with the greatest and tenderest affection. 'How sweet are Thy words unto my palate, more than honey to my mouth! Thy word is a lamp to my feet and a light to my path! Thy words have I hidden in my heart, that I should not sin against Thee!' These, and other expressions in the Psalms, speak the feelings of souls who are drawn by our Lord to that intimate union with Him which leads to the most exact and loving observance of all His precepts.

Again, it is to such souls that He reveals Himself familiarly in other ways, which are in themselves extraordinary and unusual. From the earliest pages of Sacred Scripture to the last, we see that God has always from time to time favoured souls that were dear to Him with special visitations, angelic apparitions, and the like, as in the case of Noe, Abraham, Jacob and Joseph, Moses, Josue, Samuel, David, and the whole line of prophets, and this method of dealing familiarly with those who are peculiarly honoured by Him has been repeated with far greater frequency and copiousness in the New Testament and in the history of the Church. Under the same head of the spiritual instructions and illuminations which our Lord bestows upon certain souls, must come the whole vast range of His action by means of secret inspirations, sudden interior lights and movements of the will or the affections, by which He so often manifests His presence, a range of action to which it is difficult to set any limit at all, except what may be required by the principle of His government not to force any soul beyond the extent of its own free-will in correspondence to grace. Thus He addresses Himself in one way to the souls whom He loves so much when they are in sin, to induce them to leave their misery and listen to Him, and in another way to the imperfect, to warn them or frighten them from tepidity, sloth, and negligence ; and again in another to such as have been faithful to Him up to a certain point, but whom He now calls higher and nearer to Himself, as Abraham, or St. Antony, or thousands of others. And in these cases it is essential that the faithful soul should obey the inspiration at once, as otherwise there is danger of the grace being withdrawn in order to be passed on to another soul which may show less hesitation, as we never hear that the rich young man, whom our Lord so graciously called to the state of perfection, had another opportunity afforded him after he had gone away sorrowful at the invitation.

Another part of our Lord's care of the souls which are so highly favoured by Him, consists in His watchful providence, by which He guards them against all wants and shields them in any danger to which they may be exposed in His service. The contemplation of the manner in which God provides for all His creatures is indeed wonderful and full of consolation, much more that of His special care for the souls which He regards as His own in this tender manner, as we see in the instance of Jacob, Joseph, Tobias, Elias, and others, and in numberless instances in the lives of Christian saints. The scriptural type of this care is the love shown by Assuerus for his Queen Esther, when she had exposed her life to danger, and he held out his sceptre to her, and leapt from his throne to support her and calm her fears. Another head of the same consideration, is the manner and degree in which our Lord communicates His own goods and rights to His spouses, whether we look at His dealings with the Church in this respect, or at His treatment of the saints. For the Church is endowed with royal power over the things of this life as far as is consistent with her spiritual character and mission, and much more over the treasures of the other world, the fruits of our Lord's sufferings, His merits and stores of sanctity, which are enshrined in the sacraments and other means of grace, and she has the power of binding and loosing, of retaining sins or forgiving them, and the sentence which she passes on earth is ratified in heaven. And her children, in proportion as they are faithful to grace and loyal to their heavenly Spouse, enter into a share of this royal power, for He allows immense efficacy to their prayers, and from time to time graces them with marvellous gifts, such as prophecy and miracles, and in the next life He is to give them a share in His heavenly power and glory limited only by the capacities of their nature and the extent of the merits with which He has here enriched them. All are to be kings and princes in His kingdom, and to some in particular He has promised that they shall 'sit on thrones, judging the twelve tribes of Israel.'

Other heads may be added, such as our Lord's way of providing comfort and consolation for those whom

He calls near to Himself, so that they feel they have a hundred-fold in this present life for all that they have had to sacrifice for His sake, and if that hundred-fold is to be accompanied by persecutions, still, these very persecutions are precious gages of His love, and He supports them under their sufferings with a peace and joy of conscience which is far more blessed than all the pleasures and triumphs of the world. Penance, humiliation, the struggle and conflict of self-conquest, have a happiness attached to them which comes from this tender care of Jesus Christ, and the solid joy of the soul, which becomes habitual when the exercises of prayer and contemplation are faithfully performed, is not marred or taken away by the occasional visitations of desolation and dryness, by the cloud of temptations, or the purifying annoyance of scruples.

In all these blessings, which are the lot of souls drawn especially near to our Lord, it is His Presence, His Voice and Touch, as it were, which cause the happiness which is felt, and there can be no one standing between the soul and our Lord if such intercourse is to be made possible. It is to be noted that our Lord has not only made Himself our complete and perfect pattern in the practice of every virtue, and especially in all that falls under the head of our relations to God Himself, but He has also provided us, in His saints who stand around Him in the history of His Life on earth, with models and patterns which teach us both how to imitate Him and how to behave towards Him. Our Blessed Lady, St. Joseph, St. John Baptist, the Apostles, St. Magdalene, and the other New Testament saints are our examples in this last respect as to different phases and conditions of our relations to Him, and it seems to be especially the office of the blessed Forerunner to show us how those are to act and feel who have any share of the work in which he bore so large a part, that of bringing souls to Him and helping them in their dutiful love and obedience to Him.   In burning zeal for His glory, in prudence and courage in setting forth the truth and witnessing to it, in preparing the way for Him and then retiring, in leaving room for His action on the soul, and in care not to forestall His work, not to take too strong an initiative, to rule and guide too much, or to take any place at all but that of the humblest of servants, St. John is the great pattern provided for us in the Gospel history.   He was above all things the friend of the Bridegroom, rejoicing most of all when the Bridegroom came into possession of His rights, glad as he had never been before when the time came for himself to decrease and for our Lord to increase, and when, if he could not absolutely send his own disciples, on account of their own imperfections, to our Lord, he could at least take opportunity after opportunity of bearing witness to Him, and of putting them in the way of those powerful influences by means of which it was in the counsels of God that men should be drawn to Him.   We shall find him later on, almost at the end of his earthly course, taking one more occasion to put them within the range of our Lord's special attractiveness, as soon as he heard that He was manifesting Himself as the Messias, by the evidence of which the prophets had spoken, the evidence of a large number of the most splendid miracles of healing.   Meanwhile the Providence of God was preparing his reward for him, and him for his reward. There could be no Christian martyrs, properly so called, before our Lord Himself, the King of Martyrs, had suffered.   But by an arrangement of the Divine Counsels which no one could certainly have foreseen, the glorious crown of martyrdom, for the sake of the law of God, was being prepared for St. John, and the first steps which were to lead to this glorification of the Forerunner of Jesus Christ were taken almost at the same time at which he gave his last great witness to Him.

CHAPTER XXIII.

The Samaritan Woman.

St. John iv. 1-26; *Vita Vitæ Nostræ*, § 26.

IMMEDIATELY after the account of the last testimony of St. John the Baptist to our Lord, given, as we shall see, on the very eve of his own imprisonment, St. John the Evangelist relates the journey of our Blessed Lord Himself, with His small band of companions, into that Galilee which was soon to become the scene of His most active preaching. The reason which is assigned for this change of place is, that our Lord came to know that the religious authorities at Jerusalem had now had their attention directed pointedly to Himself, not merely on account of His miracles and of the authority which He had assumed at the late feast at Jerusalem, but also because He had taken on Himself that same formal administration of Baptism which was the ground of their suspicious questionings of His Forerunner. To baptize was, as has been said, to assume a sacerdotal or prophetical office, and involved the formation of a body of disciples and adherents who were distinguished by their having received the sacred rite at the hands of their Master. It may perhaps have been one of the reasons why our Lord committed baptism at this time to His disciples, and did not perform the ceremony Himself, that He wished thus to make Himself less prominent. The Pharisees, as we have seen, had already endeavoured to sow discord between the followers of our Lord and those of St. John, or at least to excite the latter to some jealousy of the former. To avoid this, and to shun the annoyance and hindrance to which His work might be exposed if He remained longer in the jurisdiction of the priests at Jerusalem, our Lord determined to return to Galilee, where His course of public preaching was to begin, and where all fear of apparent rivalry between Himself and St. John was soon to end, on account of the imprisonment of the Baptist by Herod.

The time of the year at which this journey was taken was apparently towards the middle of May, when the barley harvest was over and the harvest of wheat ripening. Our Lord would thus have remained in Judæa for about a month after the conclusion of the Paschal Feast, at which He had wrought His miracles and received the visits of Nicodemus. Of the two possible routes from Judæa to Galilee, He chose the shortest and most direct, through Samaria; it was probably chiefly on occasions when the Galilæans went up in large caravans to the feast at Jerusalem that the road by the other side of the Jordan was usually adopted. Our Lord was in the north of Judæa when He determined to start for Galilee by way of Samaria. Several hours of travelling brought the party to the neighbourhood of the fertile plain near the modern Nablous, where the mountains of Ebal and Gerizim recede from each side of the pass which divides them, and make room for the beautiful valley or level of Shechem or Sichem. Here the traveller is still shown a heap of ruins, stones, and broken columns, in the midst of which lies a deep well, now unprotected and more than half choked up, but which in our Lord's time was still in use, and sheltered by an arcade or alcove, in which would have been a few stone seats. It was 'Jacob's Well'—the plot of ground in which it stands, outside the valley, had been bought by the Patriarch after his return from Mesopotamia, in the early days of his sojourn in the Holy Land with his family and herds. There were many springs in the valley, but Jacob seems to have been afraid to have to depend on others for water, and he dug this famous well, building also in this neighbourhood an altar to God. Before his death, he left the piece of ground as a special possession to his son Joseph.[1] The Samaritan town was at some little distance, and our Lord sent His disciples thither to purchase some food while He Himself remained sitting by the well, wearied with His long walk under the broiling sun, through a country where there was but little shade.

St. John tells us that it was about the 'sixth' hour, and as he wrote for the Asiatic Christians, and as there is some evidence that a computation of hours like our own was in use in Asia, we are, at least, free to adhere to the opinion which fixes the evening as the time of the interview which immediately followed. It would indeed have taken nearly a full day to journey on foot from the frontier of Judæa to Sichem. The well is at a spot nearer to the ancient town than to the modern Nablous, but there were other springs still nearer to the town, and so it happened that on this evening there was but one woman who came out to fill her pitcher with the water from this well. He of Whom the Church sings—

Quærens me sedisti lassus,

was waiting for her, and it was the will of His Father that He should begin with her that conversation, which, as it is recorded by the Beloved Disciple, seemingly

[1] Gen. xlviii. 22.

from her own vivid recollections, is the type and model and sanction of thousands of similar pleadings with wandering souls brought across their paths by what appear accidents, by which the followers and ministers of our Lord have been enabled in His strength and by His grace to work the same holy work which He now wrought in the soul of that poor woman. These Apostolical conversations, as they may be called, on the part of our Lord, are characteristic of the Gospel of St. John—nowhere have we such details preserved to us in as much fulness and beauty as in the reports given by the last Evangelist of our Lord's dealings with Nicodemus, with this Samaritan woman, and even with the Roman governor, Pilate. A more entire contrast could hardly be found than that which existed between the learned and timid and hesitating doctor of the law whose conversation with our Lord we have lately been considering, and this poor peasant child of nature, the first of many such wanderers from the path of virtue whom our Lord's intense compassion laboured to bring home to God. We have now to see how He Who had spoken so directly to the heart of Nicodemus, was even more directly and immediately successful in His dealings with this poor outcast.

This woman was living in a state of sin, with a man to whom she was not lawfully married, though we do not gather from our Lord's words that the intercourse was openly adulterous. The great laxity which prevailed among the Jews as to divorce must have been even exceeded among the Samaritans, and this woman had had five husbands. She was kind-hearted, open, simple, and frank, easily impressed, her heart not hardened against appeals to her conscience, and ready to receive instruction and light on matters of faith. Here, as in the case of Nicodemus, it seems most natural to suppose that the account which is given us of the conversation is meant to report only its most salient and characteristic points. The Stranger Who was sitting by the well, a weary and footsore traveller, was clothed with an air of attractive majesty which drew her attention at once. Who was He? He was evidently a Jew, and, as it seemed, a Teacher or Rabbi. He could have no dealings with her; perhaps He might even refuse if she offered Him to drink. But to her surprise, He was the first to break silence, not to revile or reprove her, but to beg of her a favour. 'Give Me to drink!' He had taken on Him the infirmities of our fallen condition, and He allowed His Body, to which the glory and impassibility of beatitude were due, to suffer pain and weariness, hunger and thirst. On this occasion, as on the Cross, we cannot doubt that the thirst which was most keenly felt by our Blessed Lord was the spiritual thirst for the salvation of the souls which He had come to redeem, and that yet at the same time His actual thirst was great and burning. 'Give me to drink!'— they were the words of Eliezer to Rebecca, as she may have remembered, and they put the person to whom they were addressed in a position of honour, as one of whom a great favour is asked. The woman was astonished at the condescension and affability of His address, and asked Him in her wonder how it was—'How is it that Thou, being a Jew, askest drink of me, who am a woman of Samaria?' The Jews held no intercourse with the Samaritans; intercourse, as it seems to be meant, of courtesy and friendship. They were allowed to buy of and to sell to the Samaritans, and even the Gentiles, but their attitude to them was of such determined hostility as to forbid them putting themselves under an obligation to them.[2] Thus at the very time

---

[2] See Lightfoot, *ad loc.*

that the disciples of our Lord were purchasing food in the town, the woman is astonished at His asking from her the common favour, so seldom refused in the East, of a drink of cold water.

Our Lord had thus already won her interest and kindly feeling by putting Himself in the attitude of a suppliant before her. He proceeded to draw her on by great hopes and promises. 'If thou knewest the free gift of God, and Who He is that saith to thee, Give Me to drink, thou wouldst have asked of Him, and He would have given thee living water.' The free gift of God, the gift properly and fully so called, is the Holy Ghost, of Whom our Lord spoke later on at the Feast of Tabernacles,[3] 'He that believeth on Me, as the Scripture saith, out of his belly shall flow rivers of living water.' Living water; water gushing up from the spring and not cut off from it, as He says a little later to the woman, 'a fountain of water springing up into eternal life.' The woman understood nothing of the spiritual meaning of our Lord's words, but His manner and presence over-awed her, as well as attracted her, and she answered in her simple literal way, showing at the same time an increase of reverence each time she addressed Him. 'Lord, Thou hast nothing to draw with, and the well is deep: Whence, then, hast Thou the living water? Or art Thou greater than our father Jacob, who gave us the well, and himself drank of it, and his sons and his herds?' Our Lord continues to kindle her desire of the precious gift of which He spoke, by dwelling on its wonderful qualities. 'Every one who drinketh of this water shall thirst again: but whoso drinketh of the water which I will give him, shall not thirst for ever, but the water which I will give him shall become in him a spring of water leaping up into eternal life.'

[3] St. John vii. 38.

The qualities of the gift of God on which He insists, are therefore three. First, whoso drinketh of this water shall never thirst again. For the grace of God and the presence of the Holy Ghost in the soul extinguish the fires of concupiscence, avarice, ambition, covetousness, the craving for sensual delights and satisfactions, all which objects of thirst have their power over us because our hearts are not filled with the possession of the true food for which they were made. We are not, indeed, as yet in the possession of all that we desire, but the presence of the Comforter gives us a certain hope, even now, of the glory of the blessed; it is a kind of 'earnest,' as St. Paul calls it, a pledge of what is promised to us and what we are heirs to, and the longer it abides in us, the more near does it lead us on to the actual possession for which we yearn. The fulness of satiety, when there is no longer any thirst or craving at all, is in heaven. There the blessed do indeed desire God for ever, but their craving is after a thing which is present to them, not after a thing from which they are debarred and separated; it is after a thing, the full enjoyment of which is always theirs. Such is the first quality of the gift of which our Lord speaks. The second is, that it is like a spring or fountain, which is the unfailing, ever-living source of fresh supplies of its pure and living water. He who has such a fountain in his garden has no need to store up for the future, or to be anxious about any failure. What he wants he has; he can draw when he likes; he can never exhaust his resources. If he needs much, he can reckon on much. His treasure is as rich after he has taken largely from it as it was before. Such is the gift of God; inexhaustible, ever ready day by day, as the manna in the wilderness, as the spiritual rock which followed the Israelites. Those who are thus enriched have no reason to take thought for the morrow; they carry with them an unfailing principle of grace which answers every need as it arises. And again, not only is the gift of God thus like to a living spring, but it is a spring which leapeth up to no lower a level than that of eternal life. The manna did not fail, the rock which supplied the Israelites did not fail; but yet they supplied nothing but physical wants: their effects were limited and humble, though their abundance day by day was inexhaustible. The gift of God is divine in its effects as it is unfailing in its ever-abiding fecundity, rising ever higher and higher in the souls in which it dwells, and raising them from strength to strength, from virtue to virtue, from grace to grace, until they find themselves at the summit of perfection to which God calls them, in the full and entire possession of Him their Creator and Lord Who has made them for Himself, and made Himself the end of their being, both naturally and supernaturally.

The woman still clung to the simple literal meaning of our Lord's words, though the thought of eternal life might have raised her mind to something higher. 'Lord,' she said, 'give me this water, that I may not thirst, nor come hither to draw.' In her simple unenlightened way, she had now become in her turn, as our Lord had said she would, a petitioner to Him, and He proceeded at once to pierce her conscience as by a ray of light, showing that His eye read her through and through. If she was to be a partaker of this divine gift of which she had spoken so wonderfully, it was necessary, according to the law of God, that her sin, the obstacle to grace, should be removed by confession and contrition. 'Go, call thy husband and come hither.' The words might in an ordinary case have been merely a hint that if He was to have more familiar dealings with her, it was right that her husband should be present and join in the interview; but to one in her state of sin, they touched with the utmost gentleness and delicacy the wounds of her soul. 'I have no husband.' Her confession was good and sorrowful as far as it went, but it did not cover the whole of her guilt, and our Lord, with immense charity and kindness, supplied what she was afraid as yet to add. 'Thou hast well said that thou hast no husband: for thou hast had five husbands, and now he whom thou hast is not thy husband. This thou hast truly said.'

'Lord, I perceive that Thou art a prophet.' Thus she acknowledged the truth of the severe charges which He had brought against her, and by so doing completed the confession of her own guilt. As nothing is told us of further conversation as to the state of her own soul or as to that heavenly gift which our Lord had promised her when he bade her fetch her husband and come to Him, we may suppose that the Evangelist passes on to the next head of instruction on which our Lord dwelt, which is indeed closely connected with the former. For the Samaritan woman had now been led on to the confession of her sinful state, and the internal obstacle to the grace of the Holy Ghost had been removed thereby. But penitence and a right faith are the conditions of acceptance with God through Jesus Christ, and thus the whole question of the position of the Samaritans in regard to the covenant of salvation necessarily followed upon the conviction and confession of sin. In the case of any one whose heart is touched by penitence, but who is externally an alien to the Church, the question immediately arises as to the conditions of that communion with her on which the state of grace depends for those who are conscious of the obligation. Thus the question of the Samaritan woman was not an idle indulgence in religious controversy, to which she had recourse in order to divert the conversation from the subject of her own sins, but the natural and logical fruit of the arousing of her conscience. Our Lord may have spoken to her, as we have said, at greater length with regard to her own state and duties, and the steps she was to take in order to reconcile herself to God and separate herself from all sinful connections. Indeed, something of the kind is hinted at in her own words when she says to the men of the town that our Lord had told her all· things she had ever done. This conversation would naturally lead up to the controversy between the Jews and the Samaritans as to the true religion and the right place and manner of worshipping God.

'Our Fathers adored in this mountain, and you (the Jews) say that in Jerusalem is the place where we ought to adore.' The controversy as to the place in which sacrifice and worship ought to be offered to God, filled the place under the older dispensation which under the Christian law is occupied by the question as to Unity. The mountain of Gerizim overhung the spot on which our Lord and the woman were conversing, and although the Samaritan temple was now in ruins, it was still to the people of the country the centre of their schismatical religion. She had been brought up to believe that Mount Gerizim was the place chosen by God to place His name there, and there were not wanting many old associations connected with the place which might have been appealed to in order to give it an apparent holiness and even a pre-eminence above Jerusalem itself. Shechem was, in truth, the oldest and most historical shrine in Palestine. It was the place on which Abraham had first pitched his tent, and built an altar to God. Jacob had dwelt there, and had left the piece of ground which he had bought there as a special legacy to his darling son Joseph. Joseph's bones were brought by the Israelites from Egypt and buried there; they are probably there to this day. Shechem was the centre of the Holy Land, and of the possessions of the great tribe of Ephraim; it was there that after the war of possession was over, Josue gathered all the people and the princes of the tribes together,[4] and made a solemn protestation and covenant with them in the name of God. Later on, Shechem was connected with the history of Abimelech and Jeroboam, whose schism was consummated there, and it then became the real centre of the rebellious kingdom of Israel, the historical type of the many schisms which have endeavoured to rend the robe of the Bride of Christ, and separate fragments of Christendom from Catholic unity. And it is curious that the Samaritans, who answer so completely to the more 'orthodox' Protestants who have not altogether degenerated into rationalism, were famous for their natural virtues, their honesty and hospitality. They held to the Pentateuch and rejected the Prophets and the whole system of worship and sacrifice at Jerusalem, exactly as people are now found who hold to the Bible and reject the later Church and the organisation which has its centre in the See of St. Peter. It cannot be doubted that numberless souls among them were in perfect good faith, and so had manifold graces to help them. By a curious anticipation of the language of many of those Christian communities which have separated themselves from the centre of Christian unity, this woman speaks in the most perfect simplicity and good faith of her fathers having worshipped in that mountain, as if the authority of antiquity and early tradition were on the Samaritan side of the controversy. The Samaritans, indeed, professed above all things to

<hr>

[4] Judges xxiv.

hold to antiquity, as against the claims of more modern developments, just as we constantly hear the Apostolic Church or the Primitive Church or the Church of the four first centuries adduced as authorities and sanctions for persons or communities who are in rebellion against the Church of the present day. The living authority is denied, and appeal is made to authority which cannot speak, and which all may interpret for themselves. The Church of our 'fathers,' the Church of Scripture, the Church of the nation—such are the words constantly in the mouths of those who are external to the Church, which is the same now as in the beginning, and in which alone abides the Presence of the Holy Ghost.

Our Lord's answer is addressed to the twofold error with which her mind was darkened. She imagined that the sort of worship of which she spoke, the worship of external rites and sacrifices, paid in one particular spot in the world to the exclusion of all others, was the true worship required by God of His creatures, to whom He was now about to impart the marvellous supernatural gift of a new relationship to Himself, making them His own children by means of the Incarnation of His only-begotten Son in their human nature. To her it was a question between Jerusalem and Gerizim, and she had no notion of the new and true worship which was to grow out of the assumption of Humanity by the Eternal Word. Besides this ignorance, she was also in error as to the very controversy of which she had spoken, for under the old dispensation which was so soon to be superseded, Jews and Samaritans were not on an equality, much less were the Jews wrong and the Samaritans right. The Jews formed the body in communion and covenant with God; they had, as St. Paul expresses it, 'the adoption of children, and the glory, and the testament, and the giving of the law, and the service or worship of God, and the promises, theirs were the fathers, and of them was Christ to be according to the flesh, Who is over all things, God blessed for ever.'[5] The Samaritans were rebels and schismatics; they rejected a part of the revelation of God to the chosen people, acknowledging only the Pentateuch; they were 'aliens from the commonwealth of Israel,' from the Temple in which God dwelt, from the priesthood which He had established, from the law which He had given, and they had, moreover, mingled much of heathenism with those fragments of Judaism which they had preserved. They were, as has been said, famous for their natural virtues, their kindness, hospitality, generosity: but all these did not lift them over the line which girt round the people of God, as the line which separated light from darkness in that famous plague of Egypt when all the rest of the land was clothed in night, 'but where the children of Israel dwelt, there was light.'[6]

The first part of our Lord's answer sets right the first error of the two of which we have been speaking. 'Woman, believe Me, that the hour cometh, when neither in this mountain nor in Jerusalem shall you adore the Father.' The worship which you pay here in this mountain to God shall cease, and the worship which now is offered in the Temple of Jerusalem shall cease, and shall be superseded by a truer and more universal worship, wherewith the Father shall be worshipped by men whom He has raised to the condition of His adopted children, and who will have a knowledge of and familiarity with Him corresponding to so high a state. He then corrects her second error: 'Jews and Samaritans are on an equality so far, that the worship of neither shall continue, but each shall be superseded by something far more perfect. Yet there is a difference

[5] Rom. ix. 4.   [6] Exod. x. 23.

between them now, for you worship what you do not know, we worship what we know, for salvation is from the Jews.' Everywhere outside the pale of the true Church, beyond the circle of light which fences in those who are in covenant with God, there is ignorance concerning Him. Men either know Him not at all, or they think many things wrongly of Him, or there are many things concerning Him which are revealed which yet they do not know. St. Paul began his address to the Athenians, the most cultivated and philosophical community in the heathen world, by speaking to them of the truth to which they had so unconsciously borne witness by their altar to the Unknown God. And to all religions but one, God is still more or less unknown, even as to that degree of knowledge which is attainable by men in this stage of their being. All forms of error and heresy, even within the range of Christianity, are so far forms of ignorance of God, for to deny unity, or not to recognise the authority of the Church, or to fall short of the true Catholic doctrine of the Sacraments, the Sacrifice, the means of grace, the power of the Saints, and the like, is to show ignorance of God as much as to deny the Three Persons in One Divine Nature. It is as much ignorance of God not to see what He has done and provided in His manifold arrangements for the salvation of souls, as it is ignorance of God not to know what He has revealed concerning His own nature and attributes.

It would seem that the Samaritans had not only inadequate, but false, notions concerning God, for they regarded Him, as it seems, as a sort of local deity, and believed that they might associate others with Him as objects of worship. Again, denying the whole of the Revelation except what was contained in the books of Moses, they did not recognise all that teaching concerning Himself which was contained in the magnificent cycle of the prophetic books, as well as in His historic dealings with the chosen people, and the other nations and Empires with which they had been brought in contact. Their knowledge of the promises of God, and, consequently, their expectations as to Jesus Christ and the fulfilment of the prophecies in Him, must have been slender and vague, although we find this very Samaritan woman looking forward and almost appealing to the Messias, Who was foretold in the Pentateuch, though not with all that minuteness and copiousness which characterise the stream of prophecy as it flows on and swells in volume. It must also be remembered that it is an ascertained fact in the history of various phases of religious belief, that a less knowledge of God is always a less knowledge of those attributes in Him which are the most apt to generate confidence, love, hope, the familiar affectionate intercourse which is natural between children and their Father. The higher we rise in theology, properly so called, the more do the infinite lovableness and condescension and tenderness, the communicativeness of God, His love of giving Himself and what is His, the intensity of His regard for His creatures, the way in which He employs all the resources of His wisdom and power for their good and salvation, and His compassionateness towards them even when they have offended Him, dawn upon us with continually increasing brightness until our eyes are dazzled by His mercifulness not less than by His majesty. All forms of belief outside the Church represent God as far less loving than He is known to be by her children ; and this law holds good of heathenism and of such imperfect vestiges of belief as was the Samaritan religion in comparison with Judaism. We shall only know God's goodness to the full extent of the capacity of creatures such as we are, when, by that same goodness, we are allowed to behold Him in heaven. And He can only be known as far as He may be known here on earth within the pale of that true faith which He has Himself given.

These considerations may help us to understand these pregnant words of our Lord, 'You adore what you do not know, we adore what we know.' However imperfect and partial was the knowledge of God, of His law, of His will, of His ways, which was possessed by the Jews, it was true and pure as far as it went; whereas the Samaritans had no living authorities among them who spoke in the name of God, they had a mangled and garbled version of His law, His action in history was a blank to them, and they had ideas concerning Him which lowered and darkened His nature to their minds, and made them feel at a distance from Him, almost as much as the Gentiles, of whom St. Paul speaks as 'having no hope in the promise and without God in the world.'[7] Thus, notwithstanding the many means of divine knowledge which they shared with the heathen, and the still more promising opportunities which they possessed in their partial Judaism, the Samaritans worshipped what they did not know, whereas the Jews worshipped what they knew.

'For salvation is from the Jews.' These words give the reason for the favour with which God regarded the nation. It had been decreed in His Providence that the salvation of all the world should come from them. The promise made to the seed of the woman at the time when the sentence of punishment and exile was laid upon our first parents, had been continually repeated in history, to Noe, to Abraham, to Jacob, and later

[7] Ephes. ii. 12.

on it had been settled still more precisely to the tribe of Judah and the family of David. The eternal counsel of God required that there should be a chosen nation in which the truth of revelation should be stored up until the coming of the Christ, which should be prepared for Him by its divinely given law and sacrificial rites and the long chain of types, personal and real, as well as of prophecies, by which that coming had been heralded. That nation lay at the centre of God's plan for the redemption of the world, and having been so long preserved and so jealously guarded during the centuries of expectation, it was at last to receive the crowning boon of the Incarnation taking place in the midst of it. That gift constituted the one incommunicable privilege, in which all others were bestowed on the nation. As it had been, more especially during the centuries immediately preceding the Incarnation, a great source of light and means of preparation for the fuller truth to the heathen world around it, large portions of which had been, as it were, leavened by the existence of numerous Jewish communities in the midst of them, either as captives or as immigrants, so when the Incarnation had taken place, the Jewish nation was to be the means and instrument through which the light from heaven was to spread all over the world. The word was to go forth from Jerusalem, there was to be given the great Pentecostal Gift. Jews were to be the first preachers and Apostles and lawgivers of the Church, which was to be in its origin a Jewish community. Such being the disposition of God's Providence, it was reasonable and even necessary that the truth concerning Him should be granted and guaranteed in a special manner to the chosen people in whom all the nations of the earth were to be blessed.

Not content with barely settling the question between

the Jews and the Samaritans, our Lord goes on to instruct the woman as to that worship and religion which He was sent to introduce, and which was to supersede Judaism and Samaritanism alike. 'But the hour cometh, and even now it is come, when the true adorers shall adore the Father in spirit and in truth.' Not only shall the worship at Jerusalem and Gerizim cease, but there should be a new and true worship introduced, in which God shall be known and adored as the Father, and instead of this worship being confined to any one spot, it shall be rendered everywhere in spirit and in truth. The characteristic privilege of the new dispensation shall be the new relationship between God and His creatures as that of Father and children, on account of the adoption granted to them by the communication of the Sonship of Jesus Christ to those who are His, to whom He giveth power (authority) to become the sons of God. And all the tender intimacy, the familiar converse, the confidence of present protection and future inheritance which the name of Father implies to us, all is contained in the rich privileges of this adoption, by virtue of which the Holy Ghost, Who is the bond and link between the Father and the Son in heaven, is sent into the hearts of the earthly children of the Father, to be at once the tie of the new relationship and to teach them its laws, to fill them with love and confidence, and to make them eloquent with the language which it is natural for the children of such a Father to use to Him in heart and tongue.

The fruit of this new adoption shall be—and it already is, because it has already been imparted to some—that there shall be true worshippers worshipping the Father in spirit and in truth. In spirit, not merely with an outward material service such as that which was offered in the Temple at Jerusalem, and in truth, not with an ignorant, mistaken, unenlightened service, such as was paid to God on Mount Gerizim. The worship of God must be spiritual and must be true; there must be no hollow, external worship, without the life of spiritual devotion to animate it; much more must there henceforth be no falsehood or error as to God in the minds of His worshippers. A spiritual worship does not exclude a material worship, rather it requires it as its outward vestment and manifestation; but the true doctrine concerning God excludes entirely all semblance of error. 'The Father seeketh such to adore Him.' If He has from the beginning of the world accepted the external sacrifices and worship which have always been rendered to Him by those to whom He was in any way known: if in later days he gave an elaborate system of ceremonial observances and holy rites to the people whom He had chosen, it was with the end that the heart might always accompany the action in sacrifice, prayer and praise, that the outward observances which He accepted might help on the interior worship which He desired. And the whole range of His provisions in this respect has had for its end to prepare the people, and lead their minds and hearts to the recognition of Him Whom He was to send to establish the true and spiritual worship over the whole face of the earth. Nay, His own glory was His end in His creation of man and of all the universe, and in all that He has done since. He has made angels and men of a spiritual nature like His own, that they might have the capacity of glorifying Him on earth and in heaven by this spiritual adoration. And now, in the fulness of time, He hath sent His Son to gather together those that are His all over the world, that they may at last give to Him the kind of honour and worship which He requires. 'God is a Spirit, and they who adore Him must adore Him in spirit and in truth.' His own nature is the rule of the worship which must be offered to Him, and thus the service of the material universe, which has no share in His spirituality, cannot satisfy Him. Man is the true priest of the universe, because in him meet the two orders of existence of which the universe is made up, the spiritual and the material order. Man is united to God in Jesus Christ, and thus human nature, and with it the whole universe which is summed up on it, is elevated and made capable of rendering to God a worship worthy of Himself. Jesus Christ is the one true Worshipper and Priest of His Father, but His Sonship in this, as in other of its privileges, is now imparted to others, and those who are incorporated into His mystical Body have a share in His worship and priesthood, and so can worship the Father in spirit and in truth.

The answer of the Samaritan woman to this divine teaching was perhaps not so much an appeal from Him Who was speaking to her to the authority to which the Samaritans as well as the Jews were taught to look forward, as a timid question, suggested by her growing faith, whether He were not Himself that great authority. She had been drawn on one step after another, during the conversation, with ever-increasing reverence and awe, from wondering respect to an overwhelming astonishment at the knowledge of her heart and life which our Lord had displayed, to confession of her sinfulness and to a humble seeking at His hands for that knowledge which was necessary to her for her amendment. She may have been growing ready to receive Him as the Messias from the moment when He revealed to her the secrets of her conscience, and yet she could not venture to ask Him directly Who He was. 'She said to Him : I know that the Messias cometh (Who is called Christ);

when therefore He cometh, He will tell us all things.' And our Lord did not hesitate to put her faith at once to the highest trial, by declaring Himself with a plainness and directness and fulness which He did not use to the Jews, and which He had not used even to so good a heart as Nicodemus. He had begun the work in her soul when He asked her to give Him to drink, and now He crowns it, showing us how humble condescension makes men willing to open their consciences, how a conscience convinced of sin and a contrite heart are ready to be the receivers of divine communications, and that He can dispense with miracles and other legitimate evidences as titles to faith, when the soul has felt His incommunicable power of reading it to its depths, and making it feel His eye penetrating to its most hidden corners. Jesus saith to her, 'I am He, Who speak to thee.'

The eye of the Evangelist is, as it were, so entirely riveted upon our Lord in this narrative, that he does not tell us in so many words how the Samaritan woman answered this appeal to her faith. Or rather, he takes it for granted that we shall understand how the powerful grace of God moved her heart at the time when this external call fell on her ears, and gave her the light and strength which were needed for the confession which was the end sought by our Lord in the whole conversation. She was at once, in her delight and astonishment, to become an Apostle to her own townsfolk, and to be full of zeal to spread the knowledge of the treasure which she had so unexpectedly found by the side of the holy well.

CHAPTER XXIV

Sowers and Reapers.

St. John iv. 27-43 ; *Vita Vitæ Nostræ*, § 26.

THE conversation between our Lord and the Samaritan woman must have lasted for some considerable time, and the disciples as they returned from the town, where they had been buying food, must have seen Him as they approached sitting with her at the well. The rules as to such conversations were very strict among the Jews, and in this case there were two circumstances which would ordinarily have enforced them still more stringently than was usual, for our Lord was now known in the character of a Rabbi or religious teacher, and was thus bound, according to the common Jewish notions, to be more reserved than other men with women. Moreover, the woman with whom He was talking was evidently a Samaritan, a resident on the spot. 'And immediately His disciples came, and they were wondering that He was talking with the woman. Yet no one said, What dost Thou seek ? or, Why dost Thou talk with her ?' for their respect for our Lord was too great to allow them to question anything that He did, and there was a majesty and purity about His whole demeanour and look that was a far better guardian of decency than any rules or customs whatsoever. The woman, however, withdrew from them, though not from Him, and leaving her pitcher by the well, she went into the town, where, if it was evening, the men would be collected for conversation and recreation, and bade them 'come and see a Man Who has told me all things whatsoever I have done. Is not He, think you, the Christ?' She must have been well known, and perhaps, even in that Samaritan community, her character did not stand high, though all may not have known her whole history. But her simple earnestness was enough to make them listen to her, and they came forth from the city and approached our Lord and His disciples.

Meanwhile, the disciples were offering to our Lord the food which in His weariness He had so much needed. But now they found that He would not eat. Fatigue and hunger seemed to have passed away. He had said to Satan in the wilderness, 'Not by bread alone doth man live, but by every word that proceedeth out of the mouth of God,' and now the fervour and love with which He had carried out the particular work which His Father had set Him to do, with regard to the soul of the Samaritan woman, had been to Him as the food which had restored the strength of the body, while the desire of His Heart, His hunger and thirst after the souls which God had given to Him, had been fed and satisfied. 'I have food to eat,' He said to them, 'which you know not of.' And the disciples, taking His words, as they were wont, in the literal sense, asked one another, 'Hath any one given Him to eat?' astonished as they were at the vigour and force which seemed to have been breathed into Him. Our Lord told them at once how it was. 'My food is, that I do the will of Him Who hath sent Me, and accomplish His work.' This, then, was spoken not only in general, of the refreshment which He always found in doing the will of His Father, but in particular of the work of the conversion of the Samaritan woman, which He had just accomplished.

This had been committed to Him at that time, and thus their wonder, at His having so far departed from the rules of behaviour which were considered binding on religious teachers, was answered and satisfied.

Our Lord went on in a strain of prophecy, speaking of the fruit which was to result from the seed which He had been sowing in the heart of the woman, considering its rapid growth and future fecundity as a type and specimen of the richness with which His Father would bless, not that work alone, but all the work of Apostolical conversation and instruction which He had now been inaugurating. Already the words of the woman had stirred up the hearts of her fellow-townsmen ; they were already on their way to put themselves at His feet, to open their homes to Him, and give Him the opportunity of more special and continued instruction ; and the sojourn which He was to make among them was, in the course of time, to produce the further result of their admission to the full privileges of His Church, when His Passion had broken down the wall of separation between Jerusalem and Gerizim, and the gift of the Holy Ghost been sent from heaven to spread far and wide the adoption of the children of God. The work of God was swift, swifter than all expectation, and yet it had its laws, the law of charity and participation in the good work, in which some were to be beginners and others finishers, and yet all were to share together the joy and the reward. There was, it seems, a Jewish proverb, founded on the interval of four months which in that climate is the usual period between the sowing and the reaping—'Four months, and the harvest cometh, but one soweth and another reapeth.' Our Lord made the two members of the proverb the ground of His instruction to the future Apostles. 'As for the first, indeed, you say that yet four months and harvest comes, whereas if you lift up your eyes and look on the country you will see the fields already white for the harvest.' This part of the proverb, therefore, cannot apply here. It was, as has been said, about the time of the wheat harvest, not long before Pentecost, and the plain before them was one of the richest portions of the Holy Land, especially in corn. They could have seen nothing like it in the part of Judæa which they had left that morning. Our Lord was, however, thinking of another harvest, the harvest of souls, and He had just found in the soul of the Samaritan woman a simplicity and docility which showed that the fruit which had been so long ripening in the world was ready to burst out in full maturity. Every word of His, by which He had led her on in succession through the various stages of her conversion, had been readily answered to with a faithfulness which showed the action of the Father Who had reserved it to Himself to draw men to His Incarnate Son, Whose work it was to be that Peter and His Apostles were to recognise Him as the Person Who He was. So neither in the spiritual sense did the proverb hold good. The harvest seemed to be coming before its time—for there was much to be done and suffered before the Church could be set up, and all nations made to flow into her.

Here we find, as it appears, the Heart of our Lord turning instinctively to the thought of the Cross, and all that it involved, which lay between Him and the harvest, for which He so much longed. He could only speak of it, as yet, figuratively and darkly, as He had spoken to the Jews when asked about His authority for cleansing the Temple. Now He speaks of it as the four months which had to pass before the harvest. The grain of wheat was yet to fall into the earth and die, before it could bring forth the fruit of the full admission of the Samaritans to the privileges of the Gospel. Our Lord

already saw that which was to follow after His Passion
and that Day of Pentecost which was yet three years off.
The reapers of the harvest were before Him in His
Apostles, for there were already by His side Peter and
John, who were to be 'sent to them,'[1] perhaps in memory
of this very conversation, when it became known that
'Samaria had received the Word of God.' 'He that
reapeth receiveth wages, and gathereth fruit unto life
eternal, that both he that soweth may rejoice at once,
and he that reapeth.' For the Apostles were to enter
upon fields white for harvest, the sowing of which had
not been their own work : our Lord's work was always
to have gone before theirs, and nothing that they were
to undertake could prosper and have the benediction
of fruitfulness unless they were therein treading in His
footsteps, building on His foundations, and continuing,
in close union with Him, with the same end and method
and manner, what He had first set His hand to in order
that it might be blessed to them.   He was now rejoicing
over the beginning of the work ; it was, as far as we can
gather, the first instance in which He had touched the
divine work of the salvation of souls outside the Jewish
covenant since the beginning of His Public Life.   This
Samaritan woman, and her fellow-townsmen, brought
before Him the whole of that wonderful kingdom which
He was to inherit, much as the Eastern sages represented
to Him the same kingdom at the Epiphany.   His Heart
was full of joy, as we gather from His own words, and
there was to be a reward and a fruit unto eternal life,
a fruit which would have its ripe beauty and glory in
heaven in their own hearts and souls, as well as in the
hearts of those for whom they were to labour as reapers in
the harvest, and the special charm and intensity of the
joy was to be that it was to be an entering into the joy

[1] Acts viii. 14.

of their Lord, a sharing of the overflowing and inconceivable delight with which He was now rejoicing in spirit, and should for ever rejoice.

For so it is to be in the kingdom of God. The second part of the proverb is true then, 'In this is the saying true, one is he that soweth, another is he that reapeth.' It is thought a loss on earth for the sower not to reap what he has sown, and an undeserved gain for the reaper to reap what he has not sown. But in the kingdom of God there are no such losses and no such gains, for it is the law of that kingdom that work shall be shared, that the gain of one is the gain of the other, and the joy of each intensified and enlarged by the joy of the other. It is one joy for a worker to rejoice over his own work, and another and a double joy to rejoice over the work of another, and with that other. Moreover, the kingdom of God is the kingdom of merit, merit transferred, handed on, the crown of which is inherited by those who come after him who has won it. Generation after generation is to succeed in the Church, and because she is the Communion of Saints, the blessing of the fathers is to descend upon the children, and successors are to share the gains and triumphs won by those who have been before them in the field. 'I have sent you,' that is, in prophetic language, 'I shall send you to reap what you have not laboured for: others will have laboured, and you shall enter into their labours.' The Church is founded in the fulness of time, and she is the heir of all that has been up to that time wrought in the providence of God, Who was from the beginning preparing the great work of the Incarnation, the fruits and merits of which are stored up in her. For her use the saints of old toiled and prayed and suffered, for her the patriarchs lived in faith, the prophets sang, the great cloud of witnesses of whom St. Paul speaks endured and fought; she was the heir of the Law, and lastly, our Lord Himself and His blessed Forerunner prepared the minds and hearts of the men of their generation, and she in a special manner reaped the seed which was sown by our Lord in the years of His Public Ministry, as well as all the inestimable treasures of grace won by Him in the rest of His Life, in His Passion, in His Resurrection, and Ascension.

Especially do our Lord's words hold good to us, who in the latter ages of the Church may have to labour in the same field of the Evangelical harvest, or at least to aid in that great work by our prayers and in other ways. For there is an ever-accumulating treasure of the labours, sufferings, and merits of successive generations; and when we have the true mission of those who are sent by the Church with which our Lord abides for ever, we may animate our courage and our hope by the certainty that our success will not depend upon our own strength and devotion alone, but that 'others have laboured, and we have entered into their labours.' Nowhere is the power of the Communion of Saints more marvellously revealed than in the blessing which descends upon the efforts of simple Evangelical workmen, who often find the fields white to the harvest before they expect it, and that the reward which meets them on their way immensely surpasses anything that they could have dared to hope or to aim at. And though there are many ways of accounting for the comparative sterility of the labours even of the most devoted men who are outside that blessed communion, still the true legitimate reason seems to be this, that they have no title to the fruit of those other labourers before them of whom our Lord speaks.

We are not told any details of the preaching and conversation of our Lord as addressed to the crowd of the fellow-townsfolk of the Samaritan woman. If we are to gather these details from the general statements of the Evangelists, and from the course taken by the conversation with the woman herself, we may suppose that He spoke to them of the necessity of repentance, and then, after they had been stricken with the consciousness of their own sins, of the duty of receiving or preparing to receive in faith the new Gospel as far as it was taught them. He may have given them some more correct notions about God and Himself, and some may have been baptized. 'Out of that city,' says St. John, 'many of the Samaritans believed in Him on account of the testimony of the woman who said, He told me all things that I had ever done.' This was the beginning, and led to the invitation to stay there—a natural exercise of hospitality, in any case, if the evening had now drawn on. 'When therefore the Samaritans had come to Him, they besought Him to abide there, and He remained there two days'—one of which, according to some writers, was the Sabbath. 'And many more believed in Him on account of His discourse, and they said to the woman, Now it is not on account of your talking that we believe, for we ourselves have heard and learnt that this is in truth the Saviour of the world.' Our Lord wrought no miracles here, unless indeed we take into account His display of the knowledge of the secrets of the conscience which had drawn the Samaritan woman to her confession and faith. Moreover, the power of His words and conversation is assigned by the Samaritans themselves as their ground of faith, and that of no ordinary faith, but faith in Him as the Saviour of the world. To others afterwards He was a Prophet, or Elias, or Jeremias, or, later, St. John the Baptist risen from the dead, but to these simple aliens from Israel He was the Saviour of the world, not of any particular nation, and their confession of Him rises in its distinctiveness almost to the height of that of St. Peter, that He was the Christ, the Son of the living God. Such is the grace of the Word of God in the mouth of Jesus Christ, needing no miracles to enforce it, because it is its own evidence, according to that saying of St. Paul, 'For the Word of God is living and effectual and more piercing than any two-edged sword, and reaching unto the division of the soul and the spirit, of the joints also and the marrow, and is a discerner of the thoughts and intents of the heart.' [2] And not less remarkable, in its contrast to the ordinary course of our Lord's Ministry as related by the other Evangelists, is this incident preserved to us by St. John of our Lord's sojourn for two days in the Samaritan town. It was a distinct infringement of His usual mode of action, and it foreshadowed in the most marked way the time when the external barriers which had separated the chosen people of God from the rest of the world were to be broken down by the universal diffusion of the graces of the New Covenant.

NOTE VII.

On the time of our Lord's visit to Sychar.

Those who are familiar with the critical questions which have been raised as to the chronology of our Lord's Ministry, will be well aware that the date of His visit to Sychar (or Sichem) is one of the points which has been most hotly disputed. There are only two notes of time in the narrative from which any conclusion can be drawn. One is, that our Lord left Judæa before St. John was cast into prison. The other is the note of time possibly, but not certainly, contained in His words to the disciples about 'the four months and then cometh the harvest,' and as to the fields being already white unto harvest.

[2] Heb. iv. 12.

As to the first note, the date of St. John's imprisonment is not certain, and therefore we cannot build any certain conclusion upon the fact that this visit to Sychar, or rather the departure from Judæa, took place before his imprisonment. But, although there is no certainty, there is still a preponderance of probability that St. John was imprisoned early in the year[1] of our Lord's first Pasch, and not so late as the same or even any earlier time in the spring or early summer of the year following. It is impossible in a note like this to enter upon any full discussion as to this question. The various chronological arrangements which have been suggested for the Ministry of St. John and for that of our Lord all rest upon the decisions arrived at by their advocates as to certain points of time, as the birth of our Lord, the date of His Baptism, and even that of His death. All that can be fairly required of writers on the subject is that they should be at least consistent with themselves, and should also be respectful to the Evangelists whose statements they attempt to harmonise. We cannot, therefore, as has been said, draw any conclusive argument from the words of St. John as to the imprisonment of the Baptist. As to the question before us, the alternatives which are open to critics are only two. Those who see a note of time in the 'four months before harvest' of which our Lord speaks, must suppose that St. John was not put into prison till the spring of the year in which occurred our Lord's *second* Pasch. Those who see no such note, but suppose the words to have been spoken when the fields were actually 'white unto harvest,' soon after the *first* Pasch at which our Lord was present after His Baptism, must suppose that St. John's imprisonment took place just about that time. This makes nearly a year's difference in the date which they assign to that imprisonment. And, as we have said, the probabilities are in favour of the earlier date rather than of the latter.

There is also another element in the argument which must be allowed its full weight in the settlement of the question before us, although, from the nature of the case, it does not admit of full discussion in this note. That element is the length of time which is required for the incidents of our Lord's Ministry, as they are to be gathered from the

[1] See Greswell, *Harmony*, t. iii. Diss. 10.

accounts of the four Evangelists. It is usually considered that our Lord's active Ministry occupied at least three full years, that is, that four several Paschs are included in the narrative, the first of which is that mentioned by St. John in his second chapter, and the last that at which our Lord was betrayed and crucified. In the hypothesis which makes the words about the 'four months before harvest' a note of time, eight or nine months of the first of these years are comparatively unaccounted for, and some writers have even supposed that our Lord spent them in comparative inaction. This theory practically restricts the Galilæan Ministry of our Lord to between a year and a year and a half. In the other hypothesis—which is followed in this work—the space allotted to the Galilæan Ministry is far longer, and room is there found, and—as it appears to the present writer—can only thus be found, for the variety of incidents, and, above all, for the gradual succession of the manifestations of our Lord as they undoubtedly occurred before the Confession of St. Peter and the Transfiguration. This, of course, is a peremptory argument as to the point before us only to those who recognise the necessity of the longer space of time for all that is to be gathered from the Evangelists. But the hypothesis here followed seems almost necessary to any one who is not prepared to crowd into the shorter space all the missionary circuits of our Lord, the many months during which He seems to have been comparatively unmolested by the Jewish authorities, the development of the opposition which began early in the second year of His preaching on account of His apparent disrespect for the Sabbath, and which deepened as time went on into accusations of a league with Satan and into persecution which forced Him to lead the life of a fugitive from place to place, as also the simultaneous development of His own plan of action in the selection of the Apostles, their subsequent mission, His withdrawal from open teaching and His adoption of the parabolic method exclusively, and finally, the very considerable portion of time which, after the Transfiguration, He appears to have spent in Judæa and near Jerusalem. It is well to mention this, in order to point out the importance of the question now under consideration, and also in order that Harmonists may be more aware than some of them seem to be, of the difficulties in which they may unwittingly involve themselves. The science of the Harmony of the Gospels, if we allow such a term, is of comparatively modern growth, and is indeed as yet very far from complete. We are convinced that, the more deeply it is studied, especially with a right view and due appreciation of the mutual relation between the several Gospels and the scope, method, and arrangement of each, the more difficult will it appear to postpone the commencement of our Lord's Ministry in Galilee to a point certainly within a few weeks of the second Pasch. It matters little, as far as this question is concerned, whether—as is supposed in the present work, as in so many others of the same sort—this second Pasch is the feast mentioned by St. John in the fifth chapter. At all events, the incident of the complaint of the Pharisees, grounded on the disciples rubbing the ears of corn in their hands on the Sabbath day, must have taken place soon after that Pasch, and therefore all that is prior to that incident in the Evangelical history must have been prior to the same feast. This, speaking broadly, is the period of time which, in the hypothesis which we are combating, must be limited to rather more than three months. Or, if the return to Galilee with which the three first Evangelists begin the narrative of our Lord's Ministry be postponed until after that Pasch, then there is a further shortening of time, and the persecution of our Lord as a sabbath-breaker must have been simultaneous with the beginning of His Preaching.

It may be said, however, that, after all, we must not interpret words in a particular way because of Harmonistic reasons, which are in themselves more or less uncertain. This is in a great measure true, but it is also true that any legitimate deduction from well-ascertained principles of Harmony must throw great light upon the meaning of words which are in themselves ambiguous. But in truth our Lord's words seem, when well considered, to be so plainly incapable of the meaning which is attached to them by the hypothesis of which we are speaking, that the decision of the question before us might be left to that argument alone without any Harmonistic considerations to help it. It is precisely on our Lord's words, considered all together, that we should found the conclusion that the 'four months' are not meant

as a note of time.   Our Lord's words do probably contain a
note of time, and that a very definite note.   He says not only,
'Do not you say or have you not a saying, Yet four months,
and harvest cometh?' but also, as if to correct such a statement in the present case, 'But I say to you, Lift up your
eyes, and see the countries (or the fields), that they are white
already unto harvest.'   It would be difficult to find any
passage in the Gospels in which our Lord has made a
similar appeal to natural phenomena or scenery or visible
things, when we cannot be certain that He had before His
eyes the picture from which He drew the illustration.   Our
Lord's habit of constantly using the things before His eyes
in order to draw from them some spiritual truth is so well
known that we have become accustomed to use it to throw
light upon sayings of His which are otherwise without
illustration.   Thus, for instance, when, in his seventh
chapter, St. John mentions His saying, on the last and
great day of the Feast of Tabernacles, 'If any one thirst, let
him come to Me to drink,' the saying is beautifully explained
as well as illustrated by what is known of the ceremony of
pouring out water in the Temple on that occasion.   There is
a similar illustration of the seemingly abrupt words in the
eighth chapter of the same Evangelist, where the incident of
the woman taken in adultery is immediately followed by our
Lord's declaration that He is the light of the world, for the
accusation of the woman was made while it was yet dawn, as
is especially mentioned by St. John, and the sunrise over the
Mount of Olives may very well have suggested the image
which our Lord uses.   Many other illustrations of our Lord's
habit might be quoted, and it is remarkable that St. John, in
whose Gospel those to which we have referred occur, never
mentions the fact when he gives our Lord's words referring
to the fact.   This is exactly his method here.   It seems
almost impossible to doubt that the fields in the plain of
Sichem were 'white unto harvest' when our Lord used the
words of which we are speaking.   They can only be otherwise explained in two ways.   Either our Lord meant to speak
of nothing at all which was before the eyes of His disciples
when He said, 'Lift up your eyes, and behold the countries,'
simply referring to the spiritual harvest, which could not be
a matter of perception to the eyes of man; or He meant the

disciples to look at the Samaritans, who were approaching Him from the town, having been persuaded to come to Him by the report of the woman. In the former case our Lord would use an image which would not only not be in accordance with what was before the disciples' eyes, but absolutely contrary to it, for the countries could not be white unto the harvest if it wanted four months thereto. In the second case the words would be more intelligible, but the image would hardly be appropriate, for the harvest does not come to the reaper, nor is it likely that the men of Sichem would have come out in any very large numbers. They would represent to His eyes sheep coming to their shepherd rather than fields waiting for the reaper's work. However this may be, it may be considered as quite undeniable that, if our Lord had said no more than ' Lift up your eyes and behold the countries, for they are already white unto harvest,' without any preceding reference to the 'four months,' no one would have doubted that the words which He used were directly occasioned by the fact before the eyes of the disciples, that the fields of Sichem were ready for the sickle. In that case it would have been thought a very far-fetched interpretation, to consider the reference to the approaching Samaritans as the direct explanation of the words. At the best, the words might have been so understood in a secondary sense, if the fields were white to harvest through which the Samaritans might be seen coming. In that case the figure would be more intelligible, but not in the other.

Here, then, we have a note of time which few would deny to be such, if it were not for the previous sentence about the 'four months.' This note is entirely in our Lord's usual manner, and the way in which it is introduced by St. John is also quite in accordance with the manner of that Evangelist. It remains to be considered whether these previous words contain another note of time. If this is the case, the one note must contradict the other. That is, one set of words must be understood either figuratively or proverbially, and the other must be taken as furnishing a note of time. The words about the countries being white unto harvest do not admit of a proverbial explanation. They admit of a figurative or spiritual explanation, as has been seen above, but only by supposing our Lord to appeal to the sense of sight

as having an image before it which was not before it in the
hypothesis which we are testing. A figurative or spiritual
interpretation of natural objects or phenomena is one of the
commonest things in our Lord's words in general; but it
would not be easy to find instances of such a meaning when
the external phenomena did not exist before His eyes. This
objection can only be met by understanding the external
phenomena of the harvest fields to be supplied by the
Samaritans approaching from Sichem. On the other hand,
the proverbial interpretation of the first set of words of our
Lord is perfectly natural, and is suggested both by the facts
of the case and by the form of our Lord's language. The
facts of the case are, that between the end of the last seed
time and the beginning of the first harvest the interval of
four months was common in the Holy Land.[2] Thus we

[2] The proof of this statement can hardly be put better than in the
following quotation from Greswell (*Harmony of the Gospels*, vol. ii.
p. 227, Dissertation 21). 'There were two seasons of harvest among
the Jews: the season of barley harvest, the first-fruits of which were to
be consecrated at the Passover, and the season of wheat harvest, with
which the same thing was done at the Pentecost (Philo ii. 206, l. 22–30 ;
De Decem Oraculis, 294, l. 5–195 : *De Septenario et Festis Diebus*).
Of wheat harvest in particular, Jerome on Amos : "Prohibui a vobis
imbrem, cum adhuc superessent tres menses usque ad messem, quæ
appellatur pluvia serotina, et agris Palæstinæ arvisque sitientibus quam
maxime necessaria est, ut ne quando herba turgeret in messem et triticum parturiret, nimia siccitate aresceret. Significat autem vernum
tempus extremi mensis Aprilis, a quo usque ad messem frumenti, tres
menses supersunt." Between each of these seasons, and the corresponding seed time, there was literally an interval of four months.
"Consider now from this day and upward, from the four-and-twentieth
day of the ninth month . . . is the seed yet in the barn? . . . from
this day I will bless you " (Haggai ii. 18, 19). On which Jerome : " Igitur
decimus est mensis eo tempore quo semina latitant in terra, nec futura
fœcunditas conjectari potest." Casleu, then, which in a rectified year
answered nearly to our December, was the seed time, four months before
Nisan, or the period of barley harvest ; and according to Maimonides
(*De rebus altari interdictis*, vii. 4), the wheat designed for the bread,
ad altaris ferta et libamina, was sown seventy days before the Passover,
so as to be ripe at the Pentecost, fifty days after it ; that is, the harvest
was just one hundred and twenty days, or literally four solar months
later than the sowing time. Diodorus Siculus asserts the same thing of
Egypt (Lib. i. 36). . . . Nor, as we learn from Pliny, was wheat harvest
in that country later than the month of May. At the time of the Exodus
from Egypt, when the vernal equinox coincided with April 5, the flax

have natural facts suggesting the proverb which is supposed to be contained in our Lord's words.[3] The form of the language confirms this explanation. For our Lord does not say, There are yet four months, and the rest, but, Do not you say, or, as it has been put above : Have you not a saying, 'There are yet four months, and then harvest cometh'? If the words were not proverbial, there is no reason for the expression, 'Do not you say.' On the other hand, this is the form by which our Lord habitually refers to proverbs of that

and the barley, it is said (Exod. ix. 31, 32), were both destroyed by the hail, because both were at that time ripening ; but the wheat and the rye were not destroyed, because they were neither of them arrived at maturity. The plague of hail must have taken place some time in the month of March, and very probably in its former half.' For the times of seed time and harvest, the reader may also be referred to Ackermann's *Archæologia Biblica*, § 61, 62. The importance of the rain three months before harvest, as mentioned in the passage of Amos quoted above, is mentioned by modern writers. 'Want of rain at this critical season is utterly ruinous to the hopes of the farmer. A little earlier, or a little later, would not be so fatal, but drouth three months before harvest is entirely destructive' (*The Land and the Book*, p. 395). The seed had then been a month in the ground, and moisture was wanted to swell it. The prophet therefore speaks of a chastisement sent by God on the land on account of sin.

We may supplement the passage quoted above from Greswell by another from Kuinoel, which is interesting on many accounts. Kuinoel is one of those who see a note of time in the 'four months,' and in order to account for the words, he is obliged to imagine that our Lord had before His eyes a man who was sowing seed. 'Perquam probabile est, Jesum, qui a rebus obviis et in sensum incurrentibus argumenta atque imagines desumere soleret, eminus conspexisse hominem qui sementem faceret, atque ea quæ hoc loco leguntur dixisse mense Decembri, cum hordeorum facerent sementem.' But he confirms, from other sources, the statement of Greswell and others as to the interval of four months, on which the proverbial interpretation of the words is founded. 'Alia semina maturius, alia serius, terræ committebantur. Quod hordeum attinet, illis in regionibus Orientes inter sementem et messem intervallum quatuor mensium interjectum est (vid. Walchii *Calendarium Palæstinæ*, p. 25 ; Buhlii, *Calendarium*, pp. 23, 28). Ante hordeum nihil metebatur : primitiæ hordei festo Paschatis, mense Nisan, nostro Aprili, Deo offerebantur (vid. Levit. xxiii. 10 ; Joseph. *Ant.* iii. 10), quibus oblatis falx in segetem immittebatur, et primitiæ tritici festo Pentecostes offerebantur (vid. Levit. xxiii. 17). Hordei igitur sementem faciebant mense Cisleu, nostro Decembri ' (Kuin. in l.)

[3] St. Matt. xvi. 2.

kind. Thus when He speaks of the common weather knowledge of the Jews, He says, 'When it is evening you say it will be fine weather, for the sky is red,' and the rest.[4] And to the Nazarenes, 'You will say to Me this similitude, Physician, heal Thyself;' and then He adds, exactly as in this place, 'Amen, I say to you, that no prophet is accepted in his own country.'[5] Indeed, our Lord goes on in this very place to use a similar form when quoting a proverb : 'For in this is the saying a true saying, that "one is the sower, another is the reaper."' The present writer, in the chapter to which this note is an appendage, has followed a conjecture which he proposed several years ago, that both parts of our Lord's sentence belong to one and the same proverb. Thus the fact that four months is the interval between seed time and harvest in Palestine supplies the ground for the proverb, which consists in a contrast between the uniform and certain succession of natural things, and the uncertainty of human affairs. The following verses may serve to illustrate its meaning—

> Four bright months must come and must go,
> Ere harvest shall garner the seed that we sow ;
> The corn that is reaped is the seed that is sown,
> But sower and reaper will not be one.

This, however, must be understood to be only a conjecture. Our Lord may have meant to refer to two distinct proverbs, or to one. Many other grounds for the first proverb, if there be two, may be suggested, besides that of the contrast pointed out in the verses just given. For example, it may have referred to the dependence of the harvest upon the Providential supply of the latter rain, mentioned in Amos iv., in the same way as St. Paul's words: 'I have planted, Apollo watered, but God gave the increase.'[6] The truth of the proverbial interpretation of the words before us must not be made to depend exclusively upon any single conjecture as to the origin and scope of the proverb itself.

There remains yet another kind of argument as to the question before us, which must not be left unnoticed. It must be remembered that, after all, we are engaged in endeavouring to discover the meaning of words spoken by our

[4] St. Matt. xvi. 2.

[5] St. Luke iv. 23, 24.   [6] 1 Cor. iii. 6.

Lord Himself, Who must have had a divine reason and method in all that He said. It would be presumptuous indeed to take upon ourselves to trace the sequel of His divine thoughts according to our own ideas, and we may be quite sure that whatever is merely our own conjecture on such a subject is likely to be defective, if not absolutely erroneous. But in the case before us we have our Lord's own words to the Samaritan woman to guide us as to the subject on which His thoughts were occupied when the disciples came back to Him from the city. He had just been declaring to the woman that 'the hour cometh, and now is, when the true adorer shall adore the Father in spirit and in truth.' It was no longer to be on 'this mountain, nor in Jerusalem,' but everywhere. He had just told her that He was the Messias, and she had gone away to ask her townsmen, ' Is not this the Christ?' He had had meat to eat which they knew not of, for He had done the will of Him that sent Him, that He might perfect His work. The work had prospered in His hand wonderfully, it was like the harvest time already, in the spiritual sense, as the fields before them declared it to be in the literal sense. Yet between Him and the harvest of souls on which His Heart was set there lay that barrier or gulf of the Passion, as to which He did not yet venture to speak to them openly. The 'four months' seem to cover an allusion to this, just as His words to the Jews about the destruction of the Temple, and what He had said to Nicodemus about the Son of Man being 'lifted up' like the brazen serpent, covered allusions to it. The work which He was to perfect was indeed the harvest of souls, but the harvest was to be reached by means of the Passion, which was thus, more immediately, the work which was before Him. He was just about to begin His Public Life and Ministry, and that Ministry was to lead Him directly to the Cross. From the Cross was to come the salvation of the world, the harvest of souls. At present He was not even sent to the Samaritans, but only to the lost sheep of the house of Israel. But when the interval, and all that it involved of suffering and death and merit, was over, then was to come the spiritual harvest which was already figured before their eyes by the bright corn fields of Sichem. This may be considered as the train of thought in the first part of the sentence.

But our Lord saw also another great truth in the scene before Him. The spiritual harvest of which He had been thinking was not for Him to reap Himself; He was to reap it through them, and they were to reap it through Him. Not yet were the harvesters to be let loose upon their work; He was to hold His hand, promising as the work seemed, and the law of the kingdom of God was to hold good in the difference between the sowers and the reapers which was spoken of in the second proverb, or in the second part of the proverb, as the case may have been. It is evident that this contrast is the leading thought in our Lord's mind while He is speaking the last words of the passage before us. 'He that reapeth receiveth wages, and gathereth fruit unto life everlasting, that both he that soweth and he that reapeth may rejoice together. For in this is the saying true, that it is one man that soweth and it is another that reapeth. I have sent you to reap that in which you did not labour; others have laboured, and you have entered into their labours.' The fields white unto harvest before their eyes suggested an immediate reaping, in which sower and reaper would be one. But it was not to be so. The harvest was yet, as the proverb said, four months off. And when it came He was to be gone, and they were to be in His place, inheriting His labours and reaping the fruit of His Passion, without which there could be no harvest of souls. But this was no disappointment to Him. On the contrary, it was His great delight that they should receive wages and gather fruit unto life everlasting as well as Himself, that the sower and the reaper might rejoice together.

It is easy to see that if this be the sequence of thought revealed to us by our Lord's words, the necessity of the Passion before the gathering in of the spiritual harvest supplies the reason for the mention of the 'four months.' The harvest before their eyes might be reaped at once, but it was not so with the harvest of souls. In this sense the passage is parallel to another in St. John, in which an image of the same kind seems to clothe the same allusion to the necessity of the Passion. That passage is found in the twelfth chapter,[7] where St. John tells us of the Gentiles, who wished to see our Lord at the feast. 'They therefore came to Philip, who was of Bethsaida of Galilee, and desired him, saying: Sir,

----

[7] St. John xii. 20, seq.

we would see Jesus. Philip cometh and telleth Andrew. Again, Andrew and Philip told Jesus.' Here is something analogous to the approach of the Samaritans, ready to believe, of which the passage before us speaks. But the reception of the Gentiles into the Church could not be, any more than that of the Samaritans, until after the Passion. So our Lord answers in the same strain as here. 'But Jesus answered them, saying : The hour is come that the Son of Man should be glorified.' The fields of Gentilism also are white unto harvest. 'Amen, amen, I say unto you, unless the grain of wheat falling unto the ground die, itself remaineth alone. But if it die, it bringeth forth much fruit.' Yet four months, and then cometh harvest. 'He that loveth his life shall lose it, and he that hateth his life in this world keepeth it unto life eternal.' The thought passes on, as in the Samaritan passage, to the toils and labours of the Apostles. 'If any man minister to Me, let him follow Me, and where I am there also shall My minister be.' The sower and the reaper shall rejoice together. We need not transcribe the rest of the passage, in which the thought of the Passion is more clearly prominent than in that before us, as was natural at that later period of our Lord's Ministry, and several considerations are added, especially in the closing verses, which, as might be expected, are not to be found in the words which we are explaining. In this manner, however, we gain something in the intelligence of the words of our Lord on both occasions, and they take their place in the series of covert and parabolic allusions to His work of redemption by means of the Cross, which run, like a silver thread, through the Gospel of St. John from its beginning to its end.

We trust that if these arguments are not enough to make the interpretation of our Lord's words about the four months, which has been followed in this work, certain to demonstration, they may at least be sufficient to show that it has not been adopted without solid reasons and careful consideration. Even if the argument from the sequence of our Lord's thoughts be not allowed or valid, the other more popularly intelligible considerations seem to us to be enough to settle the question. It cannot be denied that there is at first sight something attractive in the idea that we have here, perhaps alone in the Gospels, a note of time from our Lord's own lips. But that note of time is soon seen to be inconsistent with the rest of the passage, and there are plain internal reasons against considering the words, 'yet four months and harvest cometh,' to signify that when our Lord used them, the next harvest was just four months off. On other grounds the delay of our Lord's journey into Galilee to the December, or even to a later month, after the first Pasch, seems to create considerable difficulty in the arrangement of other events recorded in the Gospels. It lengthens out His early sojourn in Judæa for a number of months of which no sufficient account can be given, while on the other hand, it shortens most unduly the first period of our Lord's teaching in Galilee. It is true that that first period is not full of a great diversity of incidents, as will be seen in the next volume ; but this is quite a different thing from allowing that it cannot be shown to have been very fully crowded and occupied with incidents of a like character and with a most important course of teaching. We consider the misinterpretation of the 'four months' mentioned above as one of the most prolific causes of mistake in many arrangements of the Gospel history.

CHAPTER XXV.

The Nobleman's Son.

St. John iv. 43-54 ;　*Vita Vitæ Nostræ*, § 22

St. John tells us that after His stay of two days in the city of Sychar,[1] our Lord proceeded on His journey to Galilee, which He was now to make for some time the chief scene of His labours for the good of souls. This return to Galilee, the immediate reason for which is given in a former section, appears also to have co-

---

[1] Sychar, the name used by St. John for Sichem, is thought to be a sort of nickname, a corruption of the original. But this is very uncertain.

incided in time with the arrest of St. John Baptist by the licentious King, Herod Antipas. We shall speak of this in the concluding chapters of this volume. The Evangelist adds to his statement concerning our Lord's return into Galilee, the words—'For Jesus Himself bare witness that a prophet hath no honour in his own country.' This can be nothing but an allusion to the scene in the synagogue of Nazareth, in which our Lord did actually both in word and in deed bear witness to this law in the providence of God, as we find it related in St. Luke. This prepares us to find, in the narrative which follows, an illustration and, perhaps, a further explanation, of something which is contained in what St. Luke has there related.

'When then,' as has been said, 'our Lord was come into Galilee, the Galilæans welcomed Him, because they had seen all the things which He had done at Jerusalem on the feast-day, for they also had gone up to the feast.' It had been said, as we shall see, by other Evangelists, that our Lord's fame was already spread abroad when He arrived in Galilee, and St. John now mentions how it came to be so. There had not been a sufficient interval of time for them to forget the act of authority and zeal with which He had purged the Temple, the bold attitude which he had assumed towards the priests and rulers of the Temple, and the many miracles which had produced so much effect upon the mind of a learned man like Nicodemus. The minds of people were still full of Him, and thus it was that He found so ready a reception on His appearance in Galilee.

He first directed His steps to Cana, 'where,' as St. John says, 'He had made the water wine,' perhaps because His Blessed Mother was again there, as she had been after His first absence from her at the time of His Baptism and Temptation. Cana was further than

Nazareth from Sychar, but nearer to Capharnaum, and if our Blessed Lady had returned to her relatives there from Capharnaum during our Lord's absence, this would explain why He passed by His native city in order to join her.   At all events, His return into Galilee and His presence at Cana was quickly known.

A person of high rank at Capharnaum, holding some position of importance, as it seems, at the Court of Herod Antipas, had heard of our Lord from some of the numerous inhabitants of the place who had lately been at Jerusalem.   He may himself have been at the feast.   His son was dangerously ill of a fever at Capharnaum, and when the news came that the new Prophet and Wonder-worker was once again at Cana, the scene of His first great miracle a few weeks before this time, his own anxiety for his child and the faith of those about him suggested that our Lord should be asked to come and heal the sick lad.   It was a journey of several hours, but he did not hesitate to leave the child to the care of others, though he was apparently on the point of death, and go himself to beg that our Lord would come.   He poured out his tale and his entreaties, but at first received what seemed to be a check.   It was our Lord's way, by the use of what in His children is called the gift of counsel, to meet each case of those who addressed themselves to Him, or to whom He addressed Himself, in the manner which was most perfectly suitable to draw them on to higher things when they had begun well, or to detach them from errors or faults if they were in a state which needed such help.   He had begun with the Samaritan woman by asking of her a favour, and so putting Himself in the humble position of a suppliant to her.   To this man of rank and birth, who had so far overcome the pre-judices and haughtiness which infect such positions as his, our Lord replied in a manner to put his faith to a test by means of which it might be elevated and perfected. Why should He come down all the way from Cana to Capharnaum? Was there no other way by which He might work the miraculous cure which was asked of Him? Could not He do it where He was? and could not the father take His word for it, that all was well? 'Jesus, therefore, said to him, Except you see signs and wonders, you do not believe!' You require, then, that I should be on the spot, and that you should be present also to see Me do what you ask? Is not My word enough? Can you not believe without seeing? 'The nobleman said to Him, Lord, come down before my son die!' He was still not perfect in faith, but he did not answer our Lord's question in the negative. He had a strong wish in his heart, for the accomplishment of which he had put himself to great pains, and had even left the son whom he loved so tenderly when there was all human probability that he might never again see him alive. So he insisted on his prayer, which our Lord answered in a better way than he had hoped, at the same time requiring of him a special act of faith and submission to the will of God as to the manner in which his desire was to be carried out. 'Jesus saith to him, Go, thy son liveth.' No need for a long and anxious journey, straining ourselves to arrive in time before the child is brought to the last gasp: the work is done at this moment—'Go thy way!' At the same moment, two wonderful acts of mercy and power, very different in kind, were performed by our Lord. The watchers by the bedside of the dying boy saw a sudden change, and fever left him entirely. And the father's faith was so strengthened and enlarged, that he had no difficulty in at once believing our Lord's words and taking his departure on his homeward journey rejoicing. As soon as the cure was ascertained, some of the household started on the road to Cana to carry the news to him. They met him on the way, and when he asked them at what exact time the change had taken place, he found that it was at the same moment at which our Lord had said to him, 'Thy son liveth.' 'Yesterday, at the seventh hour, the fever left him.'

'And he himself believed and his whole house.' There was a richness and readiness of faith in the opening period of our Lord's teaching which faded away as time went on, and people became more familiar, at once with our Lord's miracles, and with the objections and calumnies which were circulated against them. The Samaritans, who believed on His mere word, the Galilæans, who welcomed Him so honourably after having seen His works at Jerusalem, and even the nobleman at Capharnaum, who was required to believe in signs and wonders without seeing them, seem to inherit the generous and simple faith which is so conspicuous in the shepherds and Eastern sages who came to honour our Lord in the cradle at Bethlehem. We have also a glimpse of the religious union between the nobleman and his servants—their eagerness to bear the good tidings to him, and to follow him in the profession which he now made of belief in our Blessed Lord. Nor, again, can we help noticing the manner in which, among the better classes of society in Capharnaum, the contagion of faith spread from one to another; for the faith of the centurion, who a year after this time thought it too much trouble to put our Lord to that He should be asked to come and heal his servant, but sent Him the message, 'Speak the word only, and my servant shall be healed,' seems to be the echo of the faith which our Lord had required of the nobleman. There were, we have seen, many in Capharnaum who had seen our

Lord's miracles at Jerusalem at the feast, and others who had heard of them: our Lord had already spent some few days in the busy little city. There was Matthew, sitting still at the receipt of custom, but his heart gradually preparing for the call which was to turn him from a publican into an Apostle and Evangelist; there was Jairus, the ruler of the synagogue, and probably many other families in which the good seed was already sown. The fields were white unto the harvest: but before our Lord began to make Capharnaum His residence, and the scene of so many miracles and of so much holy teaching, He had, according to the rule of God's providence and the guidance of His Father's will in His own particular case, to receive a great and, as it would seem to human eye, a dangerous humiliation at the hands of people who ought to have been far more ready to receive His word than the inhabitants of Capharnaum.

NOTE VIII.

On the meaning of St. John iv. 44.

It may be as well to say a few words in explanation of the meaning attached above to the words of St. John, in the place here cited, where the Evangelist says that 'after two days, He departed thence, and went into Galilee. For Jesus Himself gave testimony that a prophet hath no honour in his own country.' These words are interpreted above as referring to our Lord's rejection at Nazareth, the narrative of which is given in the following chapter.

The only other meaning that can be attached to the words of St. John would be that according to which they refer to our Lord's departure from Judæa, that being His native country, as if the return to Galilee was the witness spoken of. But if that had been St. John's intention, he would probably have made the remark, not here, but earlier, when he mentions the departure from Judæa. It is the departure from Judæa, not the return to Galilee, which in that case would be the witness. Again, we do not find that any place but Nazareth was called our Lord's own country, and we have also our Lord's own words as recorded by St. Luke, not to speak of other places, in which He applies the proverb to Nazareth. We are therefore entirely justified in rejecting as impossible the application to Judæa.

It remains to explain St. John's language, for if the words refer to the rejection at Nazareth, it seems at first sight strange that he should give that as the reason for our Lord's return into Galilee. And yet it is entirely in harmony with St. John's method throughout his Gospel that he should do so. To explain that fully would belong more properly to that part of the present work in which it is professedly treated of, but it may be well to mention here what may be sufficient for the understanding of the present difficulty. St. John throughout his Gospel constantly refers to what he supposes to be already known to his readers from other Gospels, and particularly from that of St. Luke, and it is frequently his object to supply some piece of information which may be useful in order to the full understanding of what has been said before him, sometimes even to prevent a false impression as to facts. His method is to introduce these supplementary narratives by some particle such as γὰρ or οὖν, which refers, not to what immediately precedes in his own narrative, but to what is already known to his readers. The most obvious instances of this method are to be found in his narrative of the Passion, as will be seen when that narrative is considered in relation to those of the three other Evangelists.[1] The word 'for' or 'therefore' in such places means, what we should express by some such words as 'as you know.' Thus in this place his meaning is, Jesus went into Galilee, for, as you have been told, He Himself had to bear witness to the truth that a prophet is without honour in his own country. That is, He went to Nazareth and was rejected

---

[1] The students of St. John's Gospel may perhaps be helped if we name a few of the passages in which this principle is exemplified. Such will be found in c. v. 16; xi. 2; xii. 1, 3; xiii. 1; xviii. 3, 28; xix. 1, 6, 21, 24, 28, 30, 31.

there. Then follows what has been here called a supplementary narrative, inasmuch as it not only supplies a fact which had been omitted by others, and particularly by that Evangelist who had related our Lord's rejection by the Nazarenes, but also explains something in what St. Luke has related which needs explanation. That something is to be found in the words of our Lord in the synagogue—'You will no doubt say to Me that parable, Physician, heal Thyself; those great things which we have heard done in Capharnaum, do here in thine own country.' Now, there is nothing in the narrative of St. Luke, nothing in that of St. Matthew or in that of St. Mark, which tells us of any mighty works wrought in Capharnaum before this time. St. John therefore subjoins the account of the miracle of the healing of the nobleman's son which was accomplished at Capharnaum by our Lord when at Cana, and which must have made a great stir, inasmuch as it was followed by the conversion of the nobleman and his whole family, and may very well have been spread over the country from a central point like Capharnaum, so as to be fresh in the minds of the people of Nazareth on the Sabbath day on which His rejection took place. It is, indeed, the earliest instance in which it is distinctly recorded that our Lord exercised His power in healing diseases, although we cannot doubt that most of the miracles which He had wrought at Jerusalem at the feast were miracles of healing, and the narrative here given by St. John explains at once the outburst of petty local jealousy in the Nazarenes, and the fury to which they were moved when our Lord told them that He was not going to work miracles in His own city.

CHAPTER XXVI.

The Synagogue at Nazareth.

St. Luke iv. 14-30; *Vita Vitæ Nostræ*, § 28.

It seems to have been soon after the miracle wrought on the nobleman's son at Capharnaum, that our Lord went to Nazareth. The miracle seems to have been known, and besides, on other accounts, such as the former miracle at Cana and the wonders wrought by Him at the feast at Jerusalem, as well as from the power, dignity, sweetness and penetration of His words, there was throughout the whole of Galilee a general disposition in His favour. The baptism and preaching of St. John had done much to prepare the hearts of the people for Him. There had been a great movement of penance, such a movement as makes people ready to welcome any teaching that promises peace and enlightenment, to show the path to virtue and open the door of grace and spiritual consolation. Our Lord's preaching was not different from that of the Baptist on the point of the necessity of penance and of the nearness of the kingdom of heaven; but His manner was sweet, gracious, breathing mercy and reconciliation, while His open condescension, and even His refraining from any display of outward austerity, attracted all men to Him. He now began the course which He followed generally during His years of active life, of teaching in the synagogues on the Sabbath and other days, and as St. Luke says, He was magnified by all.

Such being the disposition of men's hearts throughout the whole country, it might have been naturally supposed that if He were to be specially welcomed anywhere, it would be in the quiet retired town in which so many years of His life had been spent. The Nazarenes must have been in some measure proud of the reputation to which their town was raised by the fame of the young teacher who was known everywhere as one of themselves, and it is quite possible that, if it had been in harmony with the laws of Providence in such matters that He should have gratified their curiosity or vanity by making their town the scene of some striking manifestations of His glory, they might have become His zealous partisans and disciples. But such was not the will of the Father, Who guided all the earthly footsteps of His Incarnate Son, and Who chose rather that He should begin His Public Ministry by a great humiliation, parallel to that which had led to so much glory at His Baptism—a humiliation which should serve ever afterwards as a law and a warning to His ministers and servants, who might have been in danger, had the course of events been otherwise ordered, of clinging to their native places and their family connections, in a manner not consistent with that absolute purity and detachment which were to be required in all those in whose hands His work was to prosper.

'He came to Nazareth, where He had been brought up, and entered according to His custom into the synagogue, and stood up to read.' The meetings in the synagogues furnished our Lord, as afterwards the Apostles, with the most natural, easy, and promising opportunities of instructing the people, who were assembled there on the day of holy rest, with the blessing and the grace which are always attached to gatherings of those who are in covenant with God, united for the purposes of common prayer and worship. The services of the synagogue consisted of prayers and the reading of portions of Scripture, and there was a fixed table of select lessons, first from the Law and afterwards from the Prophets, for the successive Sabbaths throughout the year. We are told that any competent person might serve as reader, that he could not choose for himself the *parashah*, or lessons from the Law, but that he might select a passage from the Prophets, *haphtarah*, at his own discretion, different, if he pleased, from that which would come in due course, and that he might then add an explanation, commentary, or discourse of his own. Thus, when our Lord stood up to read, the clerk handed to Him the roll containing the prophecy of Isaias, in which, as it seems, the *haphtarah* for the day was to be found. Our Lord, however, found His own passage which He read out, and then, rolling up the manuscript again, and handing it back to the clerk, sat down, as was the custom of the teachers, and began to expound it. 'The Spirit of the Lord is upon Me, therefore hath He anointed Me; He hath sent Me, to preach the Gospel to the poor, to heal the bruised in heart, to announce deliverance to the captives, and sight to the blind, to send forth the broken into remission, to preach the accepted year of the Lord, the day of retribution.'[1]

Our Lord's discourse was an application of this wonderful prophecy to Himself and to them. 'He began to say to them, To-day is fulfilled this Scripture in your ears.' They, then, were the poor to whom the good tidings of salvation were to be preached, they were the bruised in heart, the captives, the blind, the afflicted who were to be relieved, and He was the Anointed of God, the Christ, on Whom the Holy Spirit rested; the time was come, the acceptable year of the Lord, and the day of retribution was at hand. The words which He

[1] Isaias lxi. 1, 2.

uttered spoke home to their consciences, probing their secret wounds, reminded them of the sins and miseries in which their blindness and poverty and captivity and affliction consisted, and they were offered, through Him, the remedy to their wounds. He did not more directly appeal to their consciences, than claim their faith in Himself. And yet it seems clear that He spoke with so much sweetness as well as so much power, that their hearts were drawn to Him. They gazed on Him at first with intense interest when He began, and as He went on their wonder and delight at the words of grace which came forth from His mouth found vent in acclamations of approval. But still it was an approval which had in it a certain patronising pride, such as people feel when one with whom they have long been familiar and of whom they have no very high opinion achieves suddenly some great success. Such a feeling is often, even among good men, narrow and unjust, involving an instinctive or half-conscious dislike to acknowledge superiority in those whom we know well, and it is a certain hindrance to our gaining that good from them which others may easily reap. 'They said, Is not this the son of Joseph?'

It would seem also that they were inclined to require that at least He should do some miraculous sign for their benefit. People were talking of what He had done at Cana, of what He had done at Jerusalem, and now all the country was full of the cure which He had wrought on a sick lad at Capharnaum, while He Himself was at a distance. What was Capharnaum to Him in comparison with Nazareth? It is never the way of God to indulge such pretensions, and it is the rule with those to whom He intrusts miraculous powers that they are not masters of them to use them as they wish, but only as He wills, when and where, and how. Our Lord, of course, had the full power of the Godhead, and was not bound to the laws by which He regulates the distribution of gifts in His kingdom. But His Human course was entirely regulated by the Providence of His Father; He had a certain definite mission, and was to do a certain work. It had been the Father's will that He should stop by the well at Sychar and talk with the Samaritan woman, and now it was the Father's will that He should work no miracle for the gratification of the pride of the Nazarenes. The choices and decisions of God are not arranged according to the conveniences of flesh and blood. He is absolutely free, and constantly shows His freedom by disappointing human calculations and the yearnings of the human spirit. Such seems to be the truth which our Lord now puts before His townsfolk, meeting by anticipation the demand which was in their hearts, if, indeed, it was not openly expressed. 'He said to them, No doubt you will say to Me this parable, Physician, heal Thyself;' use Thy craft for Thy home. 'The great things which we have heard of as done in Capharnaum, do here in thine own country. But He said, Amen, I say to you, no prophet is accepted in his own country. In truth I say to you, there were many widows in the days of Elias in Israel, when the heaven was shut up for three years, and when there was a great famine in all the land, and to none of those widows was Elias sent, but to Sarepta of Sidon, to a widow woman there. And there were many lepers in Israel in the time of Eliseus the prophet, and none of them was healed, but Naaman the Syrian.' In both these cases the extraordinary mercies of God had been vouchsafed not according to the choice of the prophet who had been God's instrument in working the miracle, not even according to what might have seemed natural and fitting, or likely to produce a great effect, and have the most fruitful results for good. They were not vouchsafed to many, though there were so many in need, but only to one or two, according to the free choice of God the giver, Whose ways and rules of action are not those of man. So it is now. I have worked miracles, and shall work miracles elsewhere, but to you and to this place and at this time I am not sent as a worker of miracles.

The same temper of pride and incredulity which had led them to welcome Him rather as a possible honour to themselves than as a messenger from God calling them to penitence, and which had had a share even in their applause and approval of Him, now lashed them into fury against Him—such fury as He had not met with anywhere, and which was not to have its parallel in Galilee, but only, after a considerable interval, among the proud, self-sufficient and envious priests at Jerusalem. Our Lord, according to His Father's will, left Himself for the time helpless and unresisting in their hands. ' And all in the synagogue were filled with anger, hearing these things. And they rose up, and cast Him out of the city, and they led Him as far as the brow of the hill on which their city was built, that they might cast Him down.' Their sudden access of fury appears to us unintelligible, but we must remember the extreme length of savageness and cruelty to which a crowd will sometimes go, even though it is made up of persons who, taken singly, would none of them commit a crime. The language of the Evangelist seems to imply that the whole congregation of the synagogue hung together around Him until He had been conducted outside the town, as if it had been their meaning solemnly to expel one who had insulted his native place. The party who took Him further still, to the overhanging brow of one of the circle of hills round Nazareth on the slope of which it is built, may have been fewer in number, delegates, as it were, of the community, whose office it was to execute the further cruelty of throwing Him from the rock.

But our Lord, ' passing through the midst of them, went His way.' He was to work no miracle, such as they could acknowledge, even in deliverance of Himself, and thus they were allowed to drag Him as they would out of the town. When they came to the place itself from which they intended to hurl Him, He quietly passed through the midst of them. How He extricated Himself, we are not told. He had once again to repeat the same action, when in Jerusalem the Jews took up stones to put Him to death. He could either make Himself invisible, or glide through them unperceived while they were in a state of confusion and excitement, crowding upon and jostling with one another in their eagerness each to have a hand in the deed of blood. So, at least, it has often been in the history of the Church and of the servants of God. They are helpless in the hands of furious enemies, and it seems as if Providence did not care to defend them, and did not hear the prayers that are made for them. And then, the very tumult and rage of their exulting foes blind them when they have brought the Church or the servants of God to the very edge of the precipice, and they find themselves baffled and mocked without any display of supernatural power, their victim is safe out of their hands, has passed through the very midst of them in calm majesty and confidence, and they are left to vent their impotent rage one upon another.

NOTE IX.

On the 'Mount of Precipitation' at Nazareth.

Some modern English and American travellers in the Holy Land seem to have no greater delight than in upsetting the ancient traditions with regard to the places connected with events in our Lord's life, and they seem generally to suppose that the sites which are fixed by tradition, have been chosen in the most gross ignorance of the text of the Evangelists. This, however, is positively unreasonable and even childish. The traditions which are found in the Holy Land are either genuine traditions from the earliest times, or they are the result of the pious devotion of Christian pilgrims in somewhat later ages, who desired to find spots which they might connect with the Gospel history, and chose the most suitable that they could find. But in the latter case, the very desire to find such sites implies a loving acquaintance with the Gospel history. And it is inconsistent with such acquaintance that sites should have been selected which that acquaintance would show to be impossible. It may fairly be said that if every traditional site in Palestine was just where modern readers and travellers would think it ought to be, that fact would constitute a far greater presumption against the genuineness of the tradition than in its favour.

What is now called the 'Mount of Precipitation' at Nazareth is an instance in point. It is just where it ought not to be, according to the superficial and supercilious criticism of modern travellers. It is about two miles from the present town of Nazareth, and the hill of which it forms an abrupt ending may be distinguished from the hill on which the town is built. But the only real objection to the site is that as it is a high hill, and the most conspicuous point of all the Nazareth range to travellers who approach it from the plain, it may have come to be pointed out to them as the hill so famous in the Gospel history on that account. The other arguments are worth very little. The position of towns, in which sanctuaries lie, has often shifted in the course of ages, buildings gathering round the sanctuary, and older parts of the town being abandoned. This is the case, notably, with Jerusalem itself, which by St. Jerome's time had gathered round the Holy Sepulchre. The other objection, as well as this, will be found answered in the following passage, by the late Father Hutchison of the London Oratory, which I am allowed by the kindness of a friend to transcribe from his unpublished note-book.

'On one of the western hills about midway between Nazareth and the Precipizio, are some rather extensive mounds and heaps of ruins, which mark the site of the ancient church *Del Tremore*, which was built to commemorate the spot on which our Blessed Lady hastened and looked on in terror while the multitude was hurrying her Son to the precipice beyond. Some say the city once reached as far as this. I doubt it, as I saw no traces of ruins or pottery. Very likely, it once stretched out in this direction, beyond its present limits, to at least as far as the depression in the western hill over which comes the road from Wady ——, and I found some pottery strewed about thus far, but not much. . . . But there seems no necessity for supposing that it extended thus far. No doubt the multitude led our Lord to the usual place of executing criminals, and this might well have been at this part of the steep precipice in this savage glen, outside the valley and out of sight of the town, thus casting Him out, not merely of the town, but out of the little domain, which might almost be called part of the place, Nazareth. Probably then as now the ravine was seldom ascended by travellers on account of the steepness of its rocky path, so that the usual approach to Nazareth from the plain is by the next valley westward. This wild and deserted spot would thus be a fit place for the execution of criminals, whose bodies might be left there to the vultures and the wolves.

'At the precipice over the Maronite Church, which has been suggested as a more likely spot, it would follow that they took Him out of the city to cast Him into it again, beside that this precipice is of no appalling height.

'As to its being said that they led Him to the brow of the hill on which the city was built, this might well be said of the Precipizio. The whole of the western hills, which have no valley between them, may be looked at as one continuous line, at the northern part of which the town was built, while at the south it ends in one precipitous brow over the plain. Not improbably the chief part of the town then was on the western side of the western hill, and afterwards spread along the foot of the northern hill on account of the sanctuary being there. But even now fully half of the town stands on the side of the western hill where it joins the northern.

'The instance of Bethany may be adduced in favour of this extended use of the word hill. It is said to be on the Mount of Olives, yet it stands, in truth, at the foot of a high hill, which is separated from Mount Olivet by deep valleys, except at one point, where a narrow neck like a bridge interrupts the valleys and unites it to Mount Olivet, about half-way up the southern side of that mountain. According to our modern way of speaking, we, who even distinguish the central mount from those on its right and left, and call that alone the Mount of Olives and those the "Prophets" and the "Viri Galilæi," should have rather given a distinct name to the hill over Bethany. Yet the Scripture includes the whole mass of these hills under the one name of Olivet. So, had the people of Bethany gone out to a precipice on the side of the Mount of Olives, supposing one to exist, it might have been said that they went out to a precipice on the brow of the hill on which their city was built.

'Again, the difficulty now felt about the distance would have been equally felt by those who, as is assumed, invented the tradition ; and, for convenience, they would most likely have selected a place nearer the town, possibly the small perpendicular face of the hill behind the Maronite Church.'

CHAPTER XXVII.

The Imprisonment of St. John Baptist.

St. Matt. xiv. 3-5 ; St. Mark vi. 17-20 ; St. Luke iii. 19, 20 ;
Vita Vitæ Nostræ, § 71.

IT cannot be doubted, from the manner in which the Evangelists speak of the imprisonment of St. John Baptist in connection with the beginning of our Lord's public preaching in Galilee, that there was not simply an accidental coincidence of time between these two events. St. Matthew tells us[1] that it was when our Lord had heard of the 'delivering up' of St. John that He returned to Galilee, left Nazareth, and took up His abode at Capharnaum. St. Mark simply says that our Lord came into Galilee after John was 'delivered up.'[2] The word does not necessarily imply betrayal, and may be simply the equivalent of St. Luke's expression, that 'Herod the tetrarch, when he was reproved by him for Herodias his brother's wife, and for all the evils which Herod had done, added this also above all that he shut up John in prison.'[3]

The numerous family of Herod the Great were in close relations with Rome and the Imperial House, and owed to them the favour which guaranteed them in the possession of those parts of the kingdom of their father which were allotted to them. The Herod of the Gospels was Herod Antipas, son of Herod the Great and Malthace. He has been already mentioned as tetrarch of

[1] St. Matt. iv. 22.
[2] St. Mark i. 14.
[3] St. Luke iii. 19, 20.

Galilee and Peræa. He was married to the daughter of the Arabian prince, Aretas, whose capital was at Petra. In one of his visits to Rome he seems to have stayed with his half-brother Philip, son of Herod the Great and Mariamne, daughter of Simon, who was married to his own half-niece, Herodias, daughter of Aristobulus, the son of Herod the Great and the Asmonean princess, Mariamne. Herod Philip had been disinherited by his father, and was living at Rome as a private person. Antipas was beyond the middle age, and Herodias had by her husband a daughter who was already more than a mere girl; but the visitor fell in love with his brother's wife, and it was arranged between them that they should divorce themselves from their present partners, and then marry. It seems that Herodias accompanied Herod Antipas in his return to Palestine, and the scandal thus became flagrant.

Herod's wife, the Arabian princess, fled to her father, and a war ensued in which Herod's troops—perhaps some of those soldiers who came to the baptism of St. John—were defeated. It is uncertain at what point of time the incestuous adultery of the tetrarch was made still more insulting to God and the consciences of the people by a pretended marriage, which gave to Herodias the position of a queen. It is certain that St. John Baptist spoke openly and strongly against the marriage, both to Herod himself and to others, and it is possible that when St. Mark says that Herod had already married his paramour, he means that he had her with him as a betrothed wife, and that St. John's efforts may have been directed to preventing the consummation of the outrage by the actual marriage. There is some reason for thinking that Herod went again to Rome about the time at which we have now arrived, and that the measure which he took of imprisoning St. John was dictated by a fear lest popular disturbances might arise in his absence on account of the strong stirring of the religious feelings of his people which was the result of the preaching of St. John. Voluptuous and tyrannical princes are always afraid of the free preaching of the Word of God, and we find them continually taking measures to intimidate preachers, or even to take into their own hands a sort of censorship of the pulpit. The statecraft of modern times has often adopted an Herodian policy. Even if St. John had never said a word about the adulterous incest of Herod, that prince would have been afraid of him, simply as a courageous and outspoken preacher of the moral law in all its branches, for such persons are always suspicious, and inclined to exaggerate their own danger from any religious movement. But when it became known that St. John had fearlessly reproved Herod himself, the tetrarch seemed to have everything to dread from the effect of this knowledge on the public mind. His partner in guilt was always at his side, stirring him up, like a second Jezebel, against the prophet to whom she bore so determined an enmity, all the more because she saw that the words of St. John had a real weight of their own on the inconstant and hesitating mind of Herod himself. The struggle ended, as such struggles usually end, at least in their first stage, by the resolution of Herod to put St. John into prison—fulfilling thereby the secret designs of Providence, as was afterwards said by the Apostles of him and others as to the part they had borne in the Passion of our Lord, ' To do what Thy hand and Thy counsel decreed to be done.'[4]

It may be true, as has been said above, that our Lord's active ministry was not to begin until that of His Forerunner had been closed; but we must not imagine that there could ever have been any true rivalry

---

[4] Acts iv. 28.

between them, or even doubt that the continuance of the ministry of St. John would in a very substantial manner have promoted and helped that of our Lord. If St. John had gone on preaching and baptizing, he would have contributed so far to prepare more and more souls for the reception of our Lord; but it is probable that the splendour of our Lord's miracles, which so soon began to be reported over the whole country, would gradually have drained away the tide of popular attention in favour of the new Teacher. But there were many purposes to be served in the counsels of God by the remaining portion of St. John's career, spent, as it was, in so different a manner from his early years or the few months of his preaching. As has already been said, he was to win a martyr's crown in defence of the law of God, and of that part of it in particular which enacted the sanctity of marriage. Before this he was to be a pattern of Apostolic boldness and open speaking in defence of that law, unquailing before the power of the prince as he was unyielding to all solicitations and endeavours to win him over, and thus to represent and witness to the truth against a public infamy on the part of the prince, at a time when it would not have been in accordance with the object for which our Lord was sent that He should bear that testimony in His own Sacred Person. We do not know that any remonstrance was made against Herod's wickedness on the part of the Jewish ecclesiastical authorities, who, indeed, had no great reason to be courageous in their rebukes to the members of his family. St. John, then, was God's witness to reprove this great and public crime, and it is significant that one who fills so high a place in the kingdom of the Incarnation should have been commissioned to lose his life on account of a protest against the profanation and violation of the laws of marriage.

The imprisonment of St. John at this time may also be considered as of much importance in showing the character of the kingdom which our Lord came to establish. The Providence of His Father was now declaring Him, in St. Paul's words, 'to be the Son of God in power,' by means of His marvellous miracles, and it was quite possible that, as at a later date, after the feeding of the five thousand, the people thought to come and take Him and make Him a King by force, so there may now have been enthusiastic hearts in the ever-increasing circle of those who were, more or less, His disciples, who may have indulged in the dream that the miraculous powers which He wielded were to be turned to the purposes of a merely human policy, that He would interfere in public affairs and set Himself on the throne of David. His Birth had, indeed, been marked by the permission on the part of God's providence of the cruel massacre of the Innocents, just after He had received the homage of the Eastern sages as the King of the Jews. No legion of angels had been sent to save those infant victims from the death which fell upon them because His shadow had but passed among them, and the Holy Family itself had been ordered to seek its safety in flight and exile, not by any preternatural means of defence. But this was past and forgotten, and now one after another the great manifestations of His power and dignity on which we have been dwelling had succeeded each other. Would our Lord use the power which He now displayed for any purposes but those of beneficence? He Who had cleansed the Temple unassisted, would He drive away the Roman armies and the mercenaries of the Herodian princes, as He had scattered the sellers and the money-changers in the sanctuary? Was the new kingdom to become a political and material power?

Such questions were to be answered by-and-by by our Lord Himself, in His words to Pilate, when He said that He was a King, but that His kingdom was not of this world, otherwise His servants would have fought that He might not be delivered to the Jews. But now, at the outset of His Ministry, they were implicitly answered by the imprisonment of St. John Baptist. The time was to come when St. Peter was to be saved from prison by an angel, but no angel was to be sent to loosen the chains of the blessed Forerunner of our Lord. The new religious movement, as it would be called in our time, was not to interfere with the powers already constituted in Palestine, even though they were alien in origin from the chosen people and the royal family of David. St. John was to be left to suffer imprisonment first and to be murdered afterwards, for he was in this also to go before our Lord's face, Who was Himself to be imprisoned against all law and justice for the sake of the truth, and to be put to an ignominious death by a ruler who could have no power against Him except it had been given him from above. And in this St. John was not only to have the blessed privilege of resembling his Lord and Master, but also that of silently preaching the doctrine of the Cross, before the time came for that doctrine to be openly declared by our Lord Himself. Meanwhile, until the time came for his martyrdom, he was restored, as it were, to his solitude, his long hours of silence, loneliness, prayer, and contemplation, and, in close union with God, in rejoicing thankfulness over the work he had accomplished, and the tidings which came to him at long intervals, perhaps, of the progress of Him to Whose manifestation he was devoted, he waited, as so many of the saints after him have waited, in obscurity and external suffering, the moment of his release by the sword of the executioner.

Our Lord's outburst, if we may use such words, of greater activity, upon the news of the imprisonment of St. John, has other aspects than that of the development of a religious movement when some restraining cause had been taken away. The seizure of St. John by Herod marked the end of the ministry of the Baptist, and it was now, .therefore, time to reap the harvest which he had sown. It was time to test the hearts of the people by a further trial, and to give those who had been truly faithful to the teaching of penitence the opportunity of coming to the light for which that teaching had made them ready by removing the obstacle of their attachment to sin. So it might have been in any case, if the ministry of the Baptist had been Providentially brought to an end in any manner or at any time. But it is characteristic of the kingdom of God which our Lord came to found that it derives strength from persecution, and fresh vigour and courage from the blows which strike down its most prominent champions. It rises upon its oppressors with a power of resistance and an indomitable tenacity faintly figured in the characteristic aggressiveness of Rome of which the poet sang.[5] And so the imprisonment of St. John is but one of a thousand similar acts of persecution of which the annals of the Church are full, which have been the signal for a greater activity and a more widespread devotion to good works on the part of her children than before. Human counsellors would have advised our Lord to retire before an unscrupulous prince, determined to stamp out any religious activity which might cast a fresh light upon the enormous public wickedness by which his daily life was stained, and to

---

[5] Duris ut ilex tonsa bipennibus
Nigræ feraci frondis in Algido,
Per damna, per cædes, ab ipso
Ducit opes animumque ferro.

whom bloodshed was no more a matter of hesitation than to his father Herod the Great. Instead of this, it was in the territory of this same Herod, and in the neighbourhood of his splendid residence at Tiberias, that our Lord was now to begin a new course of Evangelical preaching, illustrated by the most stupendous miracles, with which the whole country was soon to ring, and before the splendour of which the great fame even of St. John Baptist was to fade from the minds of men.

Harmony of the Gospels as to the Ministry of St. John.

§ 16.—*Preaching of St. John Baptist.*

Matt. iii. 1–12.	Mark. i. 1–8.	Luke iii. 1–18.
	The beginning of the Gospel of Jesus Christ the Son of God.	
Now in those days came John the Baptist preaching in the desert of Judea, and saying, Do penance ; for the kingdom of heaven is at hand.		Now in the fifteenth year of the reign of Tiberius Cæsar, Pontius Pilate being governor of Judea, and Herod being tetrarch of Galilee, and Philip his brother tetrarch of Iturea and the country of Trachonitis, and Lysanias tetrarch of Abilina, under the high priests Annas and Caiaphas : the word of the Lord came to John, the son of Zachary, in the desert. And he came into all the country about the Jordan, preaching the baptism of penance for the re-

Matt. iii. 3–6.

For this is he, who was spoken of by Isaias the prophet, saying: A voice of one crying in the desert: Prepare ye the way of the Lord; make straight his paths.[1]

And John himself had his garment of camel's hair, and a leathern girdle about his loins; and his food was locusts and wild honey.[2] Then went out to him Jerusalem and all Judea, and all the country about Jordan: and they were baptized by him in the Jordan, confessing their sins.

Mark i. 2–6.

As it is written in Isaias the prophet: Behold, I send my angel before thy face, who shall prepare thy way before thee.[3] The voice of one crying in the desert: Prepare ye the way of the Lord; make his paths straight.[4] John was in the desert baptizing, and preaching the baptism of penance for the remission of sins.

And there went out to him all the country of Judea and all they of Jerusalem; and were baptized by him in the river of Jordan, confessing their sins. And John was clothed with camel's hair, and a leathern girdle about his loins: and he ate locusts and wild honey.

Luke iii. 3–6.

mission of sins, as it is written in the book of the words of Isaias the prophet: A voice of one crying in the wilderness: Prepare ye the way of the Lord: make his paths straight: Every valley shall be filled: and every mountain and hill shall be brought low: and the crooked shall be made straight, and the rough ways plain: and all flesh shall see the salvation of God.[5]

[1] Isaias xl. 3. [2] Kings i. 8 (of Elias). [3] Mal. iii. 1.
[4] Isaias xl. 3. [5] Isaias xl. 3–5.

Matt. iii. 7-10.	Mark i.	Luke iii. 7-13.
And seeing many of the Pharisees and Sadducees, coming to his baptism, he said to them : Ye brood of vipers, who hath showed you to flee from the wrath to come? Bring forth, therefore, fruit worthy of penance : and think not to say within yourselves : We have Abraham for our father : for I tell you, that God is able of these stones to raise up children to Abraham. For now the axe is laid to the root of the trees. Every tree, therefore, that yieldeth not good fruit, shall be cut down, and cast into the fire.		He said, therefore, to the multitudes that came forth to be baptized by him : Ye offspring of vipers, who hath showed you to flee from the wrath to come? Bring forth, therefore, fruit worthy of penance ; and do not begin to say : We have Abraham for our father. For I say to you, that God is able of these stones to raise up children to Abraham. For now the axe is laid to the root of the trees. Every tree, therefore, that bringeth not forth good fruit, shall be cut down, and cast into the fire. And the people asked him, saying : What then shall we do? And he, answering, said to them : He that hath two coats, let him give to him that hath none : and he that hath meat, let him do in like manner. And the publicans also came to be baptized, and said to him : Master, what shall we do? But he said to

Matt. iii. 11, 12.	Mark i. 6–8.	Luke iii. 13–18.
		them : Take nothing more than that which is appointed you. And the soldiers asked him, saying : And what shall we do ? And he said to them : Do violence to no man : neither calumniate any man : and be content with your pay.
I, indeed, baptize you with water unto penance : but he who is to come after me, is stronger than I, whose shoes I am not worthy to carry : he shall baptize you with the Holy Ghost and with fire. Whose fan is in his hand ; and he will thoroughly cleanse his floor, and gather his wheat into the barn ; but the chaff he will burn with unquenchable fire.	And he preached, saying : There cometh after me one mightier than I, the latchet of whose shoes I am not worthy to stoop down and loose. I have baptized you with water : but he shall baptize you with the Holy Ghost.	And as people were of opinion, and all were thinking in their hearts of John, that perhaps he might be the Christ : John answered, saying to them all: I, indeed, baptize you with water, but there shall come one mightier than I, the latchet of whose shoes I am not worthy to loose : he shall baptize you with the Holy Ghost, and with fire : whose fan is in his hand : and he will purge his floor, and will gather the wheat into his barn : but the chaff he will burn with unquenchable fire. And many other things, exhorting, did he preach to the people.

§ 17.—*Baptism of Jesus Christ.*

Matt. iii. 13-17.	Mark i. 9-11.	Luke iii. 21-23.

Then cometh Jesus from Galilee to the Jordan, unto John, to be baptized by him.

And it came to pass, in those days, that Jesus came from Nazareth of Galilee: and was baptized by John in the Jordan.

But John stayed him, saying: I ought to be baptized by thee; and comest thou to me? And Jesus, answering, said to him: Suffer it now: for so it becometh us to fulfil all justice. Then he suffered him:

And Jesus, being baptized, went up presently out of the water: and, behold, the heavens were opened to him: and he saw the Spirit of God descending, as a dove, and coming upon him. And, behold, a voice from heaven, saying: This is my beloved Son, in whom I am well pleased.

And forthwith coming up out of the water, he saw the heavens opened and the Spirit, as a dove descending, and remaining on him. And there came a voice from heaven: Thou art my beloved Son; in thee I am well pleased.

Now it came to pass, when all the people were baptized, that Jesus also being baptized, and praying, heaven was opened: and the Holy Ghost descended in a bodily shape as a dove upon him: and a voice came from heaven: Thou art my beloved Son; in thee I am well pleased. And Jesus himself was beginning about the age of thirty years: being (as it was supposed) the son of Joseph.

§ 18.—*Fasting and Temptation of Jesus Christ.*

Matt. iv. 1-11.

Then Jesus was led by the Spirit into the desert, to be tempted by the devil. And when he had fasted forty days and forty nights, he was afterwards hungry.

And the tempter, coming, said to him : If thou be the Son of God, command that these stones be made bread. But he answered, and said : It is written : Man liveth not by bread alone, but by every word that proceedeth out of the mouth of God.[1]

Then the devil took him up into the holy city, and set him on a pinnacle of the temple. And said to him : If thou be the Son of God, cast thyself down ; for it is written : That he hath given his Angels charge of thee, and in

Mark i. 12, 13.

And immediately the Spirit drove him out into the desert. And he was in the desert forty days and forty nights ; and was tempted by Satan : and he was with beasts ; and the Angels ministered to him.

Luke iv. 1-13.

And Jesus being full of the Holy Ghost, returned from the Jordan : and was led by the Spirit into the desert, for the space of forty days; and was tempted by the devil. And he did eat nothing in those days : and when they were ended, he was hungry.

And the devil said to him : If thou be the Son of God, command this stone that it be made bread. And Jesus answered him : It is written : That man liveth not by bread alone, but by every word of God.

And the devil led him into a high mountain, and showed him all the kingdoms of the world in a moment of time : And he said to him : To thee will I give all this power, and the glory of them : for to me they are delivered ; and to

1 Deut. viii. 3.

Matt. iv. 6-11.	Mark i.	Luke iv. 6-13.

their hands shall they bear thee up, lest, perhaps, thou hurt thy foot against a stone.[2] Jesus said to him: It is written again: Thou shalt not tempt the Lord thy God.[3]

Again the devil took him up into a very high mountain; and showed him all the kingdoms of the world, and the glory of them. And he said to him: All these will I give thee, if, falling down, thou wilt adore me. Then Jesus saith to him: Begone, Satan: for it is written: The Lord thy God thou shalt adore, and him only shalt thou serve.[4] Then the devil left him; and, behold, Angels came and ministered to him.

whom I will, I give them. If thou, therefore, wilt adore before me, all shall be thine. And Jesus, answering, said to him: It is written: Thou shalt adore the Lord thy God, and him only shalt thou serve.

And he brought him to Jerusalem, and set him on a pinnacle of the temple; and said to him: If thou be the Son of God, cast thyself down from hence. For it is written, that he hath given his Angels charge over thee, that they keep thee: and that in their hands they shall bear thee up, lest thou dash thy foot against a stone. And Jesus answering, said to him: It is said: Thou shalt not tempt the Lord thy God. And when all the temptation was ended, the devil departed from him for a time.

---

[2] Psalm xci. 11, 12. [3] Deut. vi. 16. [4] Deut. vi. 13.

§ 19.—*The Testimony of St. John Baptist to the Pharisees.*

John i. 19-28.

And this is the testimony of John, when the Jews sent from Jerusalem priests and Levites to him, to ask him: Who art thou? And he confessed, and did not deny, and he confessed, I am not the Christ. And they asked him: What then? Art thou Elias? And he said: I am not. Art thou the prophet? And he answered: No. Then they said to him: Who art thou, that we may give an answer to them that sent us? What sayest thou of thyself? He said: I am the voice of one crying in the wilderness, Make straight the way of the Lord, as the prophet Isaias said.[1] And they that were sent were of the Pharisees. And they asked him, and said to him: Why then dost thou baptize, if thou be not Christ, nor Elias, nor the prophet? John answered them, saying: I baptize in water: but there hath stood one in the midst of you, whom you know not. The same is he that shall come after me, who is preferred before me; the latchet of whose shoe I am not worthy to loose. These things were done in Bethania beyond the Jordan, where John was baptizing.

---

§ 20.—*St. John points out the Lamb of God.*

John i. 29-34.

The next day John saw Jesus coming to him; and he saith: Behold the Lamb of God; behold, he who taketh away the sin of the world! This is he of whom I said: After me cometh a man, who is preferred before me, because he was before me. And I knew him not: but that he may be made manifest in Israel, therefore am I come baptizing in water. And John gave testimony, saying: I saw the Spirit coming down as a dove from heaven, and he remained upon him. And I knew him not; but he, who sent me to baptize in water, said to me: He upon whom thou shalt see the Spirit descending, and remaining on him, he it is that baptizeth with the Holy Ghost. And I saw; and I gave testimony that this is the Son of God.

---

[1] Isaias xl. 3.

§ 21.—*Some disciples of St. John join our Lord.*

John i. 35-51.

Again, the following day, John stood, and two of his disciples : and looking upon Jesus as he was walking, he saith : Behold the Lamb of God !

And the two disciples heard him speak ; and they followed Jesus. And Jesus turning, and seeing them following him, saith to them : What seek you ? They said to him : Rabbi (which is to say, being interpreted, Master), where dwellest thou ? He saith to them : Come and see. They came, and saw where he abode ; and they stayed with him that day : now it was about the tenth hour.

And Andrew, the brother of Simon Peter, was one of the two who had heard of John, and followed him. He first findeth his brother 'Simon, and said to him : We have found the Messias (which is, being interpreted, the Christ). And he brought him to Jesus. And Jesus, looking upon him, said : Thou art Simon the son of Jona : thou shalt be called Cephas (which is interpreted, Peter). On the following day he would go forth into Galilee ; and he findeth Philip. And Jesus said to him : Follow me. Now Philip was of Bethsaida, the city of Andrew and Peter.

Philip findeth Nathanael, and said to him : We have found him of whom Moses in the law, and the prophets, did write, Jesus the son of Joseph of Nazareth. And Nathanael said to him : Can anything of good come from Nazareth ? Philip saith to him : Come and see. Jesus saw Nathanael coming to him ; and he saith of him : Behold an Israelite indeed, in whom there is no guile ! Nathanael said to him : Whence knowest thou me ? Jesus answered, and said to him : Before that Philip called thee, when thou wast under the fig-tree, I saw thee. Nathanael answered him and said : Rabbi, thou art the Son of God ; thou art the King of Israel. Jesus answered and said to him : Because I said unto thee, I saw thee under the fig-tree, thou believest ? greater things than these shalt thou see. And he saith to him : Amen, amen I say to you, you shall see the heaven opened, and the Angels of God ascending and descending upon the Son of Man.[1]

[1] Gen. xxviii. 12 (Jacob's Ladder).

§ 22.—*The First Miracle of Christ at the Marriage Feast.*

John ii. 1–12.

And the third day there was a marriage in Cana of Galilee : and the mother of Jesus was there. And Jesus also was invited, and his disciples, to the marriage.

And the wine failing, the mother of Jesus saith to him : They have no wine. And Jesus saith to her : Woman, what is to me and to thee ? my hour is not yet come. His mother saith to the waiters : Whatsoever he shall say to you, do ye.

Now there were set there six water-pots of stone, according to the manner of the purifying of the Jews, containing two or three measures apiece. Jesus saith to them : Fill the water-pots with water. And they filled them up to the brim. And Jesus saith to them : Draw out now, and carry to the chief steward of the feast. And they carried it. And when the chief steward had tasted the water made wine, and knew not whence it was, but the waiters knew who had drawn the water ; the chief steward calleth the bridegroom, and saith to him : Every man at first setteth forth good wine ; and when men have well drunk, then that which is worse : but thou hast kept the good wine until now.

This beginning of miracles did Jesus in Cana of Galilee: and he manifested his glory ; and his disciples believed in him. After this he went down to Capharnaum, he and his mother, and his brethren, and his disciples : and they remained there not many days.

---

§ 23.—*The Feast of the Pasch at Jerusalem.*

John ii. 13–25.

And the pasch of the Jews was at hand, and Jesus went up to Jerusalem.

And he found in the temple them that sold oxen and sheep and doves, and the changers of money sitting. And when he had made, as it were, a scourge of little cords, he drove them all out of the temple, the sheep also and the oxen, and the money of the changers he poured out, and the tables he overthrew. And to them that sold doves he said : Take these things hence, and make not the house of my Father a house of traffic. And his disciples remembered, that it was written : The zeal of thy house hath eaten me up.[1]

The Jews, therefore, answered, and said to him : What sign dost thou show unto us, seeing thou dost

---

[1] Psalm lxvii. 9.

John ii. 19-25.

these things? Jesus answered and said to them: Destroy this temple, and in three days I will raise it up. The Jews then said: Six and forty years was this temple in building; and wilt thou raise it up in three days? But he spoke of the temple of his body. When therefore he was risen again from the dead, his disciples remembered that he had said this, and they believed the scripture, and the word that Jesus had said.

Now when he was at Jerusalem, at the pasch, upon the festival day, many believed in his name, seeing his signs which he did. But Jesus did not trust himself unto them, for that he knew all men. And because he needed not that any should give testimony of man; for he knew what was in man.

---

§ 24.—*Our Lord and Nicodemus.*

John iii. 1-21.

And there was a man of the Pharisees, named Nicodemus, a ruler of the Jews. This man came to Jesus by night, and said to him: Rabbi, we know that thou art come a teacher from God; for no man can do these signs which thou dost, unless God be with him.

Jesus answered, and said to him: Amen, amen I say to thee, unless a man be born again, he cannot see the kingdom of God.

Nicodemus saith to him: How can a man be born when he is old? can he enter a second time into his mother's womb, and be born again?

Jesus answered: Amen, amen I say to thee, unless a man be born again of water and the Holy Ghost, he cannot enter into the kingdom of God. That which is born of the flesh, is flesh; and that which is born of the Spirit, is spirit. Wonder not, that I said to thee, you must be born again. The Spirit breatheth where he will; and thou hearest his voice, but thou knowest not whence he cometh, and whither he goeth; so is every one that is born of the Spirit.

Nicodemus answered, and said to him: How can these things be done?

Jesus answered, and said to him: Art thou a master in Israel, and knowest not these things? Amen, amen I say to thee, that we speak what we know, and we testify what we have seen, and you receive not our testimony. If I have spoken to you earthly things, and you believe not; how will you believe, if I shall speak to you heavenly things? And no man hath ascended into heaven, but he that descended from

John iii. 14-21.

heaven, the son of man who is in heaven.

And as Moses lifted up the serpent in the desert, so must the Son of Man be lifted up : that whosoever believeth in him, may not perish, but may have life everlasting. For God so loved the world, as to give his only-begotten Son, that whosoever believeth in him, may not perish, but may have life everlasting. For God sent not his Son into the world, to judge the world, but that the world may be saved by him. He that believeth in him is not judged. But he that doth not believe, is already judged : because he believeth not in the name of the only-begotten Son of God. And this is the judgment : because the light is come into the world, and men love darkness rather than the light : for their works were evil. For every one that doth evil hateth the light, and cometh not to the light, that his works may not be reproved. But he that doth truth, cometh to the light, that his works may be made manifest, because they are done in God.

---

§ 25.—*St. John bears witness that Christ is the Son of God.*

John iii. 22-36.

After these things Jesus and his disciples came into the land of Judea : and there he abode with them, and baptized. And John also was baptizing in Ennon near Salim ; because there was much water there ; and they came, and were baptized. For John was not yet cast into prison.

And there arose a question between some of John's disciples and the Jews concerning purification : and they came to John, and said to him : Rabbi, he that was with thee beyond the Jordan, to whom thou gavest testimony, behold he baptizeth, and all men come to him.

John answered and said : A man cannot receive any thing, unless it be given him from heaven. You yourselves do bear me witness, that I said, I am not Christ, but that I am sent before him. He that hath the bride is the bridegroom : but the friend of the bridegroom, who standeth and heareth him, rejoiceth with joy because of the bridegroom's voice. This my joy therefore is fulfilled. He must increase, but I must decrease. He that cometh from above, is above all. He that is of the earth, of the earth he is, and of the earth he speaketh. He that cometh from heaven is above all. And what he hath seen and heard, that he testifieth : and no man receiveth his testimony. He that hath received

John iii. 33-36.

his testimony, has set to his seal that God is true. For he whom God hath sent, speaketh the words of God: for God doth not give the spirit by measure. The Father loveth the Son: and he hath given all things into his hand. He that believeth in the Son, hath life everlasting; but he that believeth not the Son, shall not see life; but the wrath of God abideth on him.

§ 26.—*Our Lord and the Samaritan Woman.*

John iv. 1-42.

When Jesus therefore understood that the Pharisees had heard, that Jesus maketh more disciples, and baptizeth (more) than John (though Jesus himself did not baptize, but his disciples), he left Judea, and went again into Galilee.

And he was of necessity to pass through Samaria. He cometh therefore to a city of Samaria, which is called Sichar, near the land which Jacob gave to his son Joseph. Now Jacob's well was there. Jesus being therefore wearied with his journey, sat thus on the well. It was about the sixth hour. There cometh a woman of Samaria, to draw water. Jesus saith to her: Give me to drink. For his disciples were gone into the city to buy meats.

Then that Samaritan woman saith to him: How dost thou, being a Jew, ask of me to drink, who am a Samaritan woman? For the Jews do not communicate with the Samaritans.

Jesus answered, and said to her: If thou didst know the gift of God, and who he is that saith to thee, Give me to drink; thou perhaps wouldst have asked of him, and he would have given thee living water.

The woman saith to him: Sir, thou hast nothing wherein to draw, and the well is deep: from whence then hast thou living water? Art thou greater than our father Jacob, who gave us the well, and drank thereof himself, and his children, and his cattle?

Jesus answered, and said to her: Whosoever drinketh of this water, shall thirst again; but he that shall drink of the water that I shall give him, shall not thirst for ever: but the water that I shall give him, shall become in him a fountain of water, springing up into life everlasting.

The woman saith to him: Sir, give me this water, that I may not thirst, nor come hither to draw.

Jesus saith to her: Go, call thy husband, and come hither.

The woman answered, and said: I have no husband.

John iv. 17-40.

Jesus said to her : Thou hast said well, I have no husband : for thou hast had five husbands : and he whom thou now hast, is not thy husband. This thou hast said truly. The woman saith to him: Sir, I perceive that thou art a prophet. Our fathers adored on this mountain, and you say, that at Jerusalem is the place where men must adore.

Jesus saith to her : Woman, believe me, that the hour cometh, when you shall neither on this mountain, nor in Jerusalem, adore the Father. You adore that which you know not : we adore that which we know ; for salvation is of the Jews. But the hour cometh, and now is, when the true adorers shall adore the Father in spirit and in truth. For the Father also seeketh such to adore him. God is a spirit ; and they that adore him, must adore him in spirit and in truth.

The woman saith to him : I know that the Messias cometh (who is called Christ); therefore, when he is come, he will tell us all things.

Jesus saith to her : I am he, who am speaking with thee.

And immediately his disciples came ; and they wondered that he talked with the woman. Yet no man said : What seekest thou ? or, why talkest thou with her ? The woman therefore left her water-pot, and went her way into the city, and saith to the men there : Come, and see a man who has told me all things, whatsoever I have done. Is not he the Christ ? They went therefore out of the city, and came unto him.

In the mean time the disciples prayed him, saying : Rabbi, eat. But he said to them : I have meat to eat, which you know not. The disciples therefore said one to another : Hath any man brought him to eat ?

Jesus saith to them : My meat is to do the will of him that sent me, that I may perfect his work. Do not you say, There are yet four months, and then the harvest cometh ? Behold, I say to you, lift up your eyes, and see the countries ; for they are white already to harvest. And he that reapeth receiveth wages, and gathereth fruit unto life everlasting ; that both he that soweth, and he that reapeth, may rejoice together. For in this is the saying true, That it is one man that soweth, and it is another that reapeth. I have sent you to reap that in which you did not labour : others have laboured, and you have entered into their labours.

Now of that city many of the Samaritans believed in him, for the word of the woman giving testimony : He told me all things whatsoever I have done. So when the Samaritans were come to him, they desired him that

John iv. 40–42.

he would tarry there. And he abode there two days. And many more believed in him because of his own word. And they said to the woman : We now believe, not for thy saying : for we ourselves have heard him, and know that this is indeed the Saviour of the world.

---

§ 27.—*Healing of the Nobleman's Son.*

John iv. 43–54.

Now after two days, he departed thence and went into Galilee. For Jesus himself gave testimony that a prophet hath no honour in his own country.

And when he was come into Galilee, the Galileans received him, having seen all the things he had done at Jerusalem on the festival day; for they also went to the festival day. He came again therefore into Cana of Galilee, where he made the water wine.

And there was a certain ruler, whose son was sick at Capharnaum. He having heard that Jesus was come from Judea into Galilee, went to him, and prayed him to come down, and heal his son; for he was at the point of death.

Jesus therefore said to him: Unless you see signs and wonders, you believe not.

The ruler saith to him : Lord, come down before that my son die.

Jesus saith to him: Go thy way; thy son liveth. The man believed the word which Jesus said to him, and went his way. And as he was going down, his servants met him ; and they brought him word, saying, that his son lived. He asked therefore of them the hour wherein he grew better. And they said to him : Yesterday, at the seventh hour, the fever left him. The father therefore knew, that it was at the same hour that Jesus said to him, Thy son liveth ; and himself believed, and his whole house.

This is again the second miracle that Jesus did, when he was come out of Judea into Galilee.

§ 28.—*The Sabbath at Nazareth.*

Luke iv. 14-31.

And Jesus returned in the power of the Spirit into Galilee, and the fame of him went out through the whole country. And he taught in their synagogues, and was magnified by all.

And he came to Nazareth, where he was brought up: and he went into the synagogue, according to his custom, on the Sabbath-day; and he rose up to read, and the book of Isaias the prophet was delivered unto him. And as he unfolded the book, he found the place where it was written: The spirit of the Lord is upon me; wherefore he hath anointed me to preach the gospel to the poor, he hath sent me to heal the contrite of heart, to preach deliverance to the captive, and sight to the blind, to set at liberty them that are bruised, to preach the acceptable year of the Lord, and the day of reward.[1]

And when he had folded the book, he restored it to the minister, and sat down. And the eyes of all in the synagogue were fixed on him.

And he began to say to them: This day is fulfilled this scripture in your ears. And all gave testimony to him: and they wondered at the words of grace that proceeded from his mouth, and they said: Is not this the son of Joseph?

And he said to them: Doubtless you will say to me this similitude: Physician, heal thyself: as great things as we have heard done in Capharnaum, do also here in thy own country. And he said: Amen I say to you, that no prophet is accepted in his own country. In truth I say to you, there were many widows in the days of Elias in Israel, when heaven was shut up three years and six months, when there was a great famine throughout all the earth; and to none of them was Elias sent, but to Sarepta of Sidon, to a widow woman. And there were many lepers in Israel in the time of Eliseus the prophet: and none of them was cleansed but Naaman the Syrian. And all they in the synagogue, hearing these things, were filled with anger. And they rose up and thrust him out of the city: and they brought him to the brow of the hill, whereon their city was built, that they might cast him down headlong. But he passing through the midst of them, went his way. And he went down into Capharnaum, a city of Galilee, and there he taught them on the Sabbath-days.

[1] Isaias xli. 1, 2.

PRINTED BY BALLANTYNE, HANSON AND CO.
EDINBURGH AND LONDON